Minnesota

Greg Breining
Photography by Paul Chesley

COMPASS AMERICAN GUIDES
An Imprint of Fodor's Travel Publications

Minnesota
Second Edition

Fodors and colophon are trademarks of Random House, Inc.
Compass American Guides is a trademark of Random House, Inc.
Copyright © 1997, 2000 Fodor's Travel Publications
Maps Copyright © 1997, 2000 Fodor's Travel Publications

Compass American Guides, 5332 College Avenue, Suite 201, Oakland, CA 94618, USA
ISBN: 0-679-00437-8

Editors: Kit Duane, Barry Parr, Deborah Dunn,   Designers: Christopher Burt, Deborah Dunn
    Cheryl Koehler   Map Design: Mark Stroud, Moon Street Cartography
Managing Editor: Kit Duane   Production House: Twin Age Ltd., Hong Kong
Creative Director: Christopher Burt   Manufactured in China

10 9 8 7 6 5 4 3 2 1

The Publisher gratefully acknowledges the following institutions and individuals for the use of their photographs and/or illustrations on the following pages: **Georgia State University Foundation, Pullen Library** p.43; **Lucille Handberg** p.88; **Hinckley Fire Museum** pp.217, 220; **Library of Congress** p.34; **Minnesota Historical Center** (special thanks to **Thomas O'Sullivan**, Curator of Art) pp.16, 22, 27, 30, 35, 37 (Lehman & Duval Lithograph), 39, 42, 44, 48-49, 55, 62, 73, 101, 124 (Mayo Clinic), 137, 140, 141, 144-145, 146, 153, 171, 182, 183, 203 (John Runk), 228, 248, 260, 269; **National Archives of Canada** p.31; **William J. Neill** p.46; **Pipestone County Museum** pp. 80, 81; **Underwood Photo Archives, San Francisco** pp.26, 29, 40, 47, 54, 107, 127, 163, 166, 231, 381; **University of Minnesota, James Ford Bell Library** p.275; and **Thomas Mark Szelog** p.10. The Publisher also thanks: **Candace Coar** for proofreading, **Jan Hughes** for her help with "TRAVELERS INFORMATION," **David Mahoney** for acting as professional reader, **Nicole Levine** for the index and for fact-checking, **Julie Searle** for the Minnesota history timeline, and **Michael Welch** for his essay, "Minneapolis Music."

For Kate

■ PHOTOGRAPHER'S ACKNOWLEDGMENT

A special thank you to my parents, Frank and Jean, who brought me up in Red Wing, Minnesota. It was an inspiration to return home and capture the beauty of my home state. I also want to thank Carole Lee for her extensive research and organization of the photographic shoots while we were on assignment in Minnesota.

C O N T E N T S

Facts About Minnesota 10
map of Minnesota 11
OVERVIEW 12
LANDSCAPE AND HISTORY 17
   Geology 17
   Geography and Climate 18
   History and Natural Features map 19
   Native American History 20
   Exploration and the Fur Trade 30
   America Flexes Its Might 33
   The Claim to Land 36
   Logging 38
   Settlement 40
   Civil War 41
   The Dakota War 42
   Railroads 45
   Immigration 47
   Labor and Industry 51
   Minnesotans Today 54
PRAIRIE PATH 58
   map of Southwest 59
   Continental Grassland 60
   Minnesota River Valley 66
   Minnesota River Driving Tour 67
   Coteau des Prairies 78
   Red River Valley 88
   map of the Red River Valley 91
SOUTHEASTERN HILLS 96
   map of Southeast 97
   Mississippi River History 98
   Following the Mississippi 103
   Lake Pepin 110

Wabasha, Weaver, and Winona 114
Coulee Country 117
Root River Valley 119
Trail of Trout Streams 122
Rochester and Vicinity 123
1-35: Towns Along the Way 126
TWIN CITIES: SHARED
RIVER AND HISTORY 136
   map of greater Minneapolis/St. Paul . . 138
   Early History of the Twin Cities . . . 140
   Fort Snelling 142
   The Mississippi River Today 148
ST. PAUL 156
   map of St. Paul 158
   Downtown St. Paul 158
   Historic Summit Avenue 170
   Como Area 175
   St. Paul Suburbs 176
MINNEAPOLIS 180
   St. Anthony Falls 182
   Downtown Minneapolis 188
   map of Minneapolis 188
   South Minneapolis 191
   Parks and Natural Areas 194
   University of Minnesota 196
   Minneapolis Suburbs 196
ST. CROIX RIVER 202
   St. Croix River Logging 203
   Wild and Scenic River 205
   map of St. Croix River Valley 205
   Up the River 206
   Stillwater 207

Up the River 206
Stillwater 207
Through the St. Croix Valley 210
Taylors Falls and St. Croix Dalles . . 211
Off the Beaten Path 214
Snake River 215
St. Croix State Park 221
Kettle River 221

NORTH SHORE AND
THE ARROWHEAD 223
Lake Superior 223
map of North Shore and Arrowhead. . 226
Duluth 227
North Shore Drive 236
Voyageurs' Highway 253
Boundary Waters 255
Voyageurs National Park 260
Home on the Iron Range 263
Driving Tour 267

NORTHERN REACHES 274
History, Treaties, and Angles 274
map of Northern Reaches. 276
Peatlands 278

GLACIAL LAKES 282
Down the Mississippi 283
map of Glacial Lakes region. 285
In the Beginning 287
Chippewa National Forest 289
Grand Rapids 292
Cuyuna Range 293
Brainerd Lakes 295
Mille Lacs 297
Little Falls and St. Cloud 300
Western Lakes 301

Gopher Prairie 302
Minnesota Vikings 305
Parks and Wildlife 306
Fergus Falls 310
Detroit Lakes 310

TRAVELERS INFORMATION 312
Area Codes 312
Metric Conversions 312
When to Come/Climate 312
Getting Around 313
map of restaurants and lodging 314
Food & Lodging by town 314
General Information Numbers 332
Festivals and Events 333

RECOMMENDED READING 338

INDEX 340

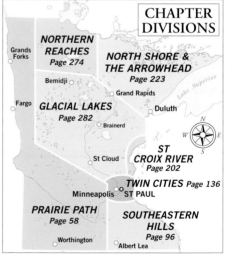

CHAPTER
DIVISIONS

NORTHERN
REACHES
Page 274

Grands
Forks

NORTH SHORE &
THE ARROWHEAD
Page 223

Bemidji

Grand Rapids

Lake Superior

Fargo

GLACIAL LAKES
Page 282

Duluth

Brainerd

St Cloud

ST
CROIX RIVER
Page 202

TWIN CITIES Page 136

Minneapolis ST PAUL

PRAIRIE PATH
Page 58

SOUTHEASTERN
HILLS
Page 96

Worthington

Albert Lea

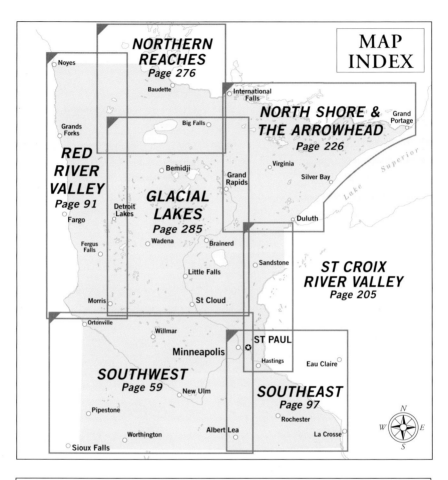

NORTHERN
REACHES
Page 276

Noyes

Baudette

Grands
Forks

Big Falls

International
Falls

NORTH SHORE &
THE ARROWHEAD
Page 226

Grand
Portage

MAP
INDEX

RED
RIVER
VALLEY
Page 91

Fargo

Fergus
Falls

Bemidji

Detroit
Lakes

GLACIAL
LAKES
Page 285

Wadena

Virginia

Grand
Rapids

Silver Bay

Duluth

Brainerd

Lake

Superior

Little Falls

Sandstone

ST CROIX
RIVER VALLEY
Page 205

Morris

St Cloud

Ortonville

Willmar

Minneapolis

ST PAUL

SOUTHWEST
Page 59

Pipestone

New Ulm

Hastings

Eau Claire

SOUTHEAST
Page 97

Rochester

Worthington

Albert Lea

La Crosse

Sioux Falls

N
W E
S

Maps

Overview 11
History and Natural Features 19
Southwest. 59
Red River Valley. 91
Southeast 97
Greater Minneapolis /St. Paul 138
Downtown St. Paul 158

Downtown Minneapolis 188
St. Croix River Valley. 205
North Shore and the Arrowhead . . 226
Northern Reaches 276
Glacial Lakes region 285
Restaurants and Lodging 314

Topical Essays

History Timeline 24–25
Places to Visit on the Mississippi River 152
Hinckley Fire 216–220
What the Land Meant 308–309
Minneapolis Music Scene 336-337

Literary Extracts

O. E. Rölvaag *on crossing the prairie* 50
Laura Ingalls Wilder *on hard times* 64
Pipestone legend 79
Diary from Woodward Farm 84
Maybelle Quarberg *on a summer evening* 93
Red River Valley 95
Howard Mohr *on talking weather* 107
Arriving in St. Paul 157
Patricia Hampl *on Summit Avenue* 170
Sigurd F. Olson *on spring* 206
WPA Guide *on the voyageurs of 1790* 250
Garrison Keillor *on Lake Wobegon* 296
Sinclair Lewis *on Sauk Centre* 304

FACTS ABOUT MINNESOTA
Land of 10,000 Lakes

Common loon

STATE NAME: Derived from two Dakota Indian words meaning "Clear Water"
NICKNAME: Gopher State, North Star State
CAPITAL: St. Paul
ENTERED UNION: May 11, 1858
STATE BIRD: Common loon
STATE FLOWER: Showy lady's-slipper
STATE TREE: Red pine
STATE FISH: Walleye

GEOGRAPHY:

Size:	84,402 sq miles, 12th largest
Highest point:	2,301' Eagle Mountain
Lowest point:	602' Lake Superior

FIVE LARGEST CITIES:

Minneapolis:	368,383
St. Paul:	272,235
Bloomington:	86,335
Duluth:	85,493
Rochester:	70,745

CLIMATE:

Hottest Day	Coldest Day	Mean annual rainfall	Mean annual snowfall
114° F	-60° F	19" northwest	70" northeast
Moorhead	at Tower	32" southeast	34" southwest
July 6, 1936	Feb. 2, 1996		

FAMOUS MINNESOTANS:

The Andrews Sisters, Warren Burger, Harry Blackmun, William O. Douglas, Bob Dylan, F. Scott Fitzgerald, Judy Garland, Jean Paul Getty, Hubert H. Humphrey, James "the Body" Ventury, Garrison Keillor, Prince, Jessica Lange, Sinclair Lewis, Charles A. Lindbergh, Jr., Walter Mondale, Jane Russell, Harrison Salisbury, Charles Schulz, Roy Wilkins

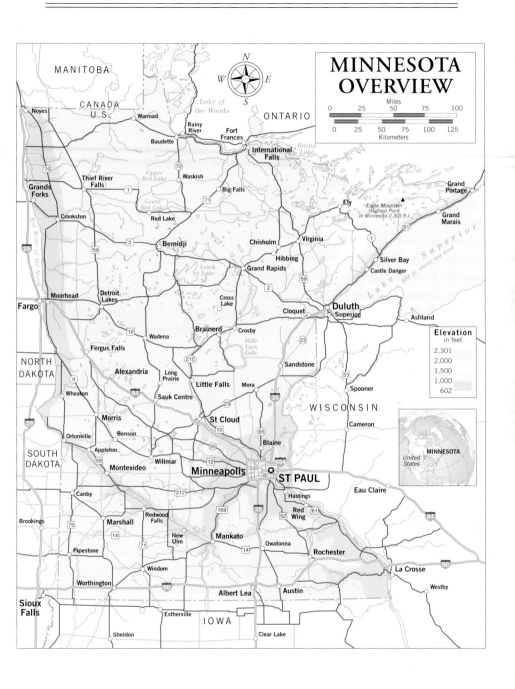

MINNESOTA OVERVIEW

O V E R V I E W

MINNESOTA'S deep woods, thousands of lakes, picturesque farmland, and progressive cities attract visitors who want to enjoy a convivial urban environment or the state's natural beauty and—secretly, perhaps—to brave the extremes of its climate. Though it boasts no mountains, Minnesota stands as a subtle topographical divide, each region distinct.

■ PRAIRIE PATH OF THE SOUTHWEST AND RED RIVER VALLEY

Once a seemingly endless grassland roamed by bison and Dakotas on horseback, the southwest is now Minnesota's richest farmland. Historic towns, monuments, and parks tell the tales of pioneers and their efforts to homestead on the prairie. *Pages 58–95*

■ SOUTHEASTERN HILLS AND MISSISSIPPI RIVER

Passed over by the last ice age, southeastern Minnesota is carved by deep river valleys. Picturesque towns from the 1800s sit in the shadows of limestone bluffs. Quick waters provide trout fishing and pleasant canoe trips. Trails and country roads make for pleasant bike routes. *Pages 96–135*

■ ST. PAUL

Born of the trade and exploration along the Mississippi River, Minneapolis and St. Paul grew up as rivals, each with its own character and sense of itself. Visit St. Paul, the state's capital, for historic sites such as the Landmark Center and the James J. Hill House, and for Victorian neighborhoods, intimate old bars, and ethnic restaurants. *Pages 156–179*

■ MINNEAPOLIS

Look to Minneapolis for its hustle and bustle, big business, and lively nightlife. Stroll the city's many lakeside parks or tour the remnants of its milling days. This is truly one of America's most "civilized" cities—friendly, safe, and clean. *Pages 180–195*

■ ST. CROIX RIVER VALLEY

Once the heart of Minnesota's white-pine logging industry, the St. Croix River Valley is today known for its natural beauty. The river was one of the nation's first designated wild and scenic rivers. Towns such as Stillwater and Taylors Falls are among the state's oldest and most picturesque. *Pages 202–222*

■ NORTH SHORE AND
THE ARROWHEAD

Lake Superior has a powerful presence.
People visit the rugged North Shore for
the crashing surf, tumultuous streams
and waterfalls, and brilliant fall color.
In the arrowhead-shaped tip of
northeastern Minnesota lie the famous
Boundary Waters Canoe Area Wilderness and the Mesabi Range, which
provided the iron that built early 20th-century America. *Pages 223–273*

■ NORTHERN REACHES

This is bog country where the landscape con-
sists of vast, wet flatlands. The Northwest
Angle, the northernmost point of the contigu-
ous United States, juts into the enormous
Lake of the Woods—a sportsman's paradise.
Pages 274–281

■ GLACIAL LAKES

When Minnesotans want to get away
they "go to the lake," often a cabin
tucked away among central Minnesota's
glacial hills and sparkling lakes. The
region caters to folks on vacation,
whether they fish, ride bikes, or play
golf. Of historic interest is the headwaters
of the Mississippi River. *Pages 282-311*

Gently rolling farmlands characterize the southern and western regions of Minnesota.

Minnehaha Falls was painted by Robert O. Sweeny in 1856. (Minnesota Historical Society)

LANDSCAPE AND HISTORY

IN NORTHERN MINNESOTA, SOMEWHERE NORTH OF HIBBING in a forest of conifers and aspen near County Road 5, lies a spot at once prosaic and remarkable. Here, at a point unmarked and for practical purposes inexact, a falling raindrop has an equal chance of draining east through a maze of tributaries to the Great Lakes and the Atlantic Ocean, north to Hudson Bay, or south down the Mississippi to the Gulf of Mexico. Because of this confluence of major divides, historian William E. Lass calls Minnesota "mother of three seas." I've never heard the phrase elsewhere, and I'm a life-long Minnesotan. But we'd do well to adopt it. It's a beautiful metaphor and symbolizes as well as anything the crossroads of geology, geography, landscapes, people, and cultures that make Minnesota the diverse state it is today.

■ GEOLOGY

Much of Minnesota sits atop rocks formed by volcanism billions of years ago, when the only life on earth were single-celled bacteria. Outcrops of gneiss in the Minnesota River Valley date to 3.6 billion years ago, making them nearly as old as any rocks discovered on earth. Greenstone, granite, and other largely igneous rocks along the Canadian border date to 2.7 billion years ago. And the cliffs of Lake Superior, remnants of a continental rift that nearly rent North America, are about 1.1 billion years old. The other prominent outcrops in the state—the bluff lands of the Mississippi south of the Twin Cities—formed hundreds of millions of years ago at the bottom of ancient seas.

Yet Minnesota looks the way it does not so much because of the ancient rock beneath it, but because of a geologic event that occurred on the threshold of the present. Less than two million years ago, changes in climate sent a series of glaciers sweeping southward from the Arctic. At intervals, ice stood more than a mile deep—five times the height of the Manhattan skyline—over much of North America, including Minnesota. The ice sheets moved earth on a continental scale, dredging up soil, sand, and gravel here and dropping it there to form ridges, hills, and gravelly plains. Glacial lakes, dammed by ice and filled with meltwater, spread across huge regions of the continent. The lakes fed torrential glacial rivers that carved deep valleys. When glacial ice melted from Minnesota a scant 10,000 years ago, much of the northern state was barren of soil. Central Minnesota was covered by rolling hills that cradled lakes in every valley. The southeast corner escaped the most recent wave of glaciation altogether, its intricate web of streams and valleys remaining intact.

■ GEOGRAPHY AND CLIMATE

If you were to climb to the top of Eagle Mountain, just a short hike from Superior National Forest Road 153, you could look across 13 miles of green forest to the infinite blue of Lake Superior. That short distance takes in Minnesota's entire topographic range. Eagle Mountain, at 2,301 feet above sea level, is the state's highest point; Lake Superior, about 602 feet, its lowest. That's all—1,699 feet from top to bottom, carried across 300 miles east to west and 400 miles north to south. Compared to many states, Minnesota is like a specimen under glass.

Yet to say that Minnesota is flat is a mistake. In the northeast, along the north shore of Lake Superior (simply the "North Shore," as any Minnesotan refers to it) rugged cliffs and hills as rough as quarry blocks rise above the lake. Rushing streams cut through narrow canyons in an irrepressible rush to the lake. A bit inland, against the Canadian border, canoe-country lakes fill basins of rugged granite. In southwestern Minnesota, the broad Minnesota River Valley seems to swallow the flat prairie and farmland that surrounds it. Along the Mississippi River, south of the Twin Cities, bluffs and coulees lie as folded and chaotic as an unmade bed.

The rumpled land left by the glaciers forms the basins of thousands of lakes. Minnesota's slogan, "Land of Ten Thousand Lakes," sells the state short. By latest count of the Minnesota Department of Natural Resources, the number of lakes 10 acres or larger is 11,842. Of those, 201 are called Mud Lake. It is the most common lake name in the state, though tourism boosters don't advertise the fact.

In Minnesota, the Great Plains and prairies of the west meet eastern woodlands and the coniferous forest of the north. The hand that paints this pattern is largely climate—especially annual rainfall and mean temperature.

Mean temperature, indeed. Minnesota's renown—in fact, a kind of perverse pride—derives from its weather. The climate is continental, with short hot summers and harsh winters. Our temperature extremes span 174 degrees—without the benefit of significant changes in elevation. Spring and fall pass as quickly as meteors. My favorite description of Minnesota's climate is this: Six months of winter; six months of tough sledding.

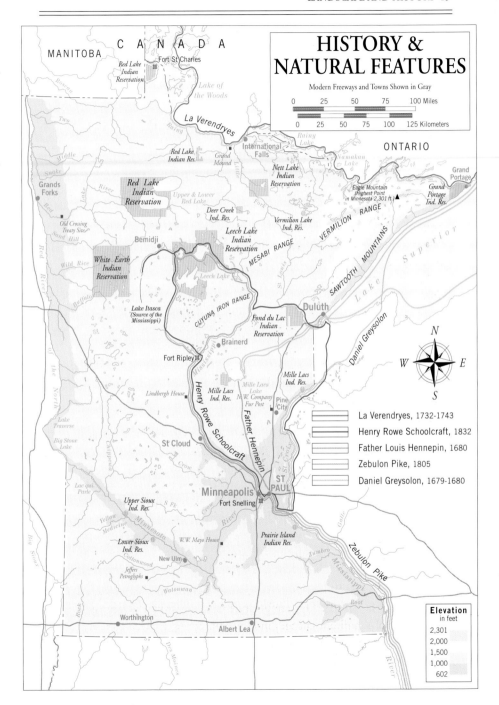

HISTORY & NATURAL FEATURES

Modern Freeways and Towns Shown in Gray

0   25   50   75   100 Miles

0   25   50   75   100   125 Kilometers

La Verendryes, 1732-1743

Henry Rowe Schoolcraft, 1832

Father Louis Hennepin, 1680

Zebulon Pike, 1805

Daniel Greysolon, 1679-1680

MANITOBA

CANADA

ONTARIO

Red Lake Indian Reservation

Fort St Charles

Lake of the Woods

Rainy Lake

Grand Portage

Red Lake Indian Res.

Grand Mound

International Falls

Namakan Lake

Nett Lake Indian Reservation

Eagle Mountain (Highest Point in Minnesota 2,301 ft.)

Grand Portage Ind. Res.

Grands Forks

Red Lake Indian Reservation

Upper & Lower Red Lake

Deer Creek Ind. Res.

Vermilion Lake Ind. Res.

VERMILION RANGE

SAWTOOTH MOUNTAINS

Old Crossing Treaty Site

Bemidji

Leech Lake Indian Reservation

MESABI RANGE

Lake Superior

White Earth Indian Reservation

Leech Lake

Lake Itasca (Source of the Mississippi)

CUYUNA IRON RANGE

Fond du Lac Indian Reservation

Duluth

Daniel Greysolon

Brainerd

Fort Ripley

Lindbergh House

Mille Lacs Ind. Res.

Mille Lacs Lake

N.W. Company Fur Post

Mille Lacs Ind. Res.

Pine City

Henry Rowe Schoolcraft

Father Hennepin

St Cloud

Lake Traverse

Big Stone Lake

Lac qui Parle

Upper Sioux Ind. Res.

Minneapolis

ST PAUL

Fort Snelling

Lower Sioux Ind. Res.

W.W. Mayo House

New Ulm

Prairie Island Indian Res.

Jeffers Petroglyphs

Zebulon Pike

Worthington

Albert Lea

N W E S

Elevation in feet
2,301
2,000
1,500
1,000
602

■ NATIVE AMERICAN HISTORY

The first "Minnesotans" were the distant ancestors of nomadic people who crossed the land bridge between what are now Siberia and Alaska in various waves of migration beginning perhaps 30,000 years ago and ending perhaps 4,000 years ago. By the close of the ice age the descendants of these early migrants had spread throughout the New World, including what is now Minnesota.

Imagine what they might have seen: To the north, glaciers still covered the land. Glacial Lake Agassiz stretched infinitely to the horizon, a virtual inland sea. The land nearest the glaciers was covered with tundra or runty spruce. These humans stepped into an unpeopled land, filled with huge beasts such as musk oxen, giant beavers, mammoths, and mastodons. By the account of scientists, early North America would have rivaled precolonial Africa for its plenitude of game.

We know these people today as Paleo-Indians. They lived in small hunting groups. They hunted with spears, tipped with finely wrought stone points, and thrown with a lever called an atlatl to give their weapons greater velocity. Their prey—the source of their food, clothes and perhaps their shelters—included the large animals of the day, including bison and, most likely, mammoths.

In the millennia following the retreat of the glaciers, many of the large herbivores vanished, possibly driven to extinction by the raw efficiency of this new bipedal hunter, perhaps done in by changes in climate and vegetation that favored some animals, such as bison, over other animals, such as mammoths. Musk oxen retreated, like the ice, into the far reaches of the north.

The economy of the ancient people changed as well. The bands became ever more skillful in adapting to their surroundings. They hunted remaining large animals, such as bison, but turned their attention also to plentiful small game. Beginning about 8,000 years ago, they discovered new ways of working stone to make axes and wood-working gouges. They discovered how to fashion the nearly pure copper nuggets, found in outcrops in the St. Croix River basin and points east, into knives and awls. We call this culture, to the extent we know them through their artifacts, the Eastern Archaic Tradition or, more specifically, the Old Copper Complex. One Old Copper site at the source of the Mississippi held the remains of a dog, the earliest evidence in Minnesota of a domestic animal. Marine shells found in Old Copper sites suggest a network of trade already had spread across North America.

The population of the region grew as people continued to become more adept at exploiting resources at hand. Beginning about 2,500 years ago the first pottery appeared, defining an era known now as the Woodland Tradition. Indians learned to harvest and store the abundant aquatic grass known as wild rice, and abandoned the atlatl and spear for the bow and arrow. Indians of the region began burying their dead in earthen mounds, occasionally with grave goods. Some mounds, such as the Grand Mound along the Rainy River, grew to huge proportions as successive generations were buried within. Tools and projectile points diversify, but copper is used more sparingly, perhaps because large pure nuggets were becoming scarce or too valuable in trade to use for tools that could be made instead from stone.

About 1,000 years ago agriculture appeared in far southwestern Minnesota and the Mississippi River Valley in the southeast, the seeds and know-how coming from agricultural tribes to the south. People of this tradition, called the Mississippian, cultivated corn, beans, squash, sunflowers, and tobacco. Hunting and fishing remained important. In the prairies of western Minnesota, bison continued as a mainstay. Tribes throughout the region made pipes of the soft catlinite stone dug by many tribes at the site now known as Pipestone National Monument.

What became of the Woodland and Mississippian Indians, or the more specific groups that were a part of them, such as the Blackduck, Selkirk, or Psinomani? Did they become the Arapaho, Cree, and Dakota of historic times? A chasm exists between the prehistoric and historic because the people who lived in North America, despite a wonderful diversity of customs and languages, did not write. Archeologists have been reluctant to bridge that chasm on the evidence of little more than stone tools, bones, and pottery.

The picture is complicated by the tremendous flux that existed between people in the days before Europeans arrived, for the white man arrived earlier than he knew. His trade goods and diseases preceded him, spreading inland shortly after Europeans landed on the Atlantic coast. By some estimates, smallpox eventually visited virtually every tribe. The initial epidemic may have killed 75 percent of the inhabitants. The European saw only "shadows of the powerful societies that had occupied the area in 1500," writes anthropologist Karl H. Schlesier. "It was easy

This portrait of Sioux chief Okee-makee-quid was painted by Henry Inman during the 1830s. (Minnesota Historical Society)

for European colonials here and elsewhere to raise flags and take possession in the names of distant kings when the original masters of the land had perished."

The push and pull of trade and the vacuum left by disease set tribes in motion across North America, perhaps as never before. The horse, introduced to the New World by Spanish conquistadors, reached the region in the 1700s. Acquisition of this marvelous new means of transportation made the buffalo easier to hunt. Tribes such as the Cheyenne, who had hunted and farmed on the western edge of Minnesota, moved west to hunt buffalo full-time as Great Plains nomads. When whites first arrived in Minnesota, the Assiniboin occupied the aspen parklands of the northwest. The Cree lived along the rocky lakes and deep forests of the north. The agricultural Oto lived along the southern border, and the Iowa along the Mississippi bluffs and bottom lands in the southeast. The Fox lived along the St. Croix River. But the great belly of the state belonged to the Dakota.

One of the best early written descriptions of the Dakota comes from Samuel W. Pond, a Congregational missionary who came to Minnesota to plow the virgin earth of pagan tribes for the Lord. He lived among the Dakota for two decades, becoming fluent in their language. He had minimal success in converting the Indians, but provided an invaluable resource in his book *The Dakota or Sioux in Minnesota As They Were in 1834.* The Dakota, also called Sioux (a term derived from the Ojibwa Indian word for viper), were closely related ethnically and culturally to the famous western Sioux tribes (known for their dialect as Lakota) that warred with the U.S. Army in the closing days of the frontier.

The Dakota, Pond wrote, lived by large lakes and rivers in summer houses made of elm bark supported by a framework of poles. During their hunting forays, the Dakota stayed in tepees of dressed bison skins.

Though the Dakota raised some corn, harvested wild plants for food and medicine, and often fished, they were hunters by tradition and necessity. Venison was their staple. Other game included muskrats, occasional elk, and bears when they were to be found. Dakota in western Minnesota killed bison.

One of their most important food-gathering ventures was the fall deer hunt when the people of the settlement split into small parties and set out in various directions. They hauled their goods and tepees on travois behind dogs and horses. The labor was grueling. "They did not contrive to live without hard labor," Pond writes.

■ HISTORY TIMELINE

1679   French explorer Daniel Greysolon, sieur Duluth, leads expedition into eastern and northern Minnesota.

1680   Father Louis Hennepin travels to southern Minnesota via the Mississippi River and sees the Falls of St. Anthony.

1727   French trading posts established as fur trade flourishes.

1763   The French and Indian War results in British control of Minnesota.

1805   Twenty-six-year-old Zebulon Pike explores the Minnesota territory established after the Louisiana Purchase of 1803.

1825   U.S. government sponsors a conference with hundreds of Indian leaders to establish land boundaries.

1832   Henry Schoolcraft, aided by an Ojibwa named Ozawindib, finds the source of the Mississippi River and names it Lake Itasca.

1857   Publisher and political writer Jane Grey Swisshelm founds the *St. Cloud Visitor*. Her editorials advocate women's rights and abolition of slavery.

1858   Minnesota joins the Union as a free state.

1859   The first commercial flour mill in Minnesota opens at the Falls of St. Anthony.

1862   Dakotas—short on food and deprived of land—rebel, killing 500 settlers and soldiers. Their uprising is crushed with disastrous results for the Dakotas.

1863   By this date, the Dakota and Ojibwa have given over nearly all of their ancestral lands through government treaties.

1876   Masses of grasshoppers devour wheat crops, consuming even laundry hanging on clotheslines as they move through fields.

1884   First iron ore shipped from the Vermilion Range. Six years later the Mesabi iron ore deposits are discovered.

1889	The first cooperative cheese factory and creamery opens in McLeod County.
1889	The Mayo family founds the Mayo Clinic in Rochester.
1927	Minnesotan Charles Lindbergh, Jr., makes non-stop solo flight across the Atlantic.
1930	Minnesota author Sinclair Lewis is first American to receive the Nobel Prize in literature.
1932	The skeleton of "Minnesota Woman," estimated to be 8,000 years old, is discovered near Pelican Rapids.
WWII	The Andrews Sisters from Minneapolis cheer troops with "Boogie Woogie Bugle Boy of Company B."
1948	Hubert Humphrey is elected State Senator as a Democratic-Farmer-Labor Party candidate. College professor Eugene McCarthy, also DFL, becomes U.S. Representative.
1940	Armistice Day blizzard buries state killing over 90 people and is considered the worst storm in state history.
1961	Baseball Player Roger Maris from Hibbing hits 61 home runs in one season.
1961	Chemist Melvin Calvin of St. Paul wins Nobel Prize for his work with photosynthesis.
1963	The Tyrone Guthrie Theatre is founded in Minneapolis.
1965-69	Hubert Humphrey serves as Lyndon Johnson's vice president.
1968	Poet Robert Bly of Madison wins the National Book Award.
1970s	Humorist Garrison Keillor describes the folks of fictional "Lake Woebegon" in his popular "A Prairie Home Companion" radio variety show, broadcast from St. Paul.
1977–80	Walter Mondale from Minnesota is U.S. vice president under Jimmy Carter.
1987	Minnesota Twins win World Series. Four years later they win again.

Obtossaway, a chief of the Minnesota Ojibwa, was photographed by the Detroit Photographic Company in 1903. (Underwood Photo Archives, San Francisco)

Continued missionary Samuel Pond:

> *In* tropical countries, where houses and clothing are not needed and food in abundance grows spontaneously, man may live without much labor, but not in Minnesota. Neither the farmer nor the hunter can get a living in this climate without working for it. . . . The Indian often went out after deer with as much reluctance as the worn-out farm laborer feels when going to the harvest field, and only went because he must hunt or he and his family would starve. . . . If the hunt proved a failure, as it sometimes did, they had little to carry home. On the upper Minnesota river, hunting parties in winter were sometimes so destitute of provisions that they ate their horses, if they had any, and numbers of Indians perished on their way home.

Dakota primacy in Minnesota wouldn't last long. For, about the time Europeans arrived in North America, a tribe known as the Ojibwa was migrating from its homeland at the mouth of the St. Lawrence River eastward toward the Great Lakes. By their own accounts, the Ojibwa suffered at the hands of their perennial and

An idealized and well-posed photograph of an Indian family titled Return of the Hunters. *(Underwood Photo Archives, San Francisco)*

powerful enemies, the Iroquois and other eastern tribes, and also suffered a sort of spiritual malaise.

The Ojibwa looked for deliverance in a vision—a great seashell that alternately rose and set in the west, leading the Ojibwa westward, according to historian William W. Warren, who tapped the tribal memory of the Ojibwa in the mid-1800s to describe the cosmology of his ancestors. Each time the shell sank from sight into yet another of the Great Lakes, "death daily visited the wigwams of our forefathers," Warren writes. Could these have been the smallpox plagues that preceded the appearance of the white man? The shell eventually led the Ojibwa around both shores of Lake Superior, where they were in continual contact with the Dakota, just as the earliest Europeans were also entering the region.

Unlike the Dakota, who moved between the prairies of the west and the woodlands of eastern Minnesota, the Ojibwa traditionally lived in deep forest. They were masters of birch-bark, using the tough covering for their wigwams, baskets, and light, durable canoes. They believed in a Great Spirit, though many lesser spirits pervaded nature. Their most important institution was the Midewiwin, roughly translated as the Grand Medicine Society. Dead were buried, usually sitting, facing west, with goods, such as gun, blanket, kettle, fire steel, flint and moccasins, to take down the "road of souls." In fact, one of the most starkly haunting expressions of grief I have encountered was recorded by missionary Joseph A. Gilfillan on the White Earth reservation. As an old Ojibwa man beheld the body of his daughter, with a sadness and sense of longing I can only imagine by thinking of my own little girl, he began, "Your feet are now on the road of souls, my daughter."

The Ojibwa called themselves Anishinabeg, "spontaneous man," according to Warren. They also used the name Ojibwa, though its origins were obscure. The word itself, Warren writes, means "to roast until puckered up." Often it is taken to refer to the distinctive toe of Ojibwa moccasins. Warren preferred to believe it referred to the torture of prisoners of war by fire, a practice not unique to the Ojibwa.

War between the Dakota and Ojibwa appears to have begun the moment the Ojibwa ventured into the territory of the Dakota. The Ojibwa, with ties farther east than the Dakota, were the first to obtain guns from traders. Better armed, they were able to drive the Fox and Dakota away from Lake Superior.

The Ojibwa weren't content to stop at Superior's shore, but carried the battle inland, slaughtering their enemies in an attack on two large Dakota settlements on Mille Lacs, in the center of what is now Minnesota. Next, the Ojibwa drove the

Dakota south through the St. Croix Valley. The French, by now trading in the territory, were desperate to put an end to hostilities. Not only were Frenchmen often killed in the crossfire, but continual battle distracted the Indians from fur trapping and trade.

During the 1700s, the Ojibwa forced the Dakota from settlements at Leech, Winnibigoshish, Cass, and Red lakes in northern Minnesota. Raid followed upon raid, retribution upon retribution, though individual bands among the two nations attempted to avoid the fray and coexist in peace. Historian William Warren writes:

> *In* these days, the hunter moved through the dense forests in fear and trembling. He paddled his light canoe over the calm bosom of a lake or down the rapid current of a river, in search of game to clothe and feed his children, expecting each moment that from behind a tree, an embankment of sand along the lake shore, or a clump of bushes on the river bank, would speed the bullet or arrow which would lay him low in death.

Frontier artist Seth Eastman painted this watercolor of Wah-Ba-Sha Village on the Mississippi, *in the mid-1840s. (Minnesota Historical Society)*

■ EXPLORATION AND THE FUR TRADE

As Indian tribes warred, France's rivalry with Britain and Spain for North America propelled its explorers through the Great Lakes region, part of what was then known as New France. Who headed the first party of Europeans to see what is now Minnesota? Possibly Pierre Esprit Radisson and Médard Chouart, the Sieur de Groseilliers, who explored the south shore of Lake Superior in 1656–57. They traveled inland to meet the Dakota Indians, and may have traveled as far west as present-day Minnesota.

Daniel Greysolon, sieur Duluth, met the Dakota at the present site of Duluth in 1679 and followed them inland to their large village on the south shore of Mille Lacs in central Minnesota. Sponsored by merchants in Montreal and Quebec, Duluth aimed to establish trade with the Dakotas. He also claimed the area for Louis XIV. Of course, it must have come as quite a surprise to the Dakota to be declared subjects of the French king.

The following year, the Dakota captured three Frenchmen on the Mississippi River. The captives included a Belgian priest named Louis Hennepin. According to Mississippi historian Timothy Severin:

An anonymous portrait of Father Louis Hennepin, circa 1694. (Minnesota Historical Society)

*F*or the next three months Hennepin and the two voyageurs were ignobly shunted up and down the river by their captors, who considered the white men something of a curiosity. Until his capture Hennepin had been boasting of his strength and physical prowess; once he fell into the hands of the Indians he wailed loudly about the agonies he endured while living their way of life. Before long he had so irritated the two voyageurs that they refused to travel in the same canoe with him.

French-Canadian canoemen of the fur trade, known as "voyageurs," were hardy individuals, capable of carrying ninety-pound packs of traders' goods across Minnesota's lakes and rivers. (National Archives of Canada)

Daniel Duluth soon negotiated Hennepin's release. When Hennepin returned to France, he wrote *Description of Louisiana,* introducing the Upper Mississippi region to Europe. According to Severin:

> *F*ather Louis Hennepin was a liar with a plainly odious personality whose writings were largely stolen from other authors. . . . His books were top-heavy with obvious inaccuracies, slanders, flattery, and boasts. . . . His readers loved it . . . Hennepin obliged them by transmuting his brief Canadian career into a breath-taking account of an intrepid priest facing impossible obstacles.

Nonetheless, Hennepin had one accomplishment to his name: He explored for Europe the Mississippi along what is now southeastern Minnesota to St. Anthony Falls, the present site of Minneapolis.

A distant force propelled events in what was to become Minnesota. That force was something as frivolous as fashion—a predilection for felt hats, which were pressed from the finely barbed underfur of the beaver. As beavers became scarce in the Old World, beaver pelts became the principal object of trade between Europeans and

Indian tribes in the New World. French traders carried woolen blankets and iron knives, axes, and kettles to the Indians. The Indians reciprocated with pelts.

To further trade and their country's imperialistic claims, French explorers sought a water route through North America to the Pacific. Among the explorers who believed this "northwest passage" ran through the Lake Superior country was Pierre Gaultier, Sieur de la Vérendrye. La Vérendrye's immediate task was to solidify the French trade route with the Indians in the country north and west of Lake Superior. The passion that burned within him, however, was the discovery of a route to the Pacific.

La Vérendrye questioned local Indians for information, among them Cree, Assiniboin, and Ojibwa. One Ojibwa, Auchagah, sketched for La Vérendrye a birch-bark map that laid out, lake by lake and portage by portage, an intricate route through the border region of northern Minnesota to Lake of the Woods and beyond. La Vérendrye followed the route in 1731, opening a major trade route to the heart of the North American continent. The Pacific, however, would always elude the explorer.

As Indians came in contact with Europeans, they universally discarded their stone knives and ceramic cookware in favor of the iron trade goods. In this respect, the commercial culture of the European was an abrasive, to which the Indian culture was absolutely without resistance. Our species is always willing to believe that we can borrow one thing without taking the rest. But soon, having taken the most treasured of trade goods, the natives were forced to take the rest—their economy turned entirely toward procuring furs for trade and their way of life was irrevocably changed. As a consequence of the trade, fur-bearers became scarce, Ojibwas invaded Dakota lands in search of game, and Indians began a growing dependence on the foreigners. Still, it was a willing dependence. Writes Ojibwa historian William W. Warren, "The Ojibwas learned to love the French people, for the Frenchmen, possessing a character of great plasticity, easily assimilated themselves to the customs and mode of life of their red brethren." The French respected rites, ceremonies, and the political rank of clans and individuals.

The tribes soon discovered there was less plasticity in the character of the British, who took control of the region in 1763 after victory in the French and Indian War. Still, while the fur trade and exploration of the region fell to the British, the French legacy persisted in names such as Mille Lacs and St. Louis, and the *chansons* of the voyageurs, French-speaking Canadians who performed the grunt work of the fur trade.

The fur trade opened up under British supervision. The Hudson's Bay Company operated on the shore of its namesake, inviting traders and Indians to deliver furs to its door. The upstart North West Company, run by a partnership of Scots, took the trade to the Indians. The company established its inland headquarters on Lake Superior at Grand Portage and sent its brigades of canoes and voyageurs along the route pioneered by countless generations of Indians and, only later, La Vérendrye.

Despite the American victory in the Revolutionary War, British companies traded with impunity in a land where the international border had not yet been clearly delineated. But the British presence in Minnesota didn't last. The British became concerned that Grand Portage would be declared American soil and subject to American tax. In 1803 The North West Company abandoned Grand Portage and withdrew to Canada, even through the British continued to maintain a few posts in Minnesota's rugged interior.

■ AMERICA FLEXES ITS MIGHT

With the acquisition of the Louisiana Purchase from France in 1803 (which included land that would become southern and western Minnesota), President Thomas Jefferson sought to learn more about this huge new addition to the United States and to build military posts to limit British influence in the area. Among the explorers sent into the new territory was 26-year-old Lt. Zebulon Pike, who started up the Mississippi from St. Louis in 1805 with a 20-man party and orders to choose sites for army posts, gather information on British traders on the Upper Mississippi, and strike a truce between Ojibwa and Dakota.

As Severin notes, the U.S. Army was parsimonious in outfitting the trip. No navigator was provided; Pike's scientific and navigational instruments consisted of a watch, thermometer, and crude device to determine latitude. He was assigned no interpreter, even though Pike was to negotiate with Indian tribes, many speaking vastly different languages.

Pike nearly swamped on windswept Lake Pepin. On at least two occasions his expedition was salvaged by Scots traders, though Pike would barely acknowledge their help. At Prairie du Chien, Pike picked up a French trader as an interpreter.

On the first day of fall, Pike camped at the confluence of the Mississippi and Minnesota rivers, and purchased the site from the Dakota Indians for what later would become the first military post in the area. Writes Severin:

> *F*rom start to finish there is something uncomfortably suspicious about Pike's dealing with the Indians. To begin with, the Sioux were notorious procrastinators. . . . Under normal conditions the Sioux would refuse to make agreements of any kind without long consultations beforehand. . . . Yet, in Pike's case, a young army lieutenant managed to force through in the space of a single day a treaty which gave the white man effective control of the upper Mississippi. . . . The most charitable conclusion, if Pike is not to be branded a cheat, is that neither he nor the Sioux sachems had any understanding of each other's motives. . . . The chiefs probably had no inkling that as a result of accepting Pike's glittering presents the U.S. Army would soon arrive to claim sovereignty and build a fort on their territory.

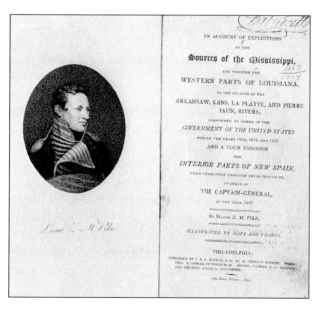

Zebulon Pike's memoir Expeditions to the Sources of the Mississippi *recounts his adventures exploring the region and his purported purchase of the site for Fort Snelling from the Dakota Indians. (Library of Congress)*

John Casper Wild's painting of Fort Snelling in 1844. (Minnesota Historical Society)

Pike continued up the Mississippi. He built sleds to haul his barges around St. Anthony Falls. He received help, advice, and food along the way from the North West Company posts scattered along the route. By winter he reached the North West Company post on Leech Lake in northern Minnesota. There, despite the help given him by the traders, he confronted the director of the Leech Lake post. He ordered his men to shoot down the British flag and warned the post's director of the consequences of operating in American territory.

America did little to back up Pike's threats. The British continued to trade. The Dakota and Ojibwa continued to war with one another. U.S. influence in the area did not truly begin until after the War of 1812. American fur trader John Jacob Astor bought North West Company posts in United States. A military fort was begun in 1819 at the strategic site Pike had purchased years earlier. Built under the command of Col. Josiah Snelling, for whom it was later named, "Fort Snelling loomed above the wilderness like a medieval fortress, its stone walls and massive towers a symbol of American strength and permanence in an area accustomed to but small and temporary fur posts," writes historian William E. Lass.

Under the protection of the fort, the fur trade continued under American traders, men like Joe Rolette (who in later years as a territorial legislator would travel by dog sled from Pembina in the northwest to the capital in St. Paul). Joseph Renville worked the Lac qui Parle area in western Minnesota, where, according to Lass, "he built a rude stockade and presided like a feudal baron." Louis Provençalle traded from his post at Traverse des Sioux on the Minnesota River. One of the young, promising traders was Henry H. Sibley, future first governor of the state. Sibley often hunted with the Dakota, who called him "walker in the pines."

Despite the presence of capable young traders such as Sibley, the era of the fur trader was drawing to a close. Fashionable European men wore silk hats now, not felt, a trend that undercut the price for furs. More important, farmers, loggers, and land speculators had designs on the land that would make fur-bearers scarce and render the old system of fur trading—with free access to open land—impossible.

"Old traders…were important characters here," Samuel Pond wrote wistfully.

> They … were almost the only representatives of the civilized world in this far-off country. The old trading posts were not regarded with indifference by the traveler, for, from one end of the land to the other, he found no other shelter from the inclemency of the weather, except the little, crowded tepees of the Indians, and they had no fixed abiding place more than the wild buffalo.

■ THE CLAIM TO LAND

If the British showed less plasticity than the French, the Americans showed least of all, for they were no mere transitory fur traders. They intended to transform the land into a garden, to make it over into their own image, and this attitude informed their dealing with the land and its original inhabitants. This new era would have dire consequences for the Indians living here, for while they could coexist with traders and even prosper through trade, their lifestyle of hunting and gathering would prove incompatible with the loggers and farmers who would stream to the territory.

George W. Featherstonhaugh explored the Minnesota River Valley in 1835. British-born, he returned to England and wrote *Canoe Voyage to the Minnay-Sotor,* the first time the future name of the state appeared prominently in print. More to the point, he characterized the frontiersmen of the region as land-hungry ruffians.

And so they were. Indeed, settlers not only were hungry for land; by their oning, the land was their destiny, expansion their crusade. To the north grew tremendous forests of tall, straight, valuable white pine. To the south and west lay fertile prairies that had never felt the steel plow. Lumbermen and immigrants looked hungrily to Minnesota. Only the Indians stood in the way.

Ojibwa historian William Warren wrote, "One of their old men . . . prophesied that the white spirits would come in numbers like sand on the lake shore, and would sweep the red race from the hunting grounds which the Great Spirit had given them."

Indeed, it was so. In 1825, the U.S. government sponsored a conference at Prairie du Chien, Wisconsin, with hundreds of Indian leaders. Ojibwa and Dakota delegations agreed to a boundary between the two groups from Chippewa Falls, Wisconsin to Moorhead, Minnesota. Peace didn't exactly break out between the two tribes. The government had no effective way of enforcing the treaty. Nor did the government, by the Indians' way of thinking, have any real role in Ojibwa-Dakota relations. The agreement, most importantly, assigned land to each tribe, preparing the way for future land cessions.

If any Dakota chiefs entertained notions of resisting the impending land grab, most were convinced by a trip to Washington, D.C., that the newcomers' numerical

View of the Great Treaty held at Prairie du Chien, Wisconsin, in September 1825.
(Lehman & Duval Lithograph, Minnesota Historical Society)

and technical superiority was overwhelming. Giving up land seemed inevitable, and a treaty was preferable to annihilation.

In 1837 Dakota bands sold all their lands east of the Mississippi (generally east of the Twin Cities). A treaty with the Ojibwa tribes in the same year opened old-growth pine lands in northern Wisconsin and east-central Minnesota to loggers. In 1851 the U.S. government negotiated what by now must have seemed inevitable: the sale for pennies an acre of all Dakota land in Minnesota (essentially all of the southwestern prairie) except a string of tiny reservations along the Minnesota River. By 1855 the Ojibwa had sold most of their land in northern Minnesota. Additional laws at the turn of the century would pry even many of these lands from the Ojibwa to the benefit of lumbermen and settlers.

■ LOGGING

From the banks of the Penobscot and Androscoggin in Maine, loggers flooded the St. Croix and Rum River valleys. According to the saying of the time, "Maineites knew logging." With the ring of the ax and song of the saw, they felled a forest

Most of Minnesota's old-growth forests were gone by the 1930s. Second growth is pictured here.

Whiteface River Drive, Spring, 1924 *by Carl Henrikson illustrates a method of moving logs downstream to be milled. (Minnesota Historical Society)*

that had never tasted steel. Virgin white pine, four feet across the trunk and more than 100 feet high, were sectioned and skidded to nearby streams. With spring freshets, the rivers carried the state's old-growth pine forests to sawmills in Stillwater, Winona, and Minneapolis, for a time the greatest sawmilling center in the world. The Mississippi carried rafts of lumber to growing cities such as St. Louis.

By 1900 Minnesota cut more wood than any other state. Mills at St. Anthony cut more lumber than any other. About 40,000 lumberjacks worked Minnesota's woods. The prevailing attitude toward our old-growth forests was embedded in Horace Greeley's remark of 1865: "This region will breathe freer when its last pine log is cut, run, sawed, rafted, and sold."

James Madison Goodhue, publisher of Minnesota's first newspaper, wrote in 1852 that the "centuries will hardly exhaust the pineries above us." But the virgin pine of the St. Croix and Rum river valleys virtually disappeared by the early 1900s. The last log raft floated down the St. Croix in 1915. By then, most lumbermen had moved on to forests in northern Minnesota. There, the virgin pine forests would last only 20 years more.

■ SETTLEMENT

According to an adage of the era, the plow follows the ax. Farmers filled the vacuum left by loggers. On the prairies of the southwest, the work of clearing the land had already been accomplished by the drier, warmer climate and the continual wildfires set by Indians to drive game, clear brush, and invigorate grazing lands for wildlife such as bison.

Because the new farmers did not know Minnesota's soil or climate, they planted a bit of everything, even tobacco. Many farmers planted wheat because it could be grown with little soil preparation. These frontier farms were small, since a farmer wielding a scythe could harvest barely more than two acres a day. Minnesota's population exploded. In 1850 about 6,000 whites lived in the territory. During the next decade, their number swelled thirtyfold.

A Minnesota farm scene in the 1870s showing an old method of stacking shocks of grain.
(Underwood Photo Archives, San Francisco)

■ CIVIL WAR

Though Minnesota entered the Union in 1858 as a free state, the issue of slavery burned in Minnesota's politics and newspaper columns in the years leading up to the Civil War. St. Anthony and Minneapolis, the two towns that grew on either side of the Mississippi at St. Anthony Falls, were popular summer retreats for southern slave owners. Should owners be allowed to bring their slaves? If so, should the slaves continue to be slaves? Those were serious issues for many Minnesotans. Proclaimed one newspaper:

> *We* don't believe in slavery, and we rejoice that Minnesota is a free state, but when people come up here from the South, and, relying upon the honor and good faith of our people, bring along with them their servants, we don't think it looks well for us to interfere.

Minnesota's most notable brush with the slavery issue stemmed from an incident that occurred in 1820, before statehood. A U.S. Army officer brought his slave from the slave state of Missouri to assignments in Illinois and later, Fort Snelling. The slave was Dred Scott. Scott eventually returned with his master to Missouri, but when the owner died, Scott sued for his freedom because he had lived in free territory where slavery was outlawed. But the U.S. Supreme Court ruled that Scott's slave status prevented him from suing in federal court. The court also ruled that territories could not prohibit slavery.

Happier circumstances prevailed in the case of Eliza Winston, a young slave who accompanied her owners on a vacation to Minneapolis. There Winston met Emily Grey, a free black woman. With the help of white friends, Grey and her husband persuaded a Minneapolis judge that Winston was held against her will in a free state. The judge agreed and sent a sheriff to the Lake Harriet home where Winston and her owners stayed. Winston won her freedom, though a proslavery mob vandalized the house where she was believed to be staying. The Greys' house, too, was mobbed. Winston, however, escaped safely to Canada.

Antislavery feelings were sufficient to rally support for the Civil War. When Fort Sumter fell to Southern troops in 1861, Minnesota's second governor, Alexander Ramsey, was in Washington, D.C. He immediately contacted Secretary of War Simon Cameron, an old acquaintance, to volunteer 1,000 Minnesota troops, the first "volunteers" of the war. Others followed and engaged in some of the bloodiest battles of the war. In all, about 24,000 Minnesotans served in the

Third Minnesota Volunteer Infantry Entering Little Rock *by Stanley Arthurs, 1910.*
(Minnesota Historical Society)

Union army. Their most famous engagement was the First Minnesota Regiment's charge at Gettysburg. No Civil War battle touched Minnesota soil. It was another war that brought bloody warfare to the state.

■ THE DAKOTA WAR

The treaties proved disastrous for the Indians, especially the semi-nomadic Dakota, who suddenly were confined to a string of tiny reservations along the Minnesota and Mississippi rivers. The Dakota were outraged when the federal government resorted to a clause in the treaty to vacate and sell the reservations on the north side of the river to satisfy land speculators and farmers. Dakota anger was further fueled by the disregard, corruption, and incompetence of the Indian agents who were supposed to (but often did not) protect the Dakotas' interest. Some Dakota

fueled by the disregard, corruption, and incompetence of the Indian agents who were supposed to (but often did not) protect the Dakotas' interest. Some Dakota relented to the government's policy of assimilating the hunters into white society, in essence, making them farmers. These "cut hairs" converted to Christianity and learned white methods of farming and, in doing so, antagonized the "blanket Sioux," who began to look for an opportunity to expel whites from the valley.

In summer of 1862, annuities to buy food didn't arrive. Starving Dakotas at the two Minnesota River agencies demanded provisions, but agents refused to open the warehouses until the annuities arrived. (One agent did later relent.) Andrew Myrick, a resident trader at Lower Sioux Agency, according to various sources, remarked "Let them eat grass."

"With one hand the government presented to them plows, and with the other [through traders] bestowed on them guns and ammunition," observed Samuel Pond.

In 1862, Sioux chief Little Crow led a rebellion against settlers in eastern South Dakota and Minnesota. (Georgia State University Foundation, Pullen Library)

*W*hich were they expected to use, the plows or the guns? . . . The plows were put in charge of white men, but the guns were put into their own hands. They were excluded from a great portion of their former hunting grounds, but were annually furnished with a superabundance of implements for hunting. They were never before so bountifully supplied with fire-arms, as at the very time when they were advised neither to hunt nor to make war. What were they expected to do with their guns?

The question was answered in August 1862. A group of young Dakota, roaming the country in search of food, murdered five white farmers. As historian Lass writes, under other circumstances the Dakota would have turned the murderers over to white authorities, but the time for such cooperation was past. Indians eager for battle managed to recruit the influential chief Little Crow (Tay-oyate-duta) to their side, even though Little Crow had traveled to Washington, knew the might of the Americans, and realized the fight was futile. But he allowed himself to be goaded into battle by the accusation he was a coward. "Tay-oyate-duta is not a coward! He is not a fool!..." Little Crow is quoted as saying.

The white men are like the locusts, when they fly so thick that the whole sky is a snowstorm. You may kill one, two, ten, yes, as many as the leaves in the forest. . . . Kill one, two, ten, and ten times ten will come to kill you. . . . You are fools. You will die like the rabbits when the hungry wolves hunt them in the hard moon. But Tay-oyate-duta is no coward. He will die with you.

Dakotas attacked the Indian agencies, looting and destroying the buildings. Among the dead was trader Myrick, his mouth stuffed with grass. The militants,

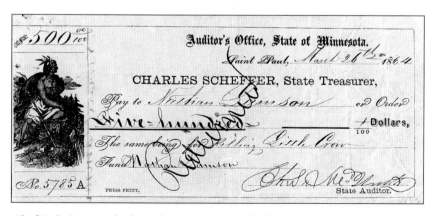

Chief Little Crow was shot by Nathan Lamson in March of 1864. He received a bounty reward of $500. (Minnesota Historical Society)

and Fort Ridgely. Chief Big Eagle later recalled, "We thought the fort was the door to the valley as far as to St. Paul, and that if we got through the door, nothing could stop us this side of the Mississippi."

During the summer, the Dakota killed nearly 500 settlers and soldiers in battles throughout the valley, but they never defeated or occupied any communities or significant fortifications. For the Dakota, militant and peaceable alike, the aftermath was disastrous. Leaders of the insurgents fled to Canada. Thirty-eight Dakota were hanged in Mankato. Many of the Indians, though they had played no part in the war, were removed to Nebraska and the Dakotas. It was the Dakotas' diaspora. Only small settlements remained along the two rivers, the Minnesota and Mississippi, that for so long had cradled the Dakota nation.

Today, four small Dakota reservations exist: Upper Sioux, Lower Sioux, Prairie Island, and Prior Lake. Ojibwa reservations are much larger. They are Mille Lacs, Fond du Lac, Grand Portage, Nett Lake (Bois Forte), Leech Lake, Red Lake, and White Earth, all in northern Minnesota.

■ RAILROADS

In 1856, Congress granted land for four railroads to radiate from St. Paul. Construction slowed during the Panic of 1857. Even a $5 million state loan in 1858 failed to get the rails laid. A political cartoon portrayed the railroad companies as top-hatted gophers, who had eaten taxpayers' money just as gophers eat farmers' crops. Ever since, Minnesota has been known as the Gopher State.

With the Indians removed, settlement resumed in earnest. There were few greater boosters of settlement than the railroads, which not only stood to profit from hauling goods and people, but also needed to sell federal land grants to recoup the cost of rail construction.

Finally, the railroads spread. Jay Cooke's Northern Pacific stretched from Duluth, across the Red River, to Bismark, North Dakota, before Cooke ran out of money. Construction resumed several years later under new ownership and the line continued westward, opening new markets for Minnesota lumber.

A pivotal figure in the development of railroads in the state was James J. Hill, the "empire builder." Hill, a Canadian, came to St. Paul when he was only 18. For years he worked in the freight business. In 1871 he started a steamboat line on the

A Northern Pacific Railroad timetable from 1881. (Courtesy of William J. Neill)

Red River. With the help of Canadian investors, Hill bid on the St. Paul and Pacific railroad, which had stalled in its construction of tracks between the Twin Cities and Winnipeg, Manitoba, and was in danger of losing its land grant. In the bullish fashion that had won him success in his earlier business, Hill crafted a deal to buy the railroad, and managed to lay tracks to Winnipeg in time to save the grant. Hill later would extend tracks into North Dakota and Montana. His railroad, rechristened the Great Northern, reached the Pacific Coast in 1893.

Hill was the archetypical 19th-century railroad baron. When a St. Paul paper supported a Populist-Democrat for president, Hill became so angered he bought the paper to change its editorial policy. Hill became the target of suspicion, even in his own state, when he joined with Edward Harriman and J. P. Morgan to form Northern Securities Co., a merger of the Great Northern, Northern Pacific and Chicago, and Burlington railroads. Minnesota filed suit under a state antimonopoly law. The protest against the monopoly brought a federal suit, which led to a U.S. Supreme Court decision in 1904 that forced the dissolution of the company. That event was the first step in building President Teddy Roosevelt's reputation as a "trust buster" and added to Minnesota's reputation for populist politics.

■ IMMIGRATION

The opening of new lands, new means of transportation, and a booming economy opened the floodgates of immigration to Minnesota.

Railroads published immigrants' guides in English, German, and Scandinavian languages, extolling Minnesota, whose "whole surface . . . is literally begemmed with innumerable lakes." Railroads made deals with steamship lines to bring immigrants to America. They helped newcomers make transfers and set up reception houses in Minnesota. Communities sprouted up instantly as whole colonies arrived.

As historian Lass notes, "everyone who had something to gain joined the chorus." James M. Goodhue, editor of the *Minnesota Pioneer,* wrote, "We have, universally, a pure, bracing, wholesome atmosphere, and Health standing up manfully under the burden of daily toil."

One of the most notable public figures of early Minnesota, Goodhue was known for his thundering editorials and tireless boosterism. "A month in Minnesota, in dog-days, is worth a whole year anywhere else," Goodhue boasted. "We

Scandinavian immigrant pioneers pose for a group portrait.
(Underwood Photo Archives, San Francisco)

"DOST THOU KNOW HOW TO PLAY THE FIDDLE?" "NO," ANSWERED THEMISTOC

Vol. I.   NININGER CITY, MINNESOT.

confidently look to see the time, when all families of leisure down South, from the
Gulf of Mexico along up, will make their regular summer hegira to our Territory;
and when hundreds of the opulent from those regions, will build delightful cottages on the borders of our ten thousand lakes and ornament their grounds with
all that is tasteful in shrubbery and horticulture, for a summer retreat."

Goodhue, observed historian Theodore C. Blegen, "intoxicated himself with his
own superlatives."

Initially, New England, New York, and other Great Lakes states provided most
of Minnesota's immigrants. New Englanders were especially influential in early
business and politics.

Emigration from Sweden began in the 1840s, as the first naive and exuberant
"America letters" trickled back to the old country. Wrote one emigrant:

> *If* it were not for the sake of my good mother and my relatives, I would
> never return to Sweden. No one need worry about my circumstances in
> America, because I am living on God's noble and free soil, neither am I a
> slave under others. On the contrary, I am my own master, like the other

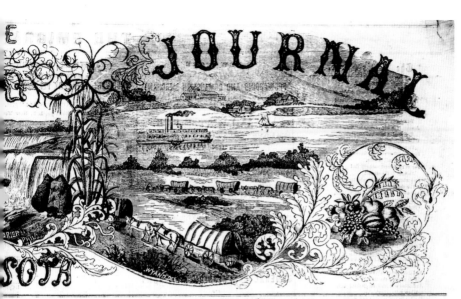

T I UNDERSTAND THE ART OF RAISING A LITTLE VILLAGE INTO A GREAT CITY."

:RITORY, DECEMBER 1, 1856.   No. 1.

The masthead of this small river-town newspaper enthusiastically invokes the words of Themistocles (ca. 524-460 B.C.), an Athenian statesman and general who lead Athens to victory over Persia at Salamis. (Minnesota Historical Society)

creatures of God. I have now been on American soil for two and a half years and I have not been compelled to pay a penny for the privilege of living. Neither is my cap worn out from lifting it in the presence of gentlemen.

During the 1860s and 1870s, immigrants arrived from throughout western and northern Europe. Despite Minnesota's reputation as a new Scandinavia, it is Germans who make up the bulk of ethnic stock. Before World War I, 70 percent of Minnesotans were foreign born, and 25 percent of these were German.

Among these immigrants were my own ancestors. My father's father arrived here from Heidelberg in the early 1900s. He married my grandmother, a descendent of English and Scots, who gave birth to my father only weeks before my grandfather was murdered in a hold-up at his butcher shop in North Minneapolis. My mother's father, the descendant of German immigrants, and Polish-speaking mother, whose parents immigrated from the fluid borderland between Germany and Poland, purchased 160 acres and a simple clapboard farmhouse, as white and neat as a starched shirt, in the rolling oak-covered hills north of Alexandria.

Germans in Minnesota exerted an influence in politics that was disproportionately tiny compared with their numbers. They remained farmers and small business owners, rarely becoming prominent as politicians. Political prowess lay with the Scandinavians, primarily Norwegians and Swedes. Since Knute Nelson's inauguration as governor in 1893, nearly four-fifths of the state's governors have been predominantly Scandinavian.

One of Minnesota's most diverse ethnic communities is northern Minnesota's Mesabi Iron Range. Because of the plenitude of jobs for the unskilled—even those who could speak no English—the "Range" became the haven of workers from every principality of want and despair in late 19th- and early 20th-century Europe. The mines attracted Croats, Slovenes, Italians, Swedes, Norwegians, Montenegrins, Germans, Serbs, and Bulgarians. Finns arrived in greater numbers than any other group. Before World War I, about three dozen ethnic groups had settled on the Range.

EMIGRANTS ON THE PRAIRIE

*T*he caravan seemed a miserably frail and Lilliputian thing as it crept over the boundless prairie toward the sky line. Of road or trail there lay not a trace ahead; as soon as the grass had straightened up again behind, no one could have told the direction from which it had come or whither it was bound. The whole train—Per Hansa with his wife and children, the oxen, the wagons, the cow, and all—might just as well have dropped down out of the sky. Nor was it at all impossible to imagine that they were trying to get back there again; their course was always the same—straight toward the west, straight toward the sky line. . . .

Poverty-stricken, unspeakably forlorn, the caravan creaked along, advancing at a snail's pace, deeper and deeper into a bluish-green infinity—on and on, and always farther on. . . . It steered for Sunset Land! . . .

—O. E. Rölvaag, *Giants in the Earth,* 1927

■ LABOR AND INDUSTRY

Between the heavily industrialized Iron Range and the manufacturing center of the Twin Cities, Minnesota's history in the 20th century was marked by the growth of the labor movement. Radical Finns led major strikes on the Iron Range and also helped organize a strike among northern Minnesota's loggers and sawmill workers.

Labor unrest continued during the Depression. During the infamous Minneapolis truckers' strikes in 1934, two special deputies were killed in May. On July 20, "Bloody Friday," two strikers were killed and dozens wounded when police opened fire on a truck carrying unarmed strikers.

The Depression also served to organize farmers and brought about the creation of the Civilian Conservation Corps and Works Progress Administration. Thousands of young men streamed from cities and towns into the woods to plant trees and build roads. The beautiful log buildings and stonework in many state parks are legacies of these Depression-era workers.

During the Depression, Minnesota's Farmer-Labor party, the protest party of the progressive era, emerged as a major party in Minnesota politics. It put forward a liberal New Deal governor, the charismatic Floyd B. Olson, who might have had a greater future had he not died of cancer at the height of his power and popularity in 1936. The legacy of this third party lives on in the unique sobriquet of Minnesota's liberal party, the "DFL," that is, the Democratic-Farmer-Labor Party.

Flour milling, which began at St. Anthony Falls, diversified to include many food products from many different companies. Aggressive promotion in this highly competitive industry gave rise to Betty Crocker, the mythic promoter of wholesomeness, homemaking, and an increasingly plentiful mix of General Mills products. Another mythic figure, the Green Giant (later bought by milling giant Pillsbury), holds sway over the Minnesota River Valley at Le Sueur. With the railroads grew meat-packing companies such as George A. Hormel and Co. in Austin, makers of famous and much-maligned Spam. Agribusiness giant Cargill, which began in 1865 as the small Iowa wheat-trading business of Will Cargill, spread a network of grain elevators across the Upper Midwest. Today, the Minnesota-based agribusiness, one of the largest privately held companies in existence, employs 76,000 at 1,000 locations in 66 countries.

The wood-products industry continues to consume Minnesota's trees, producing paper, composite building materials, and veneer. The old-growth white pine that built much of the Midwest and the fortunes of 19th-century lumber barons exists now only in scattered remnants. Principal commercial woods today (cut mostly as pulpwood for paper or particle board) are black spruce, balsam fir, jack pine, and aspen. Red pine is cut for lumber.

Corporate giant Minnesota Mining and Manufacturing, better known as 3M, survived inauspicious beginnings. The company set up shop on the north shore of Lake Superior to mine corundum to make sandpaper. The deposit, however, proved inadequate as an abrasive, so the company decided to import garnet abrasive. After a shipment of garnet aboard a tramp steamer turned out to be contaminated with olive oil, 3M started a testing facility that became its world-renowned laboratory and research system. Today the company manufactures products as varied as floppy disks and Post-It Notes.

Honeywell began as Minneapolis Heat Regulator Co., making thermostats for coal furnaces and boilers. When the company merged with Honeywell Heating Specialties Co. of Wabash, Indiana, it broadened its mission from thermostats to a variety of regulatory systems, including missile controls. By doing so, it diversified its business and has grown since the 1950s to become a corporate giant of the region and a major defense contractor.

Minnesota remains an important center for the shipment of grains and iron ore.
(right) In Duluth barley is loaded onto a ship that delivers its cargo to a brewery.

After World War II, former naval officers who had worked with early computers formed Control Data. The company's growth through the 1960s and 1970s helped establish the Twin Cities as a center for high-technology companies.

Curt Carlson rode to prominence on the strength of his idea of Gold Bond trading stamps, given out by grocery stores and redeemable for merchandise. Gold Bond Stamp Company grew phenomenally. The company, renamed Carlson Companies in 1973, has diversified. Today it is a giant in travel, hospitality, and marketing. Among its subsidiaries are Radisson Hotels International, Colony Hotels & Resorts, Country Kitchens, and TGI Friday's.

Other key industries are medical services, research, and manufacturing; tourism; printing and publishing; and finance.

■ MINNESOTANS TODAY

How to describe Minnesotans today?

We have jobs. Our unemployment rate is routinely one of the lowest in the country and the percentage of working-age adults in the labor force one of the highest.

Minnesota has the country's highest high-school graduation rate. Nearly half of the state's budget is tagged for aid to school districts and post-secondary education.

Former Democratic senator and presidential candidate Walter Mondale debates the utility of NASA'S *shuttle program in 1972 with a Republican opponent. (Underwood Photo Archives, San Francisco)*

We have the third-highest ratio of classroom computers to students of any state. Two-thirds of high-school graduates go on to post-secondary training within a year.

We are political schizophrenics. Populism sprung from the state's farmers, who blamed the railroads and vague but powerful eastern interests for the deadly combination of debt and declining prices. By the late 1800s, no longer able to look to the frontier for a fresh start, we looked to government instead. Yet these same rural populists expressed conservative social policies. So despite a reputation for progressive politics and Democratic politicians, Minnesotans often elect Republican governors and senators and produce strong conservative movements on issues such as abortion. And while we have elected only one woman to Congress, we were quite willing to elect as governor Jesse "The Body" Ventura, a one-time pro wrestler and talk-show host who told *Playboy* magazine that he wanted to be reincarnated as a double-D bra. Our strong communitarian sense may seem liberal, while a latent moralism suggests conservatism. A friend of mine, a newspaper editorial writer, once observed: "Minnesota is a liberal state full of conservative people."

Most of us—55 percent—belong to a church, far above the national average. We are predominantly Lutheran. Catholics are also numerous. But we are also many other religions—especially Protestant and Orthodox faiths brought to Minnesota during various waves of immigration.

A Republican party poster printed during a congressional campaign in 1884 warns of the perils of voting Democratic. (Minnesota Historical Society)

We are predominantly urban—half of the state's 4.4 million live in the Twin Cites or their suburbs—yet I believe we think of ourselves as rural because we grew up "on the farm," or have parents who did. We enjoy getting out in the country and imagining that we are part of nature again, as our ancestors were.

Our notion of the good life runs to the outdoors: We buy more fishing licenses per person (nearly one Minnesotan in two is an angler), have more boats per person (one in six), and more snowmobiles (one in 20) than any other state. We have the longest state trail system and the second-most hunting acreage of any state.

Although we—with other Americans—have depopulated our farms, Minnesotans grow more sugar beets than any other state and rank near the top in production of spring wheat, sweet corn, turkeys, cheese, and wild rice. The state's top crops are soybeans, corn, wheat, sugar beets, and hay. Top livestock are dairy cows, beef cattle, hogs, turkeys, and egg hens. Food and agriculture make up 17 percent of the state economy.

Minnesotans are a healthy bunch, ranking healthiest among states in a survey by Northwestern National Life Insurance Co. The state also scored high in the health and well-being of its children. Is that because of our health care system or bracing climate (a common theme of 19th-century land promotions)?

We are predominantly white—more than 94 percent so. You'd have trouble believing that in Minneapolis or St. Paul, where most of the state's minorities live. Among the most recent arrivals are Southeast Asians, who immigrated after the Vietnam War in response to a strong church-sponsorship program. The most obvious result to travelers is the existence of Asian markets and hundreds of Asian restaurants in the Twin Cities.

Despite these new immigrants, we are predominantly natives: three-fourths of Minnesota's residents were born in the state. Perhaps that statistic begins to explain two of our greatest faults: We can be a bit smug at times, a trait Sinclair Lewis so successfully lampooned in *Main Street* and *Babbitt*. And to outsiders we may seem cliquish and removed, polite but not friendly. Our Nordic chill, like the ice on our northern lakes, takes forever to thaw.

Oh, and that brings up our third big fault: We'll bore you to tears talking about the weather.

Enthusiasts turn out for the John Beargrease Sled Dog Marathan. The round-trip race between Duluth and Grand Portage covers 500 miles and takes about six days.

PRAIRIE PATH
SOUTHWEST AND RED RIVER VALLEY

■ HIGHLIGHTS

	page
New Ulm	72
Sites of the Dakota War	73
Lac qui Parle Mission	75
Pipestone National Monument	78
Jeffers Petroglyphs	85
Red River Valley	88
Hjemkomst	91
Bluestem Prairie Preserve	92

THE MIDWESTERN PRAIRIES, TREELESS GRASSLANDS stretching from horizon to horizon under a perfect hemisphere of sky, were new and strange to most of the Europeans and Americans who ventured inland during the early 1800s. These were people, after all, who lived in the shadowed forests of the East, whose ancestors had lived in the dark woodlands of Western Europe. Many seemed unsettled by a view that suddenly stretched onward to infinity.

"There is something inexpressibly lonely in the solitude of the prairie: the loneliness of a forest seems nothing to it," wrote Washington Irving.

There the view is shut in by trees, and the imagination is left free to picture some livelier scene beyond; but here we have an immense extent of landscape without a sign of human existence. We have the consciousness of being far, far beyond the bounds of human habitation; we feel as if moving into a desert world.

Charles Dickens found the prairie "oppressive in its barren monotony.... I could never abandon myself to the scene, forgetful of all else."

Visitors certainly have not been unanimous in their judgments. Judge James Hall found the prairie "striking." It "never fails to cause an exclamation of surprise. The extent of the prospect is exhilarating." Writer Sherwood Anderson recognized the power of space: "Mystery whispered in the grass," he wrote. "I can remember old fellows in my home town speaking feelingly of an evening spent on the big empty plains. It had taken the shrillness out of them. They had learned the trick of quiet."

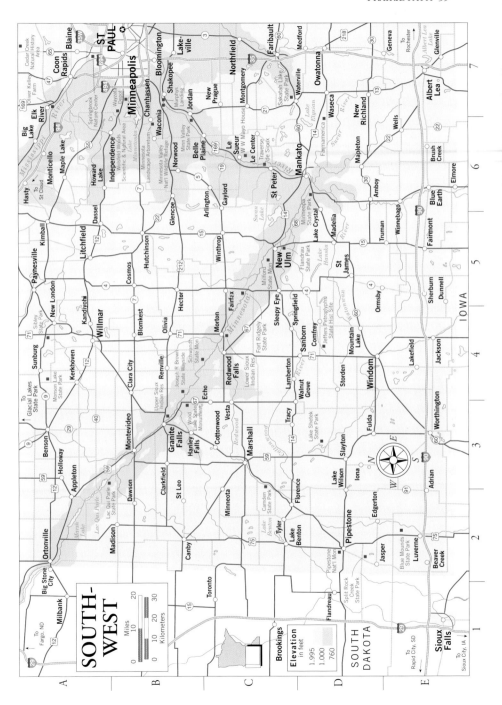

■ CONTINENTAL GRASSLAND

When settlers arrived in Minnesota, they found a broad swath of prairies across the southern third of the state and northward through the Red River Valley (where the border with North Dakota now runs). These grasslands have since been termed *tallgrass,* dominated, depending on the individual conditions of the site, by Indian grass and big bluestem—"a mighty grass," in John Madson's words.

In Minnesota, the extent of prairie was defined by two gradients: increasing average annual temperature to the southwest, and decreasing precipitation to the northwest. For thousands of years, the combination of high temperatures and low moisture dried the soil and vegetation, setting the stage for crackling wildfires, which drove trees—even hardy oak and red cedar—to the sheltered ravines. If one drives west from Minnesota, the tallgrass region, now planted largely in corn, gives way to the drier *mixed-grass plains*—now the wheat fields of the Dakotas. Farther west still, in the rain shadow of the Rockies, lie the *short-grass plains* that today are devoted largely to grazing.

I am always amazed that in a land with so much sky, with so many long views, I should spend most of the time looking at my feet. For here is an incredible diversity of plants, many distinct and beautiful. Who could resist plants with names such

Pipestone National Monument is in the center of the old tallgrass prairie.

as these: hoary puccoon, rattlesnake-master, leadplant, sneezeweed, bastard-toad-flax? Yet for all the diversity of the prairie—some 900 plant species in Minnesota alone—it is grasses that dominate, forming as much as 80 percent of the cover. "I would be converted to a religion of grass," muses writer Louise Erdrich.

Sleep the winter away and rise headlong each spring. Sink deep roots. Conserve water. Respect and nourish your neighbors and never let trees gain the upper hand. . . . Bow beneath the arm of fir . . . Provide. Provide.

The beauty of the prairie—its spring flowers and waving grasses—lies above the ground, but its substance—50 to 90 percent of its biomass—lies underground, immune to fire and grazing. Some plants, such as compass plant and heath aster, reach deep with a few long roots for deeply buried subsurface moisture, available during droughts. Others, such as little bluestem and switchgrass, absorb new water quickly with a spreading, filamentous root system. These fine roots decay easily, building prairie soil with organic matter. This organic layer accumulates to depths of several feet, creating the black soil so coveted by pioneer farmers.

Author and teacher David Costello once suggested to a student that he collect a sample of bush morning glory, including roots. Costello had made the remark in jest. "After several hours of hard digging," Costello wrote in *The Prairie World*, "he had a hole large enough to hold a cookstove, but still had not excavated the root system."

Other prairie plants show similarly remarkable adaptations: The stiff, twisted awns of porcupine-grass coil or unwind as humidity changes, driving the barbed seed into the ground—an organic seed drill.

Unlike woodland flowers—the "spring ephemerals" that bloom in early spring before leafing trees shroud them in shade—prairie flowers bloom throughout the snow-free season, changing week by week as various plants bloom and then fade from view. In early spring, delicate pasqueflowers. Then purplish white flowers of blue-eyed grass, golden Alexanders and lousewort. And so on through the year, a mutable pallet of pink, purple, yellow, white, and violet. By fall, bluestem turns its indescribable reddish color—anything but blue—and ivory-colored ladies tresses make their play for attention.

These plants, of necessity, recover quickly after fire, which for millennia has groomed the prairies, freeing plants from mats of dead vegetation, releasing nutrients, and chasing encroaching sumac and oak back to the ravines and thickets.

Prairie Near the Mouth of St. Peters—Buffalo Hunt *by Seth Eastman, 1846–48.*
(Minnesota Historical Society)

Fires were set both by lightning and by Indians. Nineteenth-century missionary Samuel Pond reported:

> *If* America had been without human inhabitants, every acre of fertile soil in the valley of the Mississippi would have been covered with dense forests. . . . In denuding the land of timber, by setting fires, to give pasturage for the buffalo, elk, and deer, the Indians did their work too thoroughly in some places; but they saved the civilized settler of the country the work of generations.

George Featherstonhaugh watched such a prairie fire in 1835 at Lac qui Parle:

> *It* is a spectacle one is never tired of looking at: half the horizon appeared like an advancing sea of fire, with dense clouds of smoke flying towards the moon, which was then shining brightly. Here I remained enjoying this glorious sight until a late hour.

Two hundred years ago, great herds of bison roamed Minnesota, grazing on the lush grass, stunting the growth of trees. Dakota Indians living in the woodlands of eastern Minnesota traveled westward up tributaries of the Mississippi for annual buffalo hunts on the prairies. It was for the traffic in Indian canoes, in fact, that a major tributary in southeastern Minnesota was called by the French *Rivière aux Canots*. Cannon River is simply the English bastardization of that name.

Gophers and badgers provide major disturbance to prairie today, grazing where biomass is greatest, underground. Other conspicuous animals on the prairie include the white-tailed jackrabbit, red fox, coyotes, and striped skunks. Conspicuous birds are meadowlarks, bobolinks, upland sandpipers, marbled godwits, red-winged and yellow-headed blackbirds, and various species of soaring hawks. Most of these species have managed to adapt to the conversion of most of the prairie to farmland, though some species—especially plants—have become rare. Two exotic species of wildlife, both popular game birds, are the ring-necked pheasant and gray (or Hungarian) partridge.

One of the most spectacular birds of the prairie is the prairie chicken, known for the male's stunning courtship display. The male struts, holding its head low, wings stiff, and the long feathers on the back of its neck erect to form a high collar. It stamps its feet like a flamenco dancer and may leap and flutter its wings. The rooster inflates its bright yellow neck sacs, producing a resonant call that can be heard a mile away. For that sound, their courting areas are called "booming grounds." They perform this display for several hours, beginning before sunrise and again at dusk. Rare in Minnesota, prairie chickens have been protected from hunting since 1935. (If you have trouble seeing a real one, you'll have no trouble at all seeing the prairie chicken monument in Rothsay, on Interstate 94 between Moorhead and Fergus Falls. It weighs four and a half tons.)

In spring, prairie wetlands comes alive with the music of chorus frogs. Many species of butterflies and skippers—including some rare ones—flit about the blooming flowers. It was another insect, however, that most concerned pioneer farmers. The prairie harbors dozens of species of grasshoppers, populations that exploded as farmers changed the composition of prairie from diverse, pest-resistant native vegetation to vulnerable monocultures. Several plagues cursed farmers during the late 1800s and early 1900s. Reported one farmer in the early 1870s:

> A large black cloud suddenly appeared high in the west from which came an ominous sound. The apparition moved directly toward us, its dark appearance became more and more terrifying and the sound changed to a deep hum. . . . We heard the buzzing; we saw the shining wings, the long bodies, the legs. The grasshoppers—the scourge of the prairie—were upon us.

HARD TIMES ON THE PRAIRIE

*D*ay after day the grasshoppers kept on eating. They ate all the wheat and the oats. They ate every green thing—all the garden and all the prairie grass.

❖   ❖   ❖

When Sunday came, Pa and Laura and Mary walked to Sunday school. The sun shone so bright and hot that Ma said she would stay at home with Carrie, and Pa left Sam and David in the shady stable.

There had been no rain for so long that Laura walked across Plum Creek on dry stones. The whole prairie was bare and brown. Millions of brown grasshoppers whirred low over it. Not a green thing was in sight anywhere.

All the way, Laura and Mary brushed off grasshoppers. When they came to the church, brown grasshoppers were thick on their petticoats. They lifted their skirts and brushed them off before they went in. But careful as they were, the grasshoppers had spit tobacco-juice on their best Sunday dresses.

Nothing would take out the horrid stains. They would have to wear their best dresses with the brown spots on them.

Many people in town were going back East. Christy and Cassie had to go. Laura said good-bye to Christy and Mary said good-bye to Cassie, their best friends.

They did not go to school any more. They must save their shoes for winter and they could not bear to walk barefooted on grasshoppers. School would be ended soon, anyway, and Ma said she would teach them through the winter so they would not be behind their classes when school opened again next spring.

Pa worked for Mr. Nelson and earned the use of Mr. Nelson's plough. He began to plough the bare wheat-field, to make it ready for next year's wheat crop.

—Laura Ingalls Wilder, *On the Banks of Plum Creek,* 1937

When white settlers arrived, nearly 20 million acres of tallgrass prairie covered Minnesota. Some settlers, on seeing the treeless plains, turned back to the familiar forest, laboring under a prevalent belief that a land that could support no trees was infertile. But many others realized the potential beneath their feet. "Such soil," remarked a Scandinavian pioneer in Ole Rölvaag's *Giants in the Earth.* "Only to sink the plow into it, to turn over the sod—and there was a field ready for seeding." Sinking the plow was easier said than done; up to 10 yoke of oxen were needed to break the soil from the tenacious roots of prairie sod. Nonetheless, the prairie rapidly turned to black fields. Reported the *Marshall Messenger* in 1878: "You can travel north, south, east, west, and everywhere you go, breaking teams are hard at work turning our rich soil." Minnesota's last wild bison was spotted in Norman County in 1880. By 1932 the native elk had vanished. Today, a century later, less than one percent of the native prairie remains. The original tallgrass has been replaced by another: corn.

Today the prairie is cut by the relentless mile-by-mile grid of country roads. Its horizon is broken by power lines and grain-storage elevators that sit by the railroad track or highway in every farm town. In fact, it is almost possible to travel from town to town by spotting these monoliths as if they were rock cairns marking a hiking trail. Of the native prairie that remains, about 48,000 acres are protected, mostly by the state Department of Natural Resources in various state parks and other natural areas, and The Nature Conservancy, a nonprofit group devoted to protecting endangered species and habitat. Some of these protected remnants are just a few acres in size. Others, such as the Conservancy's **Bluestem Prairie Preserve,** about 15 miles east of **Moorhead** *(see page 91),* total hundreds or even thousands of acres.

Giant grain elevators are ubiquitous on the plains and prairies of southwestern Minnesota.

■ MINNESOTA RIVER VALLEY

The Minnesota River, slashing across the southern third of the state, doesn't live up to its advance billing. As you approach the river at New Ulm or Mankato, the ground suddenly gives way to a yawning valley, in many places several miles wide. Surely the river that made it must be swift and mighty! Yet the stream at the bottom seems far too puny to have carved such a broad feature on the prairie landscape.

In fact, the valley was created by a much larger river, the Glacial River Warren, which existed near the close of the last Ice Age, about 14,000 years ago. At the time, Glacial Lake Agassiz covered much of northwestern Minnesota, central Saskatchewan, and western Ontario. Dammed by a glacier to the north, Agassiz crested a ridge at what is now Big Stone Lake and roared to the southeast, turned abruptly to the northeast, and then joined the Mississippi River, digging a valley befitting its huge volume of water and creating the Minnesota's distinctive elbow around the waist of the state. About 9,000 years ago, however, the dam of ice creating Glacial Lake Agassiz retreated, allowing that lake to drain north to Hudson Bay. Glacial River Warren shriveled to the much smaller river the Dakota Indians later came to call *Minnesota*.

Early whites found a valley of plenty. Explorer and tireless self-promoter Jonathan Carver described it this way:

> *W*ild rice grows here in great abundance; and every part is filled with trees bending under their loads of fruits, such as plums, grapes, and apples; the meadows are covered with hops, and many sorts of vegetables; whilst the ground is stored with useful roots, with angelica, spikenard, and ground-nuts as large as hens eggs. At a little distance from the sides of the river are eminences, from which you have views that cannot be exceeded even by the most beautiful of those I have already described.

Carver wrote this description on the basis of his travels in the valley during the *winter* of 1766–7.

According to Timothy Severin, the inaccuracies, exaggerations, absolute nonsense, and self-promotion in Carver's book, *Travels through the Interior Parts of North America,* may not have been entirely his fault. He landed penniless in London, where he tried to find a publisher for a book of his travels. He may have fallen prey to a publisher who insisted on embellishing the text to include fabricated Indian words, two-headed snakes, and a viper that shot darts from its tail. Unfortunately, the fabrications marred Carver's true accomplishments: He lived among the Dakota, 200 miles up the Minnesota River, for six months, including the long winter, far from the support of other whites. To his credit, he enjoyed his stay with the Indians and admired their customs. He learned about their tools, homes, and art, witnessed rituals for the dead and shamanism, and attended bison hunts.

Trader and known murderer Peter Pond, who visited the Minnesota River Valley in 1773–74, wrote about the area in sparse, purposeful prose ungoverned by punctuation or the rules of spelling: "The River is Destatue of fish But the Woods & Meaddoues afords abundans of annamels Sum turkeas Buffeloes are Verey Plentey the Common Dear are Plentey and Larg."

Unfortunately, the Minnesota River no longer flows with the "sky-tinted water" for which it was known by Dakota Indians. Today, it carries the muddy runoff and eroded soil of the state's richest agricultural land. Still, for the canoeist or angler, the river provides lush, forested respite from the thousands of surrounding acres, which have been thoroughly plowed and planted.

Pollution and Peter Pond's observations notwithstanding, the Minnesota is not "Destatue" of fish. In addition to walleyes and northern pike, the river provides a trophy fishery for channel and flathead catfish, which often exceed 20 pounds. In comparison to the rest of the state, the prairie region is rather deficient in lakes. Nonetheless, the large lakes that do exist provide fishing for walleyes, bass, pike, and panfish.

■ MINNESOTA RIVER DRIVING TOUR *map page 59, B&C-6&7*

Following the Minnesota River southwest out of the Twin Cities, US 169 passes a mosaic of public sites in the bottom lands, back channels, wetlands, and upland forests along the river. Many are included in the **Minnesota Valley National Wildlife Refuge. The Minnesota Valley State Recreation Area** provides hiking, camping, canoeing, horseback riding, and fishing at several locations along the Minnesota River between Shakopee and Le Sueur.

◆ LE SUEUR *map page 59, C-6*

At Le Sueur US 169 plunges deep into the Minnesota River Valley—or, according to the advertising jingle of one of the biggest businesses here, the valley of the *Jolly, ho, ho, ho, Green Giant.* On North Main Street at number 118 sits a small Gothic-

(following pages) Farmland stretches to the horizon in southwest Minnesota.

style house from which two southern Minnesota institutions emerged. The house was built in 1859 by **Dr. W. W. Mayo,** who with his sons, William and Charles, founded the world-renowned Mayo Clinic in Rochester, in Minnesota's southeast corner. From 1874 to 1920, the house was occupied by three generations of the Carson Nesbit Cosgrove family. Cosgrove helped to organize and served as president of the Minnesota Valley Canning Company, later known as the Green Giant Company. Restored and furnished in antebellum style, the Mayo house is open for tours. *118 North Main Street; 507-665-3250.* The **Le Sueur Museum,** housed in an early brick schoolhouse, contains the Green Giant Room, which recounts the history of canning and food processing in the area. *709 North Second Street.*

◆ St. Peter *map page 59, C-9*

In the years following their expulsion from northern Minnesota at the hands of the Ojibwa, the Dakota Indians settled along the Minnesota River Valley. Fur traders settled near the Dakota villages to do business with the Indians. One important gathering place was the **Traverse des Sioux,** a strategic ford of the Minnesota, where the Dakota could pass from the hardwood forests of the east to the prairies and buffalo-hunting grounds of the west. The site lies on the east side of US 169 (Minnesota Avenue), two miles north of the city of St. Peter. Also here is the **Treaty Site History Center,** operated by the Nicollet County Historical Society, with exhibits depicting the Indians and early white traders who settled the area. Among these characters was French cartographer Joseph Nicollet, who admired the Indians' descriptive names for geographic features and tried to preserve these names in original or translated form. A prominent early resident of the area was the Dakota chief Mazasha, or Red Iron. Known as kind-hearted, trustworthy, and intelligent, Mazasha adopted some white ways, planting crops, including wheat, and building a log cabin and barn. Mazasha was one of 35 Dakota chiefs who signed the treaty at Traverse des Sioux in 1851, opening 24 million acres of southern Minnesota, Iowa, and South Dakota to white settlement, and a treaty in 1858 in Washington, D.C., where he refused to wear European-style clothes for the official portraits. *Treaty Site History Center, 1851 Minnesota Avenue; 507-934-2160.*

A contemporary of Mazasha was French Canadian Louis Provençalle, who ran a trading post at Traverse des Sioux. According to the history center, Provençalle kept his ledgers in self-styled hieroglyphics so they could be read by trader and Indian alike. Historian William E. Lass is less charitable. Provençalle "epitomized the old order," writes Lass. "He entered the trade as an illiterate young man and left it as an illiterate old man."

St. Peter nearly became the state capital. In 1856–57, when Minnesota was still a territory with its capital in St. Paul, farm-country boosters prevailed in the territorial legislature with a bill to remove the capital from St. Paul. But Joe Rolette, a legislator from Pembina (now in North Dakota); stole the as-yet-unsigned bill and hid out in a St. Paul hotel until the final minutes of the legislative session. That's the lore, and Rolette is often commemorated as the man who kept the capital as St. Paul. But while Rolette did indeed disappear, the territorial governor signed a copy of the bill moving the capital to St. Peter. A federal judge ruled, however, that the action was undertaken improperly and that the capital must stay in St. Paul.

Today in St. Peter (pop. 9,400), near the historic Traverse des Sioux, are many preserved or restored homes and churches, among them the Gothic Revival E. St. **Julien Cox House** at 500 North Washington Avenue, built in 1871 and restored and furnished to the period. St. Peter is home to **Gustavus Adolphus College**, its Linnaeus Arboretum, and many sculptures by Paul Granlund. Also in St. Peter are the **Union Presbyterian Church**, one of the first churches in southern Minnesota; the **St. Peter State Hospital Museum** (formerly known as the Minnesota Hospital for the Insane); and the **Bornemann House**, a pioneer structure moved from the Traverse des Sioux after the U.S.–Dakota War.

◆ MANKATO   *map page 59, C/D-6*

Built where the Blue Earth River joins the elbow of the Minnesota River, Mankato (and North Mankato across the river) forms the commercial hub of the valley. In 1700 French explorer Pierre Charles Le Sueur collected a bluish clay from the banks of the Blue Earth in vain hopes it was copper ore. Chief industries in the past were flour milling and limestone quarrying. After the defeat of the Dakota, more than 300 Indians were sentenced to death and brought to Mankato to hang. President Abraham Lincoln commuted the sentences of simple combatants—265 in all. On the day after Christmas, 38 Indians convicted of murder or rape were hanged on a single scaffold to the cheers of a vengeful crowd of settlers and townspeople. A marker at Front and Main streets commemorates the executions. Mankato State University sits atop the south bluff of the river. Historic sites and exhibits in town include the **Blue Earth County Heritage Center**, *415 Cherry Street; 507-345-5566,* and the restored 1871 Victorian **house of Rensselaer D. Hubbard,** founder of Hubbard Milling Company; *606 South Broad Street.*

Just west of Mankato, on the bluffs overlooking the Minnesota River, **Minneopa State Park** surrounds a picturesque brace of waterfalls on Minneopa Creek, just west of Mankato. *507-389-5464.*

Mankato (pop. 31,400) is the terminus of the **Sakatah Singing Hills State Trail,** a 39-mile trail that runs east to Faribault. Built on an abandoned railroad grade, it's covered for most of its length with crushed limestone (only a few miles at either end are paved), so it's suitable for mountain bikes in summer, snowmobiles in winter. Midway along the trail is **Sakatah Hills State Park,** on the shore of Upper Sakatah Lake, with campsites and wooded hiking trails. *507-362-4438.*

◆ NEW ULM *map page 59, C-5*

The German town of New Ulm (pop. 13,100) sits on the banks of the Minnesota, as tidy as a bow tie, with neat lawns and spiffy homes, many nearly a century old.

Started in 1854–55 by two German settlement societies, New Ulm was the scene of important battles between settlers and Dakotas on August 19 and 23, 1862. Though townspeople fended off Dakota attacks, 34 of the defenders died and much of the town burned. The Greek Revival **Kiesling House** (a private home at 220 North Minnesota Street) served as a defensive site. Prominent among the stone and brick buildings along the main street is the **Brown County Historical Society Museum,** a stunning building of brick and white-glazed terra cotta and stepped gables, similar to Dutch or Flemish designs. The museum also has an Indian exhibit. *2 North Broadway; 507-233-2616.* The **Glockenspiel,** a 45-foot-tall musical clock tower with animated characters stands on the corner of Fourth and Minnesota Streets, plays three times a day.

Today, the most obvious sign of the town's Germanic heritage is the **Hermann Monument,** better known as Hermann the German, a 102-foot statue of a Germanic chief who defeated Roman conquerors in early Christian times. The monument, which you can climb, stands high on a bluff overlooking the river's broad valley. Nearby on 20th Street are the gardens, mansion, and brewery of the **August Schell Brewing Company.**

The **Alexander Harkin Store,** eight miles northwest of New Ulm on Nicollet County 21, recreates the store that once formed the hub of the bustling river town of West Newton. Restored by the Minnesota Historical Society, the store stocks its shelves with the groceries, hardware, and dry goods critically needed by settlers in the 1870s.

Swan Lake, a shallow 10,000-acre wetland just east of US 14 near New Ulm, attracts a variety of waterfowl and wading birds, including various grebe species, black-crowned night herons, Forster's and black terns, and trumpeter swans.

◆ **SITES OF THE DAKOTA WAR**   *map page 59, B&C-4&5*

From New Ulm, follow any combination of main highways and country roads northwesterly up the Minnesota River Valley. As you pass through fields of corn and soybeans on your way toward Montevideo, you'll pass many sites that are preserved to commemorate the U.S.–Dakota War of 1862. The war, often called the Sioux Uprising, was the culmination of long-simmering Dakota resentment over loss of their land and frustration with the government's failure to make timely annuity payments.

By the 1850s, the Dakota had signed treaties forcing them onto reservation along the Minnesota River, where the U.S. government tried to remake them into full-time farmers. Crops failed in 1861, and by the next year, many Dakota were starving. They gathered at the two Indian agencies that had been established along the Minnesota River to await federal payments to buy food. Promised by treaty and due in June, the annuities still had not arrived by mid-August. When the agent in charge of **Lower Sioux Agency** near Morton refused to release food from a warehouse until the payments arrived, the Dakotas' rage finally exploded. On August 18, warriors attacked the agency, a thriving town of about 100 white and mixed-blood settlers. The Indians broke into the warehouse and took food. They

Fort Ridgely under attack by the Dakota as painted by James McGrew in 1890.
(Minnesota Historical Society)

killed many of the 40 soldiers sent from nearby Fort Ridgely to restore order. During the next week, the militants among the Indians—according to all evidence, in the vast minority—killed dozens of settlers in the countryside. Today, the Minnesota Historical Society operates an interpretive center on the grounds of the old fort. The only building standing is the warehouse. *507-697-6321.*

To the northwest of the agency is the **Joseph R. Brown Wayside.** Here sits the partly reconstructed home of Joseph R. Brown, soldier, fur trader, newspaper publisher, and Indian agent for the Dakota until 1861. Some historians believe that had Brown, a man long familiar with the Dakota, remained the agent, war would not have broken out. When fighting began, the Brown family abandoned the house, which was burned by the Dakota.

The war quickly spread throughout much of the Minnesota River Valley. The Dakota laid siege to **Fort Ridgely,** an unfortified outpost—more of a police station than a fort—built on a nearly indefensible site flanked on three sides by wooded ravines. Nonetheless, a force of about 400 Dakota failed in its efforts to overrun the 180 soldiers defending the fort. Few buildings remain at the fort today. Exhibits at the fort's restored commissary, operated by the Minnesota Historical Society, tell the story of the fort and the Dakota war. The site, nine miles south of Fairfax off Route 4, lies within the borders of **Fort Ridgely State Park.** *507-426-7840.*

After fighting began, Dakota looted and burned the **Upper Sioux Agency** near Granite Falls. John Other Day, a Dakota chief, like many Indians of the Upper Sioux Agency, refused to take part in the fighting. He led many whites from the agency to safety. Today, the site of the annuity center is marked by the foundation and bricks from the original building in Upper Sioux Agency State Park. The rest of the small park, including tracts of native prairie, lies between the confluence of the Minnesota River and Yellow Medicine River, which is named for the yellow root of the moonseed plant, used by the Dakota as a medicinal herb. The park is also the resting place of Mazomani, a leader of the Wahpetonwan. In September 1862, Mazomani, whose name translates as Iron Walker, was shot in the Battle of Wood Lake, the final engagement of the war. By one report he was killed by white soldiers as he carried a white flag of truce, though the circumstances have been in some dispute. Carried to his camp, where he spent his final moments with his wife and daughter, he uttered a starkly simple and beautiful farewell: "I love you very much," he told them, "but I am going to leave you now."

◆ UPPER MINNESOTA RIVER *map page 59, A&B-3&4*

Underlying the Minnesota River Valley is the Morton Gneiss. At an estimated 3.6 billion years old, it is one of the oldest formations discovered on Earth. Sometimes called "rainbow rock" for its pink (or white) and dark bands, the gneiss crops up to the surface at several locations in the valley. Good places to view it are in the large knob of bedrock behind Morton High School and at Cold Spring Granite Company quarry in **Granite Falls**. Another exposure occurs at the **Yellow Medicine County Museum**, a half-mile south of town on Minnesota 67. The museum also includes two log homes. The **Olaf Swensson Farm Museum** northwest of town is housed in a 22-room brick farmhouse.

Machines of transportation and agriculture are the theme at **Minnesota's Machinery Museum** in **Hanley Falls**. On display are historic farm vehicles, a turn-of-the-19th-century blacksmith shop, and a farm kitchen. *First Avenue West; 507-768-3522.*

Another depiction of pioneer life among the Dakota is found at **Lac qui Parle Mission**, a Minnesota Historical Society site off US 59 near Montevideo. The Dakota had long lived at this site near the headwaters of the Minnesota River. Joseph Renville, a trader born of a French father and Dakota mother, established a post at Lac qui Parle in 1826. Soon after, he invited missionaries to the site. The missionaries sought to convert the Indians not only to Christianity, but also to agriculture and other mainstays of European culture. Renville translated many Protestant hymns into Dakota and worked with missionaries to translate the Bible into Dakota. After Renville died in 1846, Dakota resentment against the mission grew. The mission was abandoned soon after. *The Chippewa County Historical Society operates the Olaf Swensson Farm Museum and Lac qui Parle Mission; 320-269-7636.*

The **Lac qui Parle Wildlife Management Area** northwest of Montevideo and just west of Minnesota 119, is a good place for watching wildlife, especially bald eagles and deer. In the fall, more than 100,000 Canada geese congregate at this popular hunting area in preparation for their migration.

A bit to the north of the Minnesota River Valley, in **Willmar**, the **Kandiyohi County Museum** depicts local history as well as larger historical trends. An exhibit featuring a Great Northern steam locomotive describes the importance of railroads to the region. *302-235-1881.*

Monson Lake State Park northwest of Willmar contains the homesite of the Broberg family, Swedish settlers who came to the area in the 1850s and were slaughtered by the Dakota. *320-366-3797.*

Just north of Willmar are two of the largest parks in the Minnesota River Valley, **Glacial Lakes State Park**, near Starbuck, and **Sibley State Park**. They lie amid the hills that form the ragged, ill-defined boundary between prairie and the woodlands to the north and east. Among the most interesting features of both parks are the many topographic features left by the glaciers of the last Ice Age, among them, moraines and "kettle" lakes. As glaciers advanced, they acted as conveyor belts, carrying boulders, gravel, and other debris to the leading edge of the ice sheet, dropping the material as the ice melted. This deposit, or moraine, created many of the hills of western Minnesota. As glaciers retreated they left behind huge blocks of ice, buried in sand and gravel. As these blocks of ice melted, they left basins for many lakes. Both parks provide camping, high lookouts, and trails that lead through woods and prairie. *Glacial Lakes: 320-239-2860; Sibley: 320-354-2055.*

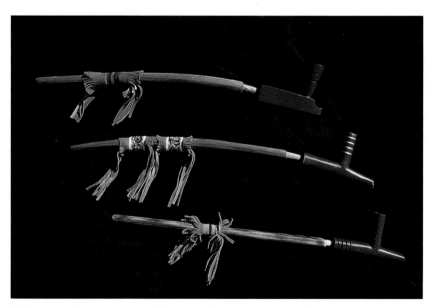

Walentyna and John Feurstein (left) make and sell honey outside their home in Lake Benton. Pipestone crafts (above) are made by local Indians. They are the only ones allowed to quarry and hand-carve the stone from Pipestone National Monument.

■ COTEAU DES PRAIRIES *map page 59, C-3*

As you drive south out of the Minnesota River Valley, even after you crest the lip of the valley itself, the land continues to rise for many miles, as though on a table tilted toward the height of the Rockies, far to the west. This persistent rise in the landscape in southwestern Minnesota and part of South Dakota is called the Coteau des Prairies. It is underlain by a bedrock core that diverted the glaciers.

If you drive south from Granite Falls on Yellow Medicine County 23, you'll soon come to **Marshall** (pop. 12,000), a big town by the standards of this agricultural region. On the east end of town near Minnesota 23 you can visit the **Southwest State University Anthropology Museum and Planetarium.**

Just southwest of Marshall lies **Camden State Park**, an oasis of hardwoods in the deep valley of a riffling stream, Camden gives the impression that a slice of southeastern hill country has migrated 200 miles west, and burrowed into the prairie farm country like a pheasant in a cornfield. You can fish for stocked trout in the Redwood River, walk trails through the wooded ravines, or tour prairie sites on the higher ground. *507-865-4530.*

Along the margins of these highlands, retreating glaciers deposited ridges and hills, among them Buffalo Ridge, near Lake Benton, where hundreds of windmills catch the southern and western winds to generate electricity.

◆ PIPESTONE *map page 59, D-2*

Far down in the southwest corner of Minnesota sits **Pipestone National Monument;** *507-824-5464.* There the downward path of Pipestone Creek intersects a long ridge of reddish Sioux quartzite bedrock, forming Winnewissa Falls. For centuries, Plains Indians gathered at the sacred site to dig the soft layer of pipestone that lies between layers of the much harder quartzite. The pipestone found its way by trade throughout North America. The quarries were already famous to European Americans when cartographer Joseph Nicollet and artist George Catlin visited in the 1830s (and for whom the stone was also called catlinite). The quarries once were held in common, but by the time Catlin visited, the Dakota controlled the land. Wrote 19th-century explorer John Wesley Powell, "It is not too much to say that the great pipestone quarry was the most important single locality in aboriginal geography and lore."

Today, Indians, mostly from the local Dakota tribes, work the quarries, following the declining layers of pipestone while piling up debris behind them as if they were gophers. Inside the interpretive center, Indian artisans work the soft, smooth

PIPESTONE LEGEND

*A*t an ancient time the Great Spirit, in the form of a large bird, stood upon the wall of rock and called all the tribes around him, and breaking out a piece of the red stone formed it into a pipe and smoked it, the smoke rolling over the whole multitude. He then told his red children that this red stone was their flesh, that they were made from it, that they must all smoke to him through it, that they must use it for nothing but pipes: and as it belonged alike to all the tribes, the ground was sacred, and no weapons must be used or brought upon it.

—Dakota account of the origin of pipestone,
recorded by George Catlin, 1835

stone into pipes and effigies, much as their ancestors have done for hundreds of years. Pipes and jewelry are available to buy.

The pipes weren't used for habitual smoking as we know it, but instead for ceremonies associated with councils, trade, declarations of war, and healing. The chief attraction to tobacco was its spiritual qualities, the spirit-like rising of smoke that suggested the Great Spirit. Occasionally pipes were buried with the dead. They were sacred and remain so to this day.

I try to imagine the ancient days at the quarry as I wander down the path past various active quarrying pits, each about the size of a living room and up to 10 feet deep. I hear the scrape of loose rock. Peering over the edge, I introduce myself. His name is Trevor Erickson, he says. He has brown hair and fair skin. "That's a Norwegian-sounding name," I say. His father is Norwegian, English, and Danish, he says. His mother is Sisseton Sioux. His grandfather, he says, was Harvey Derby, also known as Running Elk, who pioneered the reopening of the pits by Indians in the 1930s and worked at the monument as an interpreter. Since Pipestone became a national monument in 1937, quarrying has been limited to Indians. "I keep up the tradition and culture," says Erickson, who lives in nearby Pipestone and works in a boat factory. He pries loose slabs of overlying Sioux quartzite with a crowbar and tosses the rock onto a pile behind him. The sun is just reaching over the edge of the pit, and I can see he is working up a sweat. "Everything is done by hand. You can't do anything with machinery or power tools. I like this work. It's so nice and peaceful." He says he is not much involved in Dakota religion, though his brother is. "My dad's a farmer. I like to farm, too."

Next to the national monument is the town of **Pipestone** (pop. 4,560), which, as its name suggests, appears to be made of the same red stone used by Indians for pipes. In reality, the deep red building stone that forms so many historic buildings in town is the harder and more plentiful Sioux quartzite that underlies much of the area. Served by four rail lines at the turn of the century, Pipestone was a booming hub of the Coteau. Among the historic buildings at the center of town are the **Calumet Inn,** built in 1888 with Italianate features, which still serves as a hotel *(see page 324).* The **Pipestone County Historical Museum,** *1 Hiwatha Avenue; 507-825-2563,* was built in 1896 as the city hall. The three-story Beaux-Arts building now holds displays on the fur trade, pioneering, farming, and railroading. Manikins display traditional dress of Plains Indian women. The item I found most stunning was an old black-and-white photo of a pioneer sod house, taken 15 May 1889. For 13 years, according to a caption, the Conly family lived in this soddie near Jasper. Three people stand at the door, staring blankly into the camera, their eyes like windows looking out on infinity. An ax and shovel stand outside the door. A meager pile of possessions leans against an outside wall. That is all there is, except the horizon—nothing but grass stretching off to the soft edges of the

The Conly Sod Castle in Jasper, 1889. (Pipestone County Historical Society)

photograph, as though it disappears into fog, distance, and emptiness. Unlike the Indians, whose ancestors walked from the expansive steppes of Asia across the featureless tundra of North America, these people's ancestors—perhaps these settlers themselves—came from the dark cloistered forests of Europe. And, unlike the Indians, these settlers lived here without a womb of community, native culture, and sacred landmarks to shelter them from this thunderous space. Thirteen years must have seemed like a lifetime. Journals tell stories of people going mad from the emptiness. The photo recalls the words of historian Henry Steele Commager:

> *A*gainst the physical environment men can indeed struggle, and they can emerge successful. . . . But what of the souls of men here on the distant plains? What of the infinite loneliness, of the secret fears, of the primeval silences that shake the faith of men?

Or, more chilling, those of O. E. Rölvaag: "The Great Plain drinks the blood of Christian men."

The bedrock core of this area is viewed most dramatically at **Blue Mounds State Park,** south of Pipestone on US 75. There a ridge of Sioux quartzite two

The Calumet Inn, circa 1900. (Pipestone County Historical Society)

miles long, as lurid as a bruise, sprouts from the prairie, as though the god who made this place dropped a raw steak on the prairie. The bedrock was the beach of a late Precambrian sea, where waves lapped and rippled the sand perhaps a billion years ago. Today, however, not a drop of water is to be seen—just a fetch of farmland and wooded windbreaks that, on a clear day from the crest of the cliff, reaches deep into Iowa and west into South Dakota. Step back from the ridge to indulge your sense of history: The prairie grasses close around to create the impression that a robe of rippling grass stretches horizon to horizon. The illusion is furthered by a herd of about 65 bison that graze in a 120-acre pasture. They, like the patch of prairie itself, are an illusion of a world that once was, a remnant in a threadbare quilt of land that once held the full fabric of tallgrass prairie.

◆ PIONEER LIFE: MUSEUMS AND MONUMENTS *map page 59, D&E-3&4*

Several other sites scattered throughout the area provide a taste of early prairie and farm life. Several towns in southwestern Minnesota offer today's travelers a chance to understand the hardships of life on the prairie. The **Nobles County Museum** in **Worthington** exhibits 1870 furnishings. To the west, off I-90, lies the town of

Blue Mounds State Park is home to a herd of buffalo and also provides some pleasant hiking trails.

Abandoned barn on the state's southwestern plains.

Jackson, where a monument commemorates settlers slain in the U.S.–Dakota War and the **Jackson County Courthouse** displays a varied collection of fossils and Indian artifacts. **Fort Belmont,** two miles south of the US 71 and I-90 junction, is an eclectic historic museum that includes a log chapel, flour mill, and old autos. **Heron Lake Environmental Learning Center,** just north of nearby Lakefield on the west side of MN 86, offers educational outdoor activities pertaining to a shallow 8,000-acre prairie lake and wetland.

To the north is **Walnut Grove** and the **Laura Ingalls Wilder Museum,** devoted to the author whose children's books describing pioneer life inspired generations of readers, as well as television's *Little House on the Prairie.* Museum memorabilia depicts the life that Wilder described in *On the Banks of Plum Creek,* set in the area. *330 Eighth Street; 507-859-2358.* Nearby in **Tracy,** the **Wheels Across the Prairie Museum** contains a 1915 steam engine, old bicycles with wooden wheels, and tools and machinery used by settlers.

Near **Sanborn,** a mile east and a quarter mile south of the junction of highways 71 and 14, the **McCone Sod House Bed-and-Breakfast** *(see page 331)* provides an

PRAIRIE PATH

THOSE WILD ROCHESTER BOYS

In the early 1860s, Rev. Charles Woodward came as an Episcopal missionary to Rochester, Minnesota and was the first minister of Calvary Episcopal Church across the street from what is now the Mayo Clinic. To support his family, and with the aid of his young sons, he plowed 160 acres of virgin prairie and began farming. The following excerpt is from the memoirs of his son William, who was born in 1863.

*W*hile carrying on his missionary labors in Rochester, father purchased 160 acres of virgin prairie land six miles from the town, and a wood lot 40 acres in extent four miles beyond. . . .

Wild pigeons, now exterminated thru the indifference, greed and cruelty of pot hunters in those days, made their flights in myriads so many that they darkened the sky and constituted one of my first and vivid memories. The call of prairie chickens in the early morning, the mourning dove, the shrill warning whistle of the striped gopher, the howl of the prairie wolf—all these stand out in my memory together with the bitter cold of winter, so intense that life itself seemed likely to freeze, never to reawaken. The intense heat of summer, the marvelous skies, torrential thunder storms; hard work and simple living for us all.

Shivarees (Charivari) often accompanied the weddings in our section. Usually well intentioned, they often degenerated into much that was insulting to the newlyweds and altogether disgraceful. Young men and boys principally partook, assembling around the house where the young couple were located, with their tin pans, kettles, shotguns and the like. It was a matter of noise, unrestrained, until beer or something harder was handed out and even then liberties were taken, quite indefensible.

In our neighborhood lived a farmer at whose home a daughter's marriage had taken place. He gave warning no shivaree would be permitted. The night was dark. The group of noise makers assembled around the house and began their performance. The farmer appeared in the door way with a shotgun and fired several blank shells. The crowd broke and started at full speed down the road. A short distance away the farmer had fastened firmly a rope from fence post to fence post, eighteen inches from the ground. In the darkness it is safe to say that every one of the racing men and boys were brought to a stop, fell, and were bruised and shaken up; many of them seriously. On another occasion the infuriated mother-in-law poured scalding water and worse from the upper windows.

—*William F. Woodward, recalling the 1870s*

unusual opportunity to relive days of the frontier. Nineteenth-century pioneers who homesteaded the treeless prairie built their houses with walls of thick prairie sod. "People can buy an 1880s night in the sod house," says Virginia McCone. Her husband, Stan, has long been fascinated with pioneer life. His own ancestors homesteaded in a sod house in South Dakota. He built two sod houses, the first, the so-called rich man's soddie, in 1987. It is large, with a wood floor and six windows. "I think that's very extravagant," Virginia McCone says. Such a house would have cost early settlers $50 to build, mostly for the windows and scarce lumber. It is furnished with simple furniture from the late 1800s. More likely, the pioneers' first house would have been more modest, in the vein of the "poor man's dugout" that Stan McCone built the following year. Measuring only 18 square feet, with fewer windows and a dirt floor, it feels like a cellar and can't be rented out for overnight stays in these modern times. This kind of shelter might have cost $5. The sod walls, two feet thick, are hard and bristly with dried roots and grass. "It was something they were glad to get out of and put behind them," Virginia says.

◆ JEFFERS PETROGLYPHS   *map page 59, D-4*

Prairies, even the scattered remnants that survive, are transcendent places. The pull to other worlds and times is especially great at the Jeffers Petroglyphs (15 miles north of Windom on US 71, then east three miles to Cottonwood County 2). There, a lichen-encrusted sheet of Sioux quartzite spreads out over the prairie. You can see ripples in the rock from the era more than a billion summers ago when the sand changed from beach to bedrock. In more recent time Indians hammered petroglyphs into the rock. Nearly 2,000 images adorn the ridge. The images are difficult to date. The only telltale clue is the presence of atlatls, the spear-throwing levers Indians abandoned for the bow and arrow about 2,000 years ago. Many images might be much more recent, though none seem to depict horses or guns, recent arrivals on the plains. "As regards their meaning," wrote archeologist Theodore H. Lewis in 1891, "it is purely a matter of conjecture, and the reader may draw his own conclusions as to whether religious or mythological ideas entered into their construction or whether they were but casual records or idle work." *Visitors center: 507-628-5591.*

Nearly without exception, the images are very faint. Kneeling on the rock and matching my guidebook to the fissures, I run my fingers over the carvings, feeling the bison and thunderbirds, as though reading a history in Braille. There are

moments, when time turns inside out, when the past pushes aside the present, and the ghosts of those long dead speak. I imagine the rock alive with dancing shamans and warriors.

The essence of prairie is space, a confounding abstraction. "What seems flat seems empty," writes Paul Gruchow. "When we are faced with emptiness, we turn inward. . . . The prairie is like a daydream. It is one of the few plainly visible things which you can't photograph. No camera lens can take in a big enough piece of it." It is, as Gruchow notes, no more possible to walk up and touch the essence of the prairie than it is to walk up and touch the moon.

Perhaps that is the reason I turn my attention to the details at my feet rather than the immensity in the infinite, unbearable distance. I am as uncomfortable with these abstractions as I am with contemplations of God. When I allow myself to turn inward, I am left wanting. I feel a rattling emptiness impossible to console, a terrible space impossible to fill. It is the details that somehow reduce the prairie space to a scale I can comprehend.

Milkweed disperses its seeds into the steady prairie wind (above).

Jeffers Petroglyphs (left), found north of Windom, date back some 2,000 years.

■ RED RIVER VALLEY *map page 91*

There is something mysteriously stunning about absence—in the case of the Red River Valley, the complete absence of topographic relief. It's hard to believe something called a valley could spread out as flat as a lake. At times, the crown of the highway forms the highest land in sight. Driving into the valley one evening, I passed beneath a sky filled with dark thunderheads, heavy as anvils, pregnant with lightning and fury. Lightning popped, emerging from blackness, disappearing to blackness. In the distance the yellow lights of Fargo-Moorhead spread like a galaxy on the flat, black universe of the prairie. Suddenly three bolts flashed simultaneously, like tines of a pitchfork thrust to the ground, visible, I'm sure, for 30 miles in every direction. In such flatness, when the Red River rises just a few feet, it floods farmland for miles in every direction.

In fact, this great flat land did once form a lake. It was the bed of Glacial Lake Agassiz, an inland sea of continental proportions, stretching from west-central Minnesota northward nearly to Hudson Bay. Lake Winnipeg and Lake of the

An extraordinary photograph of a tornado taken by Lucille Handberg near Jasper on July 8, 1927.

Woods are but tiny remnants. When the glaciers that formed the northern shore of the lake melted, the lake drained toward Hudson Bay, leaving behind a silty and utterly flat bed that would later prove to be some of the most fertile soil in Minnesota.

The Red River of the North winds northward to Canada in endless meanders. As dirty and slow as a lame hog, it gathers the fine soils of the valley in such volumes that they billow in the opaque river like curdled cream. Despite the thick water and muddy banks, the Red provides fishing for trophy channel catfish. In fact, at a latitude where northern pike and lake trout are the most common game fish, the Red sustains one of the northernmost catfish fisheries in existence. A recent creel survey indicated the catfish taken in the Manitoba portion of the Red, just downstream from the Minnesota border, *averaged* 19 pounds. Twenty-five-pounders are common.

As historian William E. Lass notes, geographically, most of the Red River Valley lies north of Minnesota, much closer to Winnipeg, Manitoba, than to the Twin Cities. Culturally, however, it belongs more to the agricultural south than the forested north. And in many ways, it seems west in more than simply direction. It is the beginning of the Great Plains, and you are as likely to see ten-gallon hats and cowboy boots here as anywhere else in Minnesota.

◆ EARLY LIFE IN THE VALLEY

In recent centuries, various Indian tribes lived in this country—most recently the Assiniboin and Dakota. They hunted the bison that roamed the flat grasslands. Frenchmen from Canada came to the Red River Valley to work the fur trade. The mixed-blood people that descended from these European traders and resident Indians became known as métis. Among the most famous métis traders was George Bonga, the descendent of Pierre Bonga, the former slave of a British army officer, and an Ojibwa woman. Educated in Montreal, George Bonga spoke French, English, and Ojibwa. He worked as an interpreter and later grew rich as an independent trader.

In the early 1800s, disgruntled English, Scotch, and Swiss settlers fled Lord Selkirk's settlement at present-day Winnipeg, following the Red River south into the United States. Furs, bison hides, powder, shot, sugar, tea, apples, flour, liquor, bacon, canned foods, and other goods were carried between these Red River settlements and St. Paul by Red River ox carts. The two-wheeled carts were constructed entirely of wood, and were pulled by an ox or pony. Fully loaded, the ungreased wooden wheels and axles let loose a frightful scream. A train of ox carts could be heard for miles across the prairie, as they followed several trails from Fort Garry (now Winnipeg) through the Red River Valley and then southeastward to St. Paul. The Woods Trail, as its name suggests, tended to the forested area of Minnesota, roughly following the present route of US highways 59 and 10. The Middle Trail ran along the present route of Interstate 94. The Minnesota Valley Trail followed its namesake, crossing at Traverse des Sioux and leading to Mendota. In the three decades before the Civil War, the Red River ox carts made St. Paul one of the principal fur markets in the country.

Later, other European settlers flooded the Red River Valley after entering the United States at New York City. Especially prevalent along the Red River were Norwegians and Germans, who far outnumbered all other ethnic groups.

The Red River Valley became famous for cash grain, especially wheat, in the late 1800s, when the valley was known as an important breadbasket for the country. Agriculture, still the principal industry of the region, has become more diverse. Important crops are sugar beets, potatoes, wheat. Fields of sunflowers follow the sun across the sky.

Sunflowers stretch to the horizon in the Red River Valley.

♦ MOORHEAD *map opposite, E-1*

Moorhead (pop. 32,300) grew in tandem with Fargo, North Dakota, at a historic ford across the Red River of the North. The two towns were a historic hub on the Northern Pacific line from the Twin Cities. Like most prairie towns, Moorhead skitters across the prairie like grease on a skillet, with nothing in sight to contain it. The Red River is too puny to gather it close. That said, however, the old homes make a pleasant nucleus of a town.

A stunning facility is the **Heritage *Hjemkomst* Interpretive Center**, a brick and fabric-roofed building whose very outline hints at the main feature inside—a working replica of a Viking sailing ship. The *Hjemkomst* (a name that means "homecoming") was started in 1971 by Robert Asp, a junior high school counselor in Moorhead who became intrigued with the idea of building a Viking ship and sailing to Norway. He built the ship from native white oak in an old potato warehouse, rechristened the Hawley Ship Yards. Though Asp was diagnosed with leukemia shortly after building began, he finished the ship and sailed on its maiden voyage in Lake Superior, five months before his death in 1980. In 1982 a crew that included Asp's children sailed the *Hjemkomst* from Lake Superior, through the Great Lakes and down the St. Lawrence Seaway to

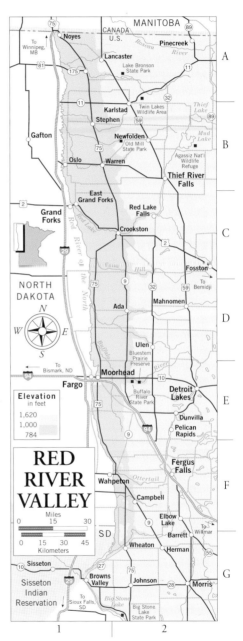

Bergen, Norway. On the Atlantic they weathered a ferocious storm that cracked the hull. Said one of the sailors, "The waves just jumped in the boat with us." Today the *Hjemkomst,* more than 76 feet long, sits at center stage of the Interpretive Center. Modeled on the 1,000-year-old Jokstad Viking warship unearthed from a Norwegian burial mound—a boat that might have made a similar journey across the Atlantic—the *Hjemkomst* seems gracefully reptilian, its long strakes like huge scales and a dragon head mounting its bow. But more than the dragon head or tail, it is the rich depth of the wood that makes it seem alive—a living testament to dreams beautiful and wild. Also located in the building are **Heritage Hall,** which displays traveling exhibits pertaining to the Red River Valley, and the expertly displayed artifacts of the **Clay County Museum.** *Heritage Hjemkomst Interpretive Center: 202 North First Avenue; 218-299-5511.*

Among the old attractive houses of Moorhead is the Victorian **Solomon G. Comstock House** at 506 South Eighth Street, built in 1883 by a partner of transportation tycoon James J. Hill. Comstock founded Moorhead State University. His daughter, Ada, became the first dean of women at the University of Minnesota and, later, the president of Radcliffe College. The house contains many of the family's original furnishings. In Moorhead is another college—**Concordia College** (Seventh Avenue), known for its music program.

◆ BUFFALO RIVER STATE PARK   *map page 91, E-2*

About 10 miles east of Moorhead along US 10, **Buffalo River State Park** offers peaceful trails through remnants of the native tallgrass prairie. A lively stream provides a stark contrast to the sluggish Red. *218 498-2124.*

Next to the park is The Nature Conservancy's **Bluestem Prairie Preserve.** Combined with the state park and Moorhead State University's Regional Science Center, this prairie totals more than 4,600 acres. To maintain the prairie, staff workers and volunteers gather native seeds and replant plowed or heavily grazed areas with native prairie plants. Following the Indian practice intended to improve hunting, the caretakers periodically burn part of the prairie to remove dead vegetation and suppress exotic species such as Kentucky bluegrass and invasive natives such as sumac.

◆ CROOKSTON   *map page 91, C-1/2*

About 60 miles north off US 75, in Crookston, a tour of the **Polk County Museum** will take you by an 1880 schoolhouse, 1872 log house, and other artifacts.

> ## SUMMER EVENINGS
> July 13, 1938
>
> *W*ashed clothes. Vacuumed upstairs. In P.M. Oscar & I went for a walk around some of the fields. It was a perfect evening. The birds were singing in the trees by Coulee (a small stream, usually flooded in spring, dry in summer). Away off we could hear a train. The fields make us happy. Even the man in the moon came up with a cigar in his mouth. One of those rare perfect moments when everything is in harmony.
>
> —Maybelle Quarberg (who farmed with her husband near Crookston)
> as reprinted in *Too Hot, Went to Lake*

Old Mill State Park, located on the banks of the Middle River north of Crookston and east on Minnesota 4, protects the site of the Larson mill, a hub of the surrounding farm community since 1886. The Larsons, immigrants from Sweden, must have been the original hard luck settlers of the area. No sooner had the family built a beautiful two-story house on their homestead than a government surveyor informed them it wasn't actually on their property. So they dismantled it and moved it on a hand-drawn sled. Their mills were the source of endless disasters. The Larsons tried water, wind, and steam power. Various mills flooded out, blew down, dried up. But the Larsons rebuilt time and again, on four different locations, grinding flour for their neighbors and attracting thousands for annual picnics. There's no denying such ingenuity and persistence. Their mill has been restored. Each summer, the steam-powered mill is started up for Grinding Days. *Old Mill State Park; 218-437-8174.*

Another large natural area in the Red River Valley is the **Twin Lakes State Wildlife Management Area** near Karlstad. In September the 8,200-acre state area is an important staging area for migrating sandhill cranes. On occasion more than 2,000 cranes are visible from Minnesota 11.

On the prairie, more than anywhere else it seems, you are likely to meet interesting people undertaking interesting projects. Why that is, I'm not sure. Perhaps simply because so little prairie is left, those of us who appreciate it tend to run into one another. I prove this to myself yet again at **Lake Bronson State Park,** about 20 miles northwest of the Twin Lakes, where I encounter Julie Otterson, a graduate student at the University of Minnesota. Unrolling a map, she explains she has toured the tallgrass prairies of the United States, from Oklahoma to this remnant of prairie in the far northwestern corner of Minnesota. She has gathered tissues and seeds of prairie plants to determine their genetic variability. "What I'd like to do is look at the evolutionary potential of plants in these fragmented prairies," she says. She hopes to determine how these plants might adapt and survive if the climate changes, such as through global warming, since they are unable to migrate or spread through the farmland that surrounds these isolated fragments of prairie.

Yet even such isolated fragments can work their magic. As Otterson drives off, I hike into the grass, a rolling savanna and prairie with acres of big bluestem and bur oaks. Such a scene, I imagine, would have been picture of heaven on earth to early hunters. In fact, evidence of prehistoric bison hunters has been excavated nearby. I can imagine a herd of elk or bison in the distance. Who knows? Even grazing mammoths, meaty targets for a small group of hunters with atlatls and spears. *Lake Bronson State Park: 218-754-2200.*

In my reverie, I think of John Madson, who wrote a very good book about the tallgrass called *Where the Sky Began* that is, by turns, informative and reflective. "The open land was calculated to turn a man in on himself," Madson wrote. "A land without echoes or shadow except the one cast by him."

This diorama depicts sandhill cranes, huge flocks of which stop on the prairies of southwestern Minnesota during their annual migration.

RED RIVER VALLEY

This early Canadian version of "The Red River Valley" tells of a young métis woman whose heart was broken by a white trader or soldier. The song was later adapted to the Red River between Texas and Oklahoma and became much more famous.

*F*rom this valley they say you are going,
I shall miss your blue eyes and sweet smile,
And you take with you all of the sunshine
That has brightened my pathway a while.

As you go to your home by the ocean
May you never forget those sweet hours
That we spent in the Red River Valley
And the love we exchanged 'mid its bowers.

There never could be such a longing
In the heart of a pale maiden's breast
As dwells in the heart you are breaking
With love for the boy who came west.

And the dark maiden's prayer for her lover
To the Spirit that rules all this world
Is that sunshine his pathway may cover
And the grief of the Red River Girl.

Chorus:
So consider a while ere you leave me
Do not hasten to bid me adieu,
But remember the Red River Valley
And the half-breed that loved you so true.

SOUTHEASTERN HILLS

■ HIGHLIGHTS

	page
Hastings History Tour	104
Red Wing	106
Lake Pepin	110
Winona	115
Lanesboro	119
Mystery Cave	122
Mayo Clinic	123
Mantorville	125

SOUTHEASTERN HILLS

TO A KENTUCKY BOY WHO GREW UP in the foothills of the Appalachians or a hillbilly from the Ozarks, the hills of southeastern Minnesota may seem common enough as country goes. But to someone like me, familiar from an early age with the lake country of central Minnesota, the canoe country along the Canadian border, and the prairie and farmland of the west, these hills seem like topsy-turvy country indeed.

For one thing, they are not so much hills as valleys—"coulee country" they call it in some parts. When you rip along in your car, windows down, wind and dust and the sound of crunching gravel in the air, winding, climbing, turning, climbing and climbing up a country road, you aren't so much surmounting a hill as just getting up out of some twisted, steep valley carved deep into the bedrock by some age-old and obscure runt of a creek. And when you break out on the summit, rather than the sweeping view from a hilltop, the panorama you might expect, you're surrounded by cornfields.

Hills or valleys, they make up some of the most rugged terrain in the state (excluding possibly the North Shore of Lake Superior). They owe their existence to the glaciers—or lack of them. During the most recent ice age—which began about 75,000 years ago and ended in Minnesota about 10,000 years ago—continental glaciers smothered nearly all of Minnesota, leveling and grinding the terrain, and leaving behind low hills and ridges formed of glacial debris. The Southeast escaped this glacial bulldozing (though it had been affected by glaciers during much older ice ages). Thus the handiwork of rivers over hundreds of thousands of years—the erosion of deep, lakeless valleys—was never erased. Indeed, it never stopped, but continues to the present.

But it is not topography alone that distinguishes the southeast from the rest of the state; the geology, flora, fauna, and history are unusual by Minnesota standards.

The soluble limestone bedrock, evident in the outcrops and cliffs that rim the river valleys, is riddled with caves and sinkholes, and cool, calcium-rich springs and trout streams. With greater rainfall than the prairie and a warmer climate than areas north, the southeastern hills are the northernmost extent of the Kentucky coffee tree, black walnut, and red mulberry. The region is a stronghold of the wild turkey. The southeast has the highest number of reptiles and amphibians in Minnesota, including the only two poisonous snakes found in the state: the relatively common timber rattlesnake in the craggy bluffs, and the much rarer massasauga in

the Mississippi backwaters. The ranges of several mid-latitude species, from bull-frogs to opossums, reach northward through the southeastern hills but peter out by the Twin Cities.

The southeastern hill country is perhaps the most engaging region of Minnesota, the best for an aimless ramble for a day or a week. It comprises picturesque valleys and historic towns (generally, the oldest in Minnesota). Paddle a canoe down one of several swift rivers. Fish for trout. Bargain for antiques or Amish furniture. Ride a bike along country roads and winding trails. The Mississippi River Valley and Southeastern Hills are especially beautiful in autumn, when the hardwood forests blaze yellow and red.

■ MISSISSIPPI RIVER HISTORY

The Mississippi River, which forms our border with Wisconsin for nearly 140 miles, is the backbone of the region. Several large tributaries—notably the Vermilion, Cannon, Zumbro, Whitewater, and Root—girdle the region and join this backbone like so many ribs.

This far along its path, the Mississippi is already a large river. In the past, its water, regulated and filtered by the well-vegetated prairies and forests, ran impressively clear, according to geologist D. D. Owen. Seeing the river at a point near the southeasternmost tip of the state in the early 1800s, he wrote, "Imagine a stream a mile in width whose waters are as transparent as those of a mountain spring, flowing over rock and gravel."

The Glacial River Warren, the deluge that flowed from Glacial Lake Agassiz to carve the Minnesota River Valley, joined the drainage from Glacial Lake Duluth at the present confluence of the Mississippi and St. Croix rivers. This combined torrent flowed along the present course of the Mississippi Valley. So deep and fast did this river erode the soft sandstone and fractured limestone bedrock that tributaries along the western shore were left perched high above the river—hanging valleys spilling their contents to the Mississippi in long falls and cataracts.

From any number of high overlooks you can imagine this scene still, though in recent millennia the tributaries have burrowed deeper into their valleys, finding their way to the Mississippi's own level. On a misty morning, when the road is quiet, between the trains that run along the shore, before the fishermen crank up their outboards, you can imagine a quieter era when the birch-bark canoes of Indians and, later, of fur traders, coursed silently on the river. No one describes this scene better than Mark Twain. No one in literature is so at home on the river:

SOUTHEASTERN HILLS

The majestic bluffs that overlook the river, along through this region, charm one with the grace and variety of their forms, and the soft beauty of their adornment. The steep, verdant slope, whose base is at the water's edge, is topped by a lofty rampart of broken, turreted rocks, which are exquisitely rich and mellow in color—mainly dark browns and dull greens, but splashed with other tints. And then you have the shining river, winding here and there and yonder, its sweep interrupted at intervals by clusters of wooded islands threaded by silver channels; and you have glimpses of distant villages, asleep upon capes; and of stealthy rafts slipping along in the shade of the forest walls; and of white steamers vanishing around remote points. And it is all as tranquil and reposeful as dreamland, and has nothing this-worldly about it—nothing to hang a fret or a worry upon.

◆ CANOES AND STEAMBOATS

Canoes were the first boats on the river. Then, in the late 1700s and early 1800s, appeared a boat uniquely American, made for the big rivers in the interior of the continent. These were keel boats, 50 to 80 feet long, gracefully tapered and pointed at both ends, propelled by sail or oars or, if necessary, towed from shore with a 1,000-foot-long rope. And, if necessary, in forging upstream where men could not easily walk the shore, they were pushed by long poles of white ash. John Madson, in *Up on the River,* describes the ordeal:

> The captain would shout: *"À bas les perches!"* and the crewmen would plant the poles in the riverbed, the knobbed ends of the poles in the hollows of their shoulders, and walk toward the stern, slowly pushing the keelboat forward. When the man farthest aft had gone as far as he could, the *patron* would bellow: *"Levez les perches!"* and the men would raise their poles, walk quickly back toward the bow, and again obey the command "Down with the poles."

This all day to make eight to twelve miles. Though they would endure for several decades more, keelboats were doomed with the arrival of the steamboat *Virginia* at Fort Snelling (now in the Twin Cities) in 1823. As Madson says, ". . . there suddenly seemed to be steamboats everywhere. They materialized as if by magic—a swelling traffic of side-wheelers and stern-wheelers that ran from Saint Louis to the head of navigation at St. Anthony Falls."

And what excitement their arrival caused in the little towns that sat on the river's shoulders. Twain again:

> *B*efore these events, the day was glorious with expectancy; after them, the day was a dead and empty thing. . . . A negro drayman, famous for his quick eye and prodigious voice, lifts up the cry, "S-t-e-a-m-boat a-comin'! . . . The town drunkard stirs, the clerks wake up, a furious clatter of drays follows, every house and store pours out a human contribution, and all in a twinkling the dead town is alive and moving. . . . The people fasten their eyes upon the coming boat as upon a wonder they are seeing for the first time. And the boat *is* rather a handsome sight, too. She is long and sharp and trim and pretty; she has two tall, fancy-topped chimneys, with a gilded device of some kind swung between them; a fanciful pilot-house, all glass and "gingerbread," perched on top of the "texas" deck behind them.

During the 1840s, a steamboat trip up the Mississippi to St. Anthony Falls became what George Catlin had originally called a "fashionable tour" to see the newly purchased West. Henry Lewis produced and exhibited his canvas "panorama" of the river between St. Louis and Fort Snelling. Measuring a staggering 1,200

View on the Mississippi *(above) by Ferdinand Reichardt, 1857. (Minnesota Historical Society)*
An aerial view (left) of the Mississippi where it flows beside Goodhue County in the southeast.

SOUTHEASTERN HILLS

yards long and 12 feet high, it showed the river's natural features, Indian villages, and settlers' towns. In New York and Boston alone, 400,000 saw Lewis's depiction of the river, so hungry were people to see the Mississippi. Soon tourists were packing steamboats bound for St. Paul.

Mississippi riverboat pilots memorized every bend, every downed tree, every shoal in order to maneuver their cargo and passengers up and down more than 2,000 miles of river. But the river was too fickle for us by far, flooding one season, drying up the next. At times the river, despite its breadth and grandeur, provided barely a yard of water in its riffles to float a boat. The average life of a steamboat, its hull abused by shoals and riddled with holes from snags, was only five years. The Corps of Engineers began to dredge the shoals and yank snags—"pulling the river's teeth," in Twain's words. Even that was not enough to satisfy shipping interests, which were losing the competition for cargo with the railroads. In the late 1800s Congress directed the Corps to build thousands of wing dams to force the Mississippi into a narrower, deeper channel. Yet even then, the railroad outstripped the Mississippi's ability to carry cargo. By 1880 the Golden Age of Steamboats was over. The river and its boats were outhustled and outcarried by the railroads that spread like spider webs across the Mississippi basin. Oh, heck, let Twain tell it:

> The new railroad, stretching up through Mississippi, Tennessee, and Kentucky, to Northern railway-centers, began to divert the passenger travel from the steamboats; next the war came and almost entirely annihilated the steamboat industry during several years, leaving most of the pilots idle and the cost of living advancing all the time; then the treasurer of the St. Louis association put his hand into the till and walked off with every dollar of the ample fund; and finally, the railroads intruding everywhere, there was little for the steamers to do, when the war was over, but carry freights; so straightway [sic] some genius from the Atlantic coast introduced the plan of towing a dozen steamer cargoes down to New Orleans at the tail of a vulgar little tug-boat; and behold, in the twinkling of an eye, as it were, the [pilots'] association and the noble science of piloting were things of the dead and pathetic past!

Lack of use and demand were not persuasive enough arguments for Congress and the Corps. Even as river traffic shriveled during the late 1800s and the early 1900s, the federal government acceded to the irresponsible demands of river boosters to spend millions to deepen and maintain the Mississippi River channel.

In 1930, Congress authorized a huge public works project that led to a system of 29 locks and dams from Minneapolis to St. Louis to pool up the river, flood her riffles, and allow the passage of heavy barges and towboats.

Still, no matter how much it's changed, its riffles flooded and current impounded, the river remains, as Twain said, a "wonderful book [with] a new story to tell every day." It floats traffic of barges and pleasure boats on its broad main channel, harbors fish in its riffles, supports wildlife in its backwaters, and carries cities along its banks. Whatever changes we have made to it, this river remains the grandest stream in our state, and most would say the nation.

■ FOLLOWING THE MISSISSIPPI   *map page 97*

Short of a ride on one of the river steamboats from St. Paul, one of the best ways to see the Mississippi is to set out on US 61, going south from St. Paul. A picture of the grand valley of the Mississippi and the southeastern hills begins to unfold as soon as you leave. A high bluff rises to the east. To the west, toward the river, a long view stretches across wetlands, backwaters, and bottomlands broad and strong enough to carry the weight of railroads and refineries.

Many of the settlers traveling to Minnesota in the mid-1800s arrived by boat via the Mississippi. As the result, the ports of call along the river developed into some of the first, and now the oldest, towns in the state. Says Twain:

> *F*rom St. Louis northward there are all the enlivening signs of the presence of active, energetic, intelligent, prosperous, practical 19th-century populations. The people don't dream; they work. . . . One breathes a go-ahead atmosphere which tastes good in the nostrils.

The people built their business districts of stately brick and stone. Owing partly to the era, partly to the steep riverine topography, the towns, even today, huddle near the river, a compact economic knot of activity, rather than spread across the land like many of the railroad and lumber towns to the north and west. As in river towns elsewhere, the slope of the valley and activity at the waterfront brought about the development of a cohesive, river-hugging downtown. The limestone bluffs provided building material of a beautiful and durable sort. Many of these towns were sawmill or flour mill towns, shipping wheat brought by railroad to large cities downstream on the Mississippi. They lie along US 61, my candidate for the most beautiful highway in the state: at its northern end, the stark beauty of Lake Superior; at its southern end, the bucolic lushness of the Mississippi River Valley. (The middle section between St. Paul and Duluth is, however, largely unremarkable.)

SOUTHEASTERN
HILLS

◆ HASTINGS *map page 97, B-2*

Hastings grew from the early river settlement of Oliver's Grove and earned its name in a drawing. Land speculators behind the town had tossed their names in a hat. The winner was Henry Hastings Sibley, fur trader and, later, first governor. *Hastings History Tour: The "Self-Guided Walk and Drive"* leads visitors to about 30 19th-century commercial buildings and houses throughout town. One of the most elaborate is the 1865 Gothic Revival **LeDuc-Simmons Mansion,** 1629 Vermilion Street. Built by Gen. William LeDuc, once secretary of agriculture to President Rutherford B. Hayes, the house has nine fireplaces, servants' quarters, and a chapel. It is now being restored by the Minnesota Historical Society. Other houses on tour include the Greek Revival **Olson House,** Italianate **Pringle House,** and the **Norrish Octagon House,** all on West Second Street in the residential district. The tour brochure is available from the Chamber of Commerce; *111 Third Street East; www.hastingsmn.org.*

The spectacular gorge and falls of the **Vermilion River** is hidden from the view of most travelers, though it lies only a quarter mile downstream of US 61 through

Cargo barges make their way up the river above Red Wing.

Hastings. A trail and park follow the river, past the falls and through a narrow gorge. About a half-mile below the falls are the remains of the state's first flour mill, built by Alexander Ramsey in 1857. On the Mississippi at the upstream end of town is **Lock and Dam 2**, which provides good fishing for a variety of game fish and a hangout for wintering eagles.

◆ CANNON RIVER VALLEY   *map page 97, B-2&3*

Heading southeastward on US 61 (or, better, Minnesota 316) you soon plunge into the valley of the Cannon River. The Cannon, by the way, has everything to do with canoes and nothing to do with heavy artillery. It was named *Rivière aux Canots* (River of Canoes) by the French because it was such a handy thoroughfare by canoe to reach the buffalo prairies to the west. English speakers later mangled the name. Nonetheless, the Cannon remains a lovely canoeing stream. You could do worse than to take a day exploring some of its treasures, by car or canoe. Launch your canoe at **Welch**, an old mill village about five miles upstream from the highway, or at **Cannon Falls**, about 12 miles farther upstream. Then enjoy a leisurely trip past tangled hardwood and bottomland forest, in the shadow of steep bluffs, down quick riffles where spunky smallmouth bass and sleek, silvery channel

All commercial river traffic must pass through a series of locks and dams such as the one pictured above near Red Wing.

catfish swim. As the Cannon slides under the US 61 bridge toward its confluence with the Mississippi, it begins to lose its way, breaking into a multitude of channels in trying to find the big river. Several years ago, when I paddled down the Cannon, its channels split and split and split again, growing smaller each time, until finally we had to use our paddles as poles to push along the grassy banks. Bald eagles sat in bare trees, waiting like vultures. Not for us, we hoped.

The **Cannon Valley Trail** provides another way to follow the river. An old railroad grade, the trail runs 19 miles from **Cannon Falls,** an old and pleasant town on the river, to Red Wing. Passing through prairie and woods, the trail is suitable for biking, in-line skating, or hiking; *651-258-4141.* If you want simply to explore the Cannon Valley by the many back roads, check out **Vasa**, a Swedish Lutheran community dating to 1855. Among the buildings in town are the Greek Revival Vasa Swedish Lutheran Church, the Vasa Museum, and 1875 town hall.

◆ RED WING *map page 97, B-3*

Approaching Red Wing (pop. 15,135), US 61 passes the usual fast-food outlets and other ubiquitous architectural dreck. But once you reach downtown, you'll see that geography and history have been kind to the city. Townsfolk have tried to capitalize on their scenic location and preserve their historic buildings. Even the local Hardee's fast-food outlet occupies a refurbished brick train depot. Cradled by limestone bluffs at one of the sharpest bends in the navigable Mississippi, the town is named for Dakota Indian chief Ta-tan-ka-mani (Walking Buffalo), also known as Koo-poo-hoo-sha (Red Wing) for the swan wing, dyed scarlet, that served as talisman for his lineage. His band of Mdewakanton Dakota lived near the present site of town, at the foot of an abrupt and distinctive hill today called **Barn Bluff.** As farms began to fill the valleys along the west side of the Mississippi in the 1860s, Red Wing became an important port for grain shipments. Briefly, Goodhue County farms produced more wheat than those of any other county in the country, and Red Wing became a leading port. Lumber barons, mill owners, and bankers built antebellum and Victorian monuments on the hillside. The centerpiece of the historic downtown is the elegant **St. James Hotel,** *406 Main Street, (See page 325),* built in 1874 to serve visitors arriving by river and rail. (A trolley tour departs from the St. James.) The hotel fell into disrepair until 1977, when it was purchased and renovated by the **Red Wing Shoe Company.** (The company, known for its hunting, hiking, and work boots, is a major employer in town, as it provides about 1,400 jobs.)

TALKING WEATHER

*I*f you can't carry on a conversation about the weather in Minnesota, you might as well pack your bags and head back to where you came from. One day the clerk at the Red Owl said to this guy ahead of me in line, "What d'ya think of this weather?" And this guy's face got red and he said,

"I don't think anything. I don't pay any attention. What weather? Are you kidding me? Do I know you?"

That was not a good reply for Minnesota.

Here are two Minnesotans getting wound up on the weather.

"What d'ya think of this weather?"

"Boy, it's something."

"I've never seen anything like it."

"You got it right."

—Howard Mohr, *How to Talk Minnesotan,* 1987

The rigors of Minnesota winters include 20-foot-deep snowdrifts. (Underwood Photo Archives, San Francisco)

◆ HISTORIC DOWNTOWN RED WING

Many other 19th-century buildings form the downtown. The "mall," situated along East and West avenues adjacent to the downtown, is ringed by churches and civic buildings, including the **T. B. Sheldon Memorial Auditorium,** built in 1904 and recently renovated. The nation's first municipally owned and operated theater, the auditorium has a neo-Renaissance exterior in the Beaux-Arts style, with small faces popping out of the exterior as if each were Scrooge's door knocker. The interior is lushly finished with curving stairways and balcony, gold-leaf, cast-plaster decorations, and painted murals. It now stages shows and concerts. *443 West Third Street.*

Red Wing has long been famous for its utilitarian ceramic pottery, including storage crocks and jars once used in households all across America.

The E. S. Hoyt House in Red Wing is a classic example of Prairie School–style architecture.

Historic houses include the unmistakable 1857 **Lawther Octagonal House at** 927 Third Street, the 1868 French Second Empire **Sprague House at** 1008 Third Street, and 1913 Prairie School–style **E. S. Hoyt House at** 300 Hill Street. The **Goodhue County Courthouse,** on Fifth Street between East and West Avenues, exemplifies the 1930s architecture of the Works Progress Administration. The Italianate **Pratt-Tabor Inn,** a bed-and-breakfast *(see page 325),* stands near the center of town. A brochure called *Footsteps through Historic Red Wing* is available at the St. James and other downtown locations.

Red Wing is also known for the crocks, jugs, and jars of the Red Wing Potteries. The company closed in 1967 after a long strike. The factory itself has been converted to a complex of stores and antique shops. The **Red Wing Pottery Salesroom** sells remaining Red Wing Potteries inventory and other name-brand pottery, including locally produced stoneware. Also here are a couple of potters who are making and selling 19th-century-style salt-glazed pottery. *1995 West Main Street near US 61; 651-388-3562, 800-228-0174.*

The **Goodhue County Historical Museum,** located up the bluff from downtown, provides a broad view of Red Wing and the Mississippi Valley. On exhibit are Red Wing pottery, a full-size Dakota tepee (like the ones that once stood in villages on the banks of the river), and information about the immigrants who arrived from Scandinavia, Germany, and the eastern United States during the mid-1800s. *1166 Oak Street; 651-388-6024.*

Upstream from Red Wing is the **Prairie Island Dakota Reservation**. Most visitors head toward **Treasure Island Casino**, which is owned by the band. But it's also possible to arrange tours of the reservation and take in demonstrations and exhibits of Dakota life at the **Heritage Village**. Near the confluence of the Mississippi and Cannon Rivers are hundreds of Indian burial mounds, one of the largest such concentrations in the state. *651-460-8050.*

Heading downstream again, US 61 leads to **Frontenac,** a small town with houses dating to the 1850s. Frontenac was the site of agricultural Indian villages 2,000 years ago. In 1727 French explorers set up Fort Beauharnois, named for the governor general of New France. Two Jesuit missionaries at the fort established what may have been Minnesota's first church, the Mission St. Michael the Archangel. The town as it appears today developed during the mid-1800s as a resort village served by steamboats. Frontenac bustled during the two decades following the Civil War, but declined as steamboat traffic dwindled.

Next to town is **Frontenac State Park,** with 15 miles of walking trails and long vistas of Lake Pepin. The park is popular with birdwatchers, who watch in early May for more than two dozen species of migrating warblers, including the brilliant yellow prothonotary warbler.

■ LAKE PEPIN   *map page 97, B/C-3*

The sandy Chippewa River, entering the Mississippi from Wisconsin, has deposited a large delta, a natural dam of the larger river that in turn has formed Lake Pepin. This riverine lake, flanked by lofty, wooded bluffs, extends from Red Wing downstream to **Reads Landing** and is more than three miles across at its widest. Pepin is popular for sailing and motorboating. It's also a good fishing hole, especially for walleyes, saugers, big northern pike, and white bass, which roam the open water in ravenous schools, pursuing bait fish. **Maiden Rock,** a town and landmark on Pepin's Wisconsin shore, is named for the legend of Winona, a Dakota maiden. Forced by her parents to marry a man she didn't love, she committed suicide by leaping from a cliff. Mark Twain in *Life on the Mississippi* quotes a riverboat passenger as calling the story "perhaps the most celebrated, as well as the most pathetic, of all the legends of the Mississippi." As Twain also notes, the Dakota had young maidens flinging themselves from cliffs up and down the Mississippi Valley, and may well have had them jumping from bridges and pitching themselves beneath the wheels of speeding trains had they had those opportunities, but the legend of Maiden Rock has a particular twist. According to the passenger's version, she not only threw herself from the rock, but landed on her parents, "and dashed them in pieces," the passenger told Twain. "She was a good deal jarred up and jolted, but she got herself together and disappeared before the coroner reached the fatal spot; and 'tis said she sought and married her true love."

◆ MINNESOTA WINE

Minnesota is hardly known for its wine, but that doesn't mean vineyards in the hills and valleys in southern Minnesota aren't trying to build a reputation. One of the state's largest vineyards is **Marshall's Great River Vineyard**, just off US 61, three miles north of Lake City. Though Great River Vineyard does not operate a winery, several Minnesota vineyards do and they welcome guests for wine tasting. *Alexis Bailly Vineyards near Hastings; 651-437-1413, Scenic Valley Winery in Lanesboro; 507-467-2958, and Northern Vineyards (see page 209).*

◆ LAKE CITY

The largest small-craft harbor and marina on this part of the river provides the focal point for **Lake City.** It was here on Lake Pepin that waterskiing was invented in 1922, when 18-year-old Ralph Samuelson strapped on eight-foot pine skis and skimmed along the lake behind a motorboat. **Riverwalk,** a three-mile-long path, follows the shore of Pepin. Hok-Si-La Park, 250 acres of city land on the shore of the lake, provides good viewing for woodland and water birds. Several Victorian homes crowd the hillside. For those with a taste for wildlife art, **Wild Wings Gallery** displays works of some of the country's most famous and successful wildlife artists.

Lake Pepin ends where the Chippewa River pours into the Mississippi at **Reads Landing.** The turbulence of the confluence prevents the river from freezing in winter, attracting dozens of bald eagles to a ready source of live and dead fish. In winter, drive along US 61, looking for open water and the telltale white heads in the gray trees of the river bottoms from Reads Landing downstream to Wabasha. Smaller flocks of wintering eagles may take up residence at Colvill Park on the riverfront in Red Wing.

(following pages) An aerial view of the bluffs which overlook both sides of the Mississippi River from Iowa to Minneapolis.

SOUTHEASTERN HILLS

■ WABASHA, WEAVER, AND WINONA

◆ WABASHA   *map page 97, C-4*

Named for a dynasty of three Dakota chiefs, Wabasha is one of the state's oldest towns. White settlement dates from the 1830s. At its quaint heart sits the **Anderson House Hotel,** *(see page 326)* distinguished as the state's oldest operating hotel (since 1856) and the only one I know of that provides cats to their visitors to take back to their rooms for the night. A guide from the chamber of commerce will lead you on a walking tour through town. Wabasha's **Old City Hall** includes a variety of shops. Wabasha is a port of call for the *Delta Queen* and *Mississippi Queen* steamboats. Two miles west on Minnesota 60, on the bluffs overlooking Wabasha, is **Arrowhead Bluffs Museum,** which exhibits mounted wildlife, Indian and pioneer artifacts, and firearms, including Winchester firearms from 1866 to the present.

◆ WEAVER   *map page 97, C-4*

Just downstream from Wabasha, near the tiny town of Weaver, lies **Weaver Bottoms,** a sprawling Mississippi backwater, part of the **Upper Mississippi River Wildlife and Fish Refuge,** a huge wildlife area that stretches more than 260 miles along the river from Reads Landing to Rock Island, Illinois. The refuge harbors more than 100 species of fish and 265 species of birds. Weaver Bottoms was legendary for waterfowl hunting in days past. This stretch of the river has lived in infamy since the Armistice Day storm of 1940. That day began unseasonably balmy, and hunters went to the river in light jackets. Later, a howling north wind brought waterfowl in numbers few hunters had ever seen. "The ducks were all over, so we just stood there and shot 'em," Ed Kosidowski told journalist C. B. Bylander in *The Minnesota Volunteer.* "We had warm clothes—extra socks and all—so we kept firing away. Oh, it was a terrible night. We didn't make it to shore until about 10 o'clock. But that shooting, oh, that shooting, you couldn't imagine it." But many hunters weren't so well prepared. Trapped on islands and remote shorelines by building waves that kept their low-cut boats ashore, they tried weathering a night when the temperature dropped to minus 9. Many died near their blinds, stretched out in the snow. The storm killed 20 hunters on the Mississippi between Red Wing and Prairie du Chien, Wisconsin.

The legendary productivity of the river has declined in recent decades as the impoundments behind the navigation dams inevitably age and fill with sediment. Nonetheless, the bottomlands still attract birds and wildlife. In November, thousands of tundra swans and canvasback ducks gather in the shallows of Weaver Bottoms, just downstream from the mouth of the Whitewater River. The refuge head-quarters is in Winona.

John A. Latsch State Park provides a sweeping overlook of the Mississippi and its bluff lands. Steamboat pilots used the overlook and the two bluffs just down-stream as important landmarks in guiding their boats. Rising 500 feet above the river, the three promontories were known on old charts as (going upstream) Mount Faith, Mount Hope, and Mount Charity. In the 1850s, a logging town and steamboat landing at the base of the three bluffs did a brisk trade, supplying timber to mills in Winona. Construction of the railroad and inundation of the shoreline by Lock and Dam 5 have obliterated traces of the town.

◆ WINONA *map page 97, D-4*

The now bustling town of **Winona** was started in 1851 as a depot to restock steamboats with firewood. It soon grew to become a prominent sawmilling town, with 10 sawmills and 1,500 mill workers. By 1915, with the exhaustion of the northern pineries, the last raft of lumber left town downstream, behind the *Ottumwa Belle*. The **Julius C. Wilkie Steamboat Center** provides a glimpse of life on the Mississippi of a century ago, as do several private buildings, built in the late 1850s and early 1860s. *Levee Park on Main Street at the river; 507-454-1254.* Two Prairie School–style banks form the hub of the town's historic downtown district. **Merchants National Bank**, built in 1912, has terra cotta ornamentation and stained glass. *102 East Third Street; 507-457-1100.* The **Winona National Savings Bank**, 1914, has an Egyptian-influenced style and Tiffany windows. *204 Main Street; 507-454-4320.* The brochure *Historic Downtown Walking Tour* produced by the chamber of commerce provides information about these and two dozen other homes and commercial buildings. *67 Main Street; 507-452-2272.*

The **Winona County Historical Society** operates two museums and a historic site in the area. **Armory Museum** in town provides exhibits of county life. Children's exhibits include a cave, tepee, and steamboat. *160 Johnson Street; 507-454-2733.* Named for a nearby stone-arch railroad bridge, the **Arches Museum of Pioneer Life**, 11 miles west of town on US 14 between Stockton and Lewiston, includes a one-room school, log house, barn, and early farm equipment and household goods. *507-523-2111.* The **Bunnell House** (just downstream from Winona in **Homer**) was built in the 1850s by the area's first permanent white settlers. Overlooking the Mississippi, the site now offers a look at early settlement.

Latch Island in Winona is the mooring place of nearly 100 boathouses and floating homes, which constitute the largest floating community in Minnesota

ters. This Winona tradition has run afoul of the state in recent years, which insists their presence violates state law.

Downstream from Winona, not far from where the Mississippi and US 61 leave Minnesota, the bluffs of **O. L. Kipp State Park** rise 500 feet above the river. To reach the park entrance, turn west off US 61 to I-90 and take Minnesota 3 north. Once inside the park, take any of several hiking trails to the tops of the river bluffs. Huck Finn would have liked it here, a perfect lookout for steamboats and pirates and all kinds of adventure in the making. Immediately below lies the delta of the Black River, entering the Mississippi in a tangle of channels and backwaters. Up and down is the long view of the river and its valley, with folded hills like rumpled blankets protecting the river. The scene is not so different from what Father Louis Hennepin saw in 1680, when he observed that the Mississippi "runs between the two chains of mountains . . . that wind with the river."

Most of us think of the river as a sluggish, soiled, fetid thing, and for some of its length, that's true. But it's also true that some of the river is far more beautiful than we imagine. And the river is a part of America itself, a place where history, legend, and identity meet. It, like the country it serves, is a contradiction. Here, John Madsons describes the Great River:

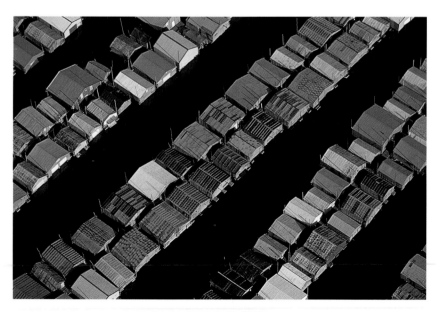

Boathouses in the Red Wing area.

*P*rey of greed and spoils politics, like us, flowing out of a hopeful past into an aimless and uncertain future, like us, the Great River embodies all our follies, fancies, and glories. . . . Like us—rich, powerful, colorful, polluted, wasted, beloved, feared, serene, brutal, ugly, and beautiful. It is not the American Ganges; the soul of America is not to be found there. It is only reflected there. And like America as a whole, it is a joyous place once you shrug off its sour detractors and find it for yourself.

■ COULEE COUNTRY

At many points in your drive down the Mississippi, it is possible to take a hard right and turn into a land of rugged hills, mysterious valleys, and quaint towns. It is a land of illusion where a road bores down into a valley to follow a creek, while bluffs separate as though the land itself is pried apart. Hills spring from valleys and cornfields from mountaintops. It is a land of rivers, carved by rivers, and inhabited by them still, as if they were spirits dwelling in the body of the land, gurgling, shifting, sliding silvery and black into the shadows of steep canyons and foggy valleys.

Place names ring with strangeness: Looney Valley, Chosen Valley, Skunk

The Anderson House Hotel in Wabasha provides cats for its guests to cuddle with.

Hollow, Paradise Valley, Wiscoy Valley, Rose Valley, Yucatan Valley, Funk Ford, New Yorker Hollow, Dog Square Ridge, Swede Bottom, Rattlesnake Ridge, Whiskey Hill, Money Creek. They seem vaguely Southern and conjure up a place old and isolated, by turns melancholy and hopeful.

◆ APPLES AND AMISH   *map page 97, D&E-5*

Head inland at **La Crescent,** just across the river from the regional hub of La Cross, Wisconsin. La Crescent is a hub of its own—for apple orchards. A scenic drive from town winds through acres of orchards. Just north of town sits **Pickwick Mill,** with some of its original machinery.

Follow Minnesota 16 and the 44 across the broad valley of the Root River and up through the hills and farmland into **Caledonia.** At the **Houston County Museum Complex,** the County Historical Society owns several historic buildings, including a log house, old school house, church, and working town hall, where the town board still meets. *East of town at the fairgrounds on Houston County 3; 507-896-3884.* **Christian Bungy Jr.'s Store** lies south on Minnesota 76 and tight against the Iowa border. The society has stocked with goods that might have been sold in pioneer times. By appointment, the county opens **The Church of the Holy Comforter, Episcopal,** built in 1869 in downtown **Brownsville** at the base of the bluffs along the Mississippi.

For an interesting side trip, drive MN 1, five miles west of Caledonia to **Beaver Creek Valley State Park,** nestled in the deep valley of Beaver Creek. The jewel of the valley is a diminutive but very productive brown trout stream. At the north end of the park is **Schech's Mill,** one of few mills in Minnesota that still operates on water power, and the only one that contains original, working millstones. The mill, still privately owned, is open for tours. *507-724-2107.*

Farther west along the main road is **Spring Grove,** the first Norwegian settlement in Minnesota. The town's heritage is evident in the beautiful rosemaling on store fronts and in its craft shops. In **Mabel,** on the Iowa border, motorheads with a sense of history will appreciate the **Steam Engine Museum,** where steam-driven tractors and other machinery are on display. *South end of Main Street in Steam Engine Park.*

Nearby **Harmony** is the center of an Amish settlement, begun in the 1970s by settlers from Ohio. About 1,000 Amish in the area work as farmers and furniture makers. Amish goods are for sale in stores throughout the area. Just south of town is **Niagara Cave.** Open for public tours, its most stunning feature is a 60-foot-high underground waterfall.

■ ROOT RIVER VALLEY *map page 97, D&E-3&4*

Perhaps no part of the southeast typifies Minnesota's hill country as well as the Root River Valley, with its lofty bluffs, craggy outcrops of limestone and dolomite, hardwood-covered hillsides, rolling farms nestled in protected valleys, and small old towns, as solid and compact as the bluffs themselves.

Secluded valleys and foggy bottomlands give rise to legends. According to one, a train crew chugging along the new Root River line in 1870 suddenly saw an Indian standing on the tracks, holding up his hand for the train to stop. The engine plunged headlong down the dark valley and seemed to run right over the man. But when the crew stopped the train and walked back up the tracks to investigate, they found no trace. Again and again this happened, each time the Indian vanishing beneath the train; each time the crew finding nothing. Finally a local Winnebago (a tribe that had recently moved to eastern Minnesota from Wisconsin) said the man on the tracks sought help to find his boy, who had drowned in the river. Ever after, long after the mysterious man stopped appearing, train crews would blow their whistle at that spot.

The track, abandoned in 1971, is now the **Root River Trail.** Cyclists, hikers, and, in winter, cross-country skiers follow the 36-mile route, which strings together some of the most picturesque small towns in the state as it winds along the Root River from **Fountain** eastward nearly to **Houston.** The Harmony–Preston Valley Trail provides a five-mile side trip.

◆ LANESBORO *map page 97, E-4*

Particularly noteworthy among these small valley towns is **Lanesboro,** founded in 1868 as a summer resort for eastern tourists. Its location in a deep fold of the river valley inspired the normally restrained authors of *The WPA Guide to Minnesota* to gush about the valley's "almost unbelievable charm." During the mid-20th century, time passed the town by, a bit of economic serendipity that preserved the historic look of its brick and stone buildings. With the construction of the trail, the town's fortunes have revived. Bed-and-breakfasts, restaurants, and other visitor services have proliferated. **The Commonweal Theatre** puts on professional productions; the **Cornucopia Arts Center** exhibits artwork and provides a center for artists. Just northwest of town is the **Forest Resource Center,** which not only will feed you, but also challenge you with an outdoor skills obstacle course and lead you on interpretive tours of the forest.

◆ WYKOFF *map page 97, E-3*

The tiny town of **Wykoff** (in the western, upstream end of the watershed) has one of the most unusual bed-and-breakfasts in the area: the **Historic Wykoff Jail Haus,** which is just what it says, renovated *(see page 327).* Also in town is a small collection of local memorabilia you have to like for the name, if nothing else: **Ed's Museum.** *507-352-4205.*

◆ FORESTVILLE *map page 97, E-3*

A town that no longer thrives is historic **Forestville,** a Minnesota Historical Society site and one of several attractions in **Forestville–Mystery Cave State Park.** Founded in the 1850s, Forestville prospered, supplying goods and services to area farmers. About 100 folks lived here in 1858, but in 1868 the railroad bypassed the community, sapping its vitality. By 1890 Thomas J. Meighen owned the entire village, which was populated by laborers who worked Meighen's farm. Today the store, Meighen's house, granary, and wagon barn are open to tourists. They are maintained much as they would have appeared at the turn of the century.

Other attractions of the park are campsites and hiking trails, which wind

Amish culture endures in historic Harmony (above).
(right) An artisan paints one of the 26 figures that make up the hand-carved carousel built and operated by L.A.R.K. Toys in Kellogg. The shop and carousel are open to the public.

through the wooded bluff country along the **South Branch of the Root River,** one of the state's premier trout streams. About five miles east of the main part of the park is **Mystery Cave,** Minnesota's largest known cave, discovered in 1937 by a local named Joe Petty, who noticed steam rising from the snowy stream bank. Shortly afterward, the owner of the land developed the cave as a tourist attraction. And so it has remained. Recently the state took over operation of the cave. Visitors can tour the largest of the natural caverns, formed over eons as natural seeps dissolved the limestone bedrock. Glacial meltwater enlarged these passages. Even today, the South Branch of the Root disappears into the maze of caverns and reappears 1.5 miles downstream at an area known as Seven Springs. Spelunkers have identified more than 12 miles of passages, given names such as Chinese Torture Chamber; Way the Hell an' Gone, Standing Room Only, Main Street, Second Avenue, Third Avenue, Fourth Avenue, Fifth Avenue, Sixth Avenue, Enigma Pit, and Carrot Sticks. In miles of passageways, Mystery is the 32nd longest cave in the United States. (Mammoth Cave in Kentucky is largest, with 300 miles of mapped passages.) *Forestville-Mystery Cave State Park; 507-352-5111.*

■ TRAIL OF TROUT STREAMS   *map page 97, C&D-3&4*

You could plan an itinerary simply around trout streams and see almost every acre of the state's hill country. The limestone hills supply the cold, clean groundwater imperative to supporting trout. Unlike the boisterous, rollicking streams so common out west, Minnesota's are small things, flowing from springs in the hills and running lightly from pool to crystalline pool, sneaking through pastures and woodlands like footpaths. Only the largest run much longer than 20 miles or wider than 30 feet. Like a glass-topped music box, they are delicate and precious, their workings open to scrutiny.

Before settlement, brook trout inhabited these streams. These native fish largely disappeared during the last century, victims of overfishing and clearcutting of the hillside forests, which caused flooding and siltation of the streams. Brook trout still inhabit the coldest and smallest of the headwaters streams down here, but the hardier and warier brown trout (a European native) now occupies the larger streams. The best of streams support self-sustaining "wild" brown trout.

Two of Minnesota's best trout streams have already been mentioned: **Beaver Creek** and the **South Branch of the Root** (and several of its tiny tributaries). **Trout Run Creek,** east of Chatfield, is another, offering more than 12 miles of top-quality water in a setting that ranges from pasture to woodland. **Hay Creek,** near

Red Wing, provides good trout fishing within an easy drive of the Twin Cities. Perhaps the epicenter of Minnesota trout fishing is the **Whitewater River** Valley, northeast of Rochester. The three branches of the Whitewater constitute one of the most productive and popular networks of trout streams in the state. At the confluence of the North Fork, Middle Fork, and South Fork of the Whitewater is the town of **Elba.** Stop in at **Mauer Brothers Tavern** in town to hear the latest fishing report and marvel at the huge fish reported each week in the bar's fishing contest.

Carley State Park, on the upper reaches of the North Fork, provides camping, hiking, and trout fishing. **Whitewater State Park,** on the Middle Fork, is a much larger park. It provides excellent trout fishing, camping, and 10 miles of hiking trails, which wind through the valley and ascend the bluffs to lookouts high above the river. *For information on both parks, call 507-932-3007.*

One of the largest and most diverse public holdings in the Whitewater Valley—indeed, in the whole southeast—is **Whitewater State Wildlife Management Area,** more than 27,000 acres of wooded hills, trout streams, waterfowl ponds, and hillside "goat" prairies, so named because they are so steep only a goat could graze them. One of the best ways to tour is to walk, bike, or drive at dawn or dusk to spot wild turkeys, wading birds, waterfowl, hawks, and many woodland birds.

For a map and more information about trout fishing in the Southeastern Hills, call the state Department of Natural Resources; *651-296-6157, 888-646-6367.*

■ ROCHESTER AND VICINITY *map page 97, D-3*

Rochester (pop. 70,230), the commercial and industrial center of the region, is best known as the home of the **Mayo Clinic,** *200 First Street Southwest,* the largest medical complex in the world and certainly one of the most sophisticated and celebrated. Author and historian Helen Clapesattle Shugg referred to the "paradox of Rochester"—that such technological sophistication and cosmopolitan nature of its visitors should be found in a "little river valley town in midwestern America." The clinic sprang from the practice of William W. Mayo, who opened his Rochester office in 1863, and his sons, William J. and Charles H. The family of doctors used innovative and successful techniques in treatment, attracting international attention to their practice. The system that evolved to coordinate the activities of physicians and treatment of patients grew to be the Mayo Clinic. Presently 16,000 people (including about 2,000 doctors and residents in training) work for the Mayo Medical Center (clinic and two affiliated hospitals), treating nearly 300,000

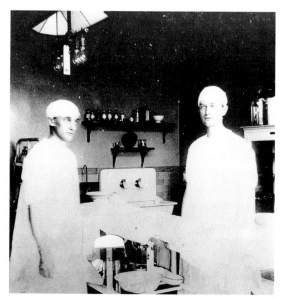

Doctors C. H. and W. J. Mayo in their first operating room at St. Mary's Hospital in 1904. (Mayo Clinic, Minnesota Historical Society)

patients a year. Research at the clinic isolated cortisone for the treatment of arthritis, designed a mask and anti-blackout suit for high-altitude test pilots, developed technology for open-heart surgery, advanced the use of lasers to destroy brain tumors, and used chemicals to dissolve gallstones without surgery. The clinic comprises more than 30 buildings, including the 19-story Mayo Building, which covers an entire block. *Tours available; 507-284-5580.*

Also in Rochester, the **Olmsted County History Center**, 1195 West Circle Drive Southwest; 507-282-9447, a large museum and educational facility, has exhibits on Indian life and pioneer settlements, and on the development of the local businesses, including the Mayo Clinic and IBM. The 1860 Stoppel Farmstead is on the grounds. The history center provides tours of **Mayowood**, a 57-room mansion built in 1911 by Charles H. Mayo at the southwest corner of town. By one story, the house was so large that the doctor's sons kept goats undetected in the basement for two weeks. Less ostentatious is the 1916 house of his brother William J. Mayo; today it is home to the Mayo Foundation. During the turn of the century, downtown Rochester was known as Saloon Alley. It has undergone considerable change since then, but many of the old building façades remain along Third Street, preserving a historic feel to the street. Thousands of giant Canada geese winter on **Silver Lake**, an old millpond near the center of town, an entertaining sight for visitors, but an annoyance for residents because of their gabbling and droppings. According to one travel guide, "Their presence adds greatly to the community." Amen.

The **Douglas State Trail** provides a 12.5-mile non-motorized route between Rochester and Pine Island to the northwest. Depending on the season, the trail is suitable for hiking, biking, horseback riding, snowmobiling, and skiing. Park and get on the trail at Olmsted County 4 on the northwest side of town, in the small town of Douglas, or in Pine Island.

◆ MANTORVILLE *map page 97, D-2*

A dozen miles west of Rochester is Mantorville, a small town notable for its many restored buildings, many dating to the 1850s. In fact, its entire downtown is on the National Register of Historic Places. Its boardwalk is reminiscent of pioneer towns. Highlights are the **Hubbell House,** built in 1856, a former stagecoach stop with many Civil War–era documents and artifacts now converted into a popular restaurant *(see page 326)*; the Victorian **Grand Old Mansion,** built in 1899 and now fully restored and open as a bed-and-breakfast *(see page 326);* the **Dodge County Courthouse,** built in 1865 and the state's oldest working courthouse; and the **Mantorville Melodramas Opera House,** built in 1918, where old-time melodramas are still performed. An 1865 log cabin stands in town.

A bas relief on the Mayo Clinic in Rochester.

SOUTHEASTERN HILLS

Flowing north from Rochester, the **Zumbro River** takes in several tributaries and soon grows into a large stream, flanked by wooded hills and filled with easy rapids. It provides yet another example of English-speaking settlers mangling a perfectly descriptive French name. The stream was originally called *Rivière des Embarras*—River of Difficulties—possibly for the many trees downed by bank erosion in the stream's lower reaches. (Pronounce *Riv-vee-air dez-ZEM-BER-A* with your best French accent and "Zumbro" doesn't seem so far fetched.) The Zumbro provides excellent canoeing downstream (north and east) of Zumbro Lake. During the summer, with low water, the many sandbars in the lower river provide pleasant places to lounge and camp. Connected as it is to the prolific Mississippi fishery, the Zumbro is a cornucopia of game fish, including channel catfish, walleyes, saugers, and especially smallmouth bass.

■ I-35: TOWNS ALONG THE WAY

Interstate 35 serves as a more accurate natural boundary than we have a right to expect from a freeway. With wooded hill country to the east, and glacial lakes and cornfields (the modern equivalent of tallgrass prairie) to the west, the freeway serves as the border of the southeastern hills. If you're not hell-bent on reaching Iowa, take your time, stopping at a few towns and taking a few back roads along the way.

◆ NORTHFIELD *map page 97, B/C-1*

Every fall, as if folks can't quite believe he's dead, Northfield defeats the latest reincarnation of the notorious James-Younger Gang in **Defeat of Jesse James Days,** a festival that draws up to 100,000 people. The tradition commemorates September 7, 1876, when townspeople shot up the real gangsters as they robbed the First National Bank. The gang killed a bank employee but got no money. Two robbers were killed in the gunfight. The surviving six fled to the woods, just ahead of a posse, 1,000 men strong. Frank and Jesse James escaped. Charlie Pitts was killed. Cole, Bob, and Jim Younger were arrested and later sent to prison for life. The Outlaw Trail Tour follows the escape route of the James brothers. The **Northfield Historical Society Bank Museum,** in the restored First National Bank, tells of the foiled heist; *507 Division Street; 507-645-9268.*

Also in Northfield, the **Archer House,** a historic hotel, is worth a short visit or overnight stay *(see page 324).* The historic and tidy downtown, its buildings clustered near the Cannon River, is a scenic place to stroll. Norwegian-American novelist O. E. Rölvaag lived in the house (private) at 311 Manitou Street. Northfield is home to two well-known universities: **St. Olaf** and **Carleton.** St. Olaf's 350-acre campus sits atop a wooded hill a mile west of the downtown. The Lutheran college, founded in 1874, is renowned for its choir, band, and orchestra. Carleton, a prestigious liberal arts college founded in 1866, sits at the opposite edge of town, on Minnesota 19. On campus is a 455-acre arboretum with hiking trails along the Cannon River. Carleton's Goodsell Observatory is housed in its original 1887 Richardsonian Romanesque building, with 19th-century astronomical instruments.

◆ FARIBAULT   *map page 97, C-1*

Back on the interstate, a few miles south, is **Faribault.** The town's namesake was French Canadian Alexander Faribault, who established a post here at the confluence of the Cannon and Straight rivers in 1826 to trade with the Dakota. His home, built in 1873, is open for tours. Exhibits of the **Rice County Museum of History** include a log cabin built in 1856, a church dating from about 1869, and an old one-room schoolhouse. *507-332-2121* Wool milling has been a key industry in town. The **Faribault Woolen Mill Company** was founded in 1865 by a young German cabinet-maker, Carl Klemer. Despite three fires in the mill's early

Mary's little lamb. Mary Sullivan of New Prague proudly shows her award-winning lamb at a livestock exhibition in the 1920s. (Underwood Photo Archives, San Francisco)

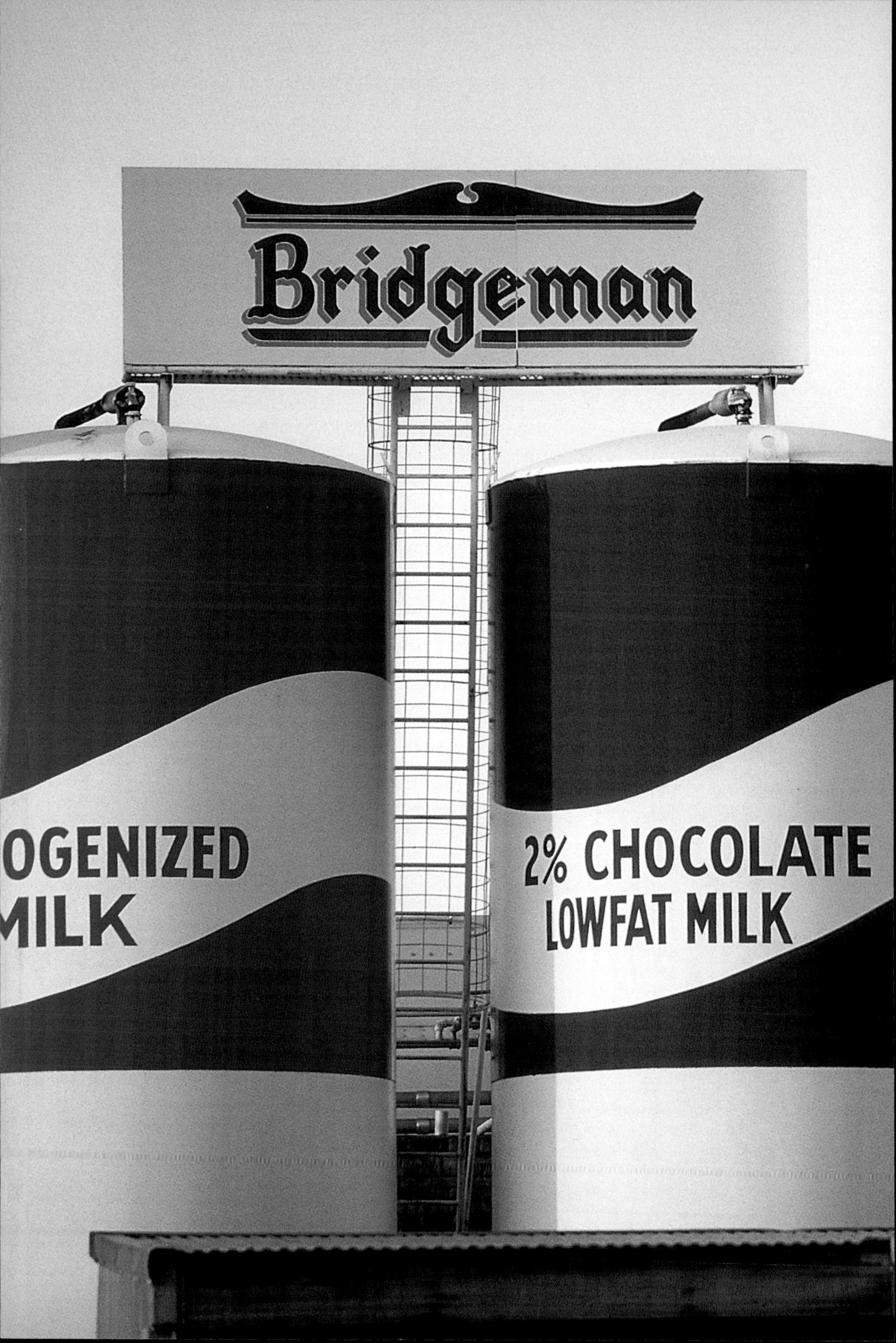
Bridgeman
OGENIZED
MILK
2% CHOCOLATE
LOWFAT MILK

days, Klemer and his sons built a reputation for quality among customers and fairness among employees. The Klemers were pioneers in providing employee benefits, starting a life insurance program for workers in 1919 and encouraging them to form an independent labor group in 1937. Located in an old brick mill on the banks of the Cannon River, the facility is a "vertical mill," capable of transforming raw wool into finished blankets under one roof. The mill still operates, with midday tours. **River Bend Nature Center,** southeast on Minnesota 30, comprises more than 600 acres of woods, prairie, and ponds along the Straight River.

◆ NERSTRAND BIG WOODS STATE PARK *map page 97, C-1/2*
Drive north and east out of town for several miles, past fields of corn and other crops. Soon you'll come to Nerstrand Big Woods State Park, remnant of a characteristic hardwood forest called the Big Woods that once stretched in patches from Minnesota into Illinois. The grove that came to be called Nerstrand Woods originally spread about 5,000 acres when white settlers arrived in 1854. They divvied the woods among themselves in five- to ten-acre woodlots, cutting wood for fuel and building but never clearing the forest. Then in the 1930s mechanized loggers began to clear-cut the woods and reduce its size. In 1945 the state established the state park to protect what remained. With less than two square miles, Nerstrand Woods is one of the largest remaining tracts of Big Woods. *507-334-8848.*

As small as it is, however, it is enough to give a sense of this old-growth hardwood forest as it once was. Huge, rough-barked trunks of sugar maple, basswood, elm, green ash, and ironwood rise from the forest floor to spread in full canopies, like umbrellas, some 100 feet high. So dense is the foliage in summer that deep shadow shrouds the forest floor, suppressing the growth of shorter plants. In spring, in the few weeks between the onset of warm weather and the explosion of leaves in the treetops, wildflowers—the aptly named "spring ephemerals"—bloom in the brief time before they once again are exiled to shadow. Thirteen miles of hiking trails wind through this deep forest and at several points cross picturesque Prairie Creek. A boardwalk keeps hikers' boots from trampling one of the rarest flowers in Minnesota—indeed, in the world. It is the Minnesota trout lily (also known as the "dwarf trout lily"), known to exist in a limited number of populations nowhere in the world except Rice and Goodhue counties. The delicate, tiny white spring ephemeral, on the federal endangered species list, grows only in rich soil on north-facing wooded slopes and flood plains.

Food processing and agriculture make up 17 percent of the state's industry and employ 4 percent of the population.

Puffed Wheat was the invention of Minnesota scientist Prof. Alexander P. Anderson.

◆ OWATONNA *map page 97, D-1*

A compact and attractive town on the banks of the Straight River, Owatonna is known for its many parks, with hiking, biking, and cross-country skiing. **Mineral Springs Park** is associated with the naming of the town. When a Dakota woman named Owatonna (a Dakota word translated as morally "straight" or honest) was healed by waters from the spring, her father Chief Wabena (or Wadena) moved the village to the *minnewakan,* or water spirit. A statue of Owatonna now watches over the spring.

A particularly striking building is the **Norwest Bank,** a Prairie School–style structure built by Louis Sullivan in 1908 as the National Farmer's Bank, *101 North Cedar Street.* With elaborate arched windows, mosaics, and terra cotta ornamentation, the building is lavishly decorated inside with ornamented chandeliers and two large murals depicting the rural countryside. According to a historical guide published by the Smithsonian Institution, "More than any other single Midwestern building, it justifies a journey." The **Owatonna Arts Center** consists of a sculpture garden, performing arts hall, and gallery. The center occupies a century-old Romanesque building that served as headquarters of a state orphanage that cared for about 20,000 children from 1886 to 1945. *435 Garden View Lane; 507-*

451-0533. Other historic buildings include the Romanesque Steele County Courthouse, built in 1891, and the 1887 Union Depot, where a steam locomotive once driven by Casey Jones now sits. The **Village of Yesteryear** maintains several 19th-century buildings. *Steele County Historical Society: 507-451-1420.*

According to local lore, the waters of the **Straight River,** a tributary of the Cannon, once had enough smallmouth bass to keep President Calvin Coolidge busily fishing for hours. The stream looks much as it did then, a riffling ribbon of shallows and pools, but recent electrofishing surveys have turned up no bass whatsoever. What happened? According to state fisheries managers, the fish were probably killed by chemical and organic runoff from the intensively farmed land in the upland portions of the watershed.

East of Owatonna on US 14, four miles west of **Waseca,** is **Farmamerica,** otherwise known as the Minnesota Agriculture Interpretive Center. Visitors tour working farmsteads that represent family farms from the 1850s to the present. On plots representing older farms, horses are used to work the fields. The exhibit on the modern farm employs a tractor, of course, and provides a forum for a discussion of farm issues.

The Louis Sullivan–designed bank in Owatonna.

◆ ALBERT LEA *map page 97, E-1*

Farther south, at the junction of I-35 and I-90, in the heart of Minnesota's corn country, Albert Lea is a peaceful town nestled between Albert Lea and Fountain lakes. Exhibits at the **Freeborn County Historical Society Museum and Pioneer Village,** *1031 Bridge Avenue; 507-373-8003,* include an early log home, schoolhouse, 1878 Gothic Revival Norwegian Lutheran church, general store and post office, and other shops as they might have existed in a 19th-century village. A number of grand Victorian houses ring the lakes. One is the **Victorian Rose Inn.** *(See page 315.)* Albert Lea is also home of the **Minnesota Festival Theatre,** which, more than most summer theaters, is devoted to the development of new plays.

Just southeast of town is **Myre Big Island State Park,** a pleasing mix of prairie, savanna, and woodland with campsites, picnic areas, and hiking trails. The park is named for a 116-acre island in Albert Lea Lake, joined to the rest of the park by a causeway. White pelicans flock to the lake, usually in early September, in their flight south. These large, gregarious birds have a wingspread of up to nine feet.

◆ AUSTIN *map page 97, E-2*

East on I-90 is **Austin,** which grew on the banks of the upper reaches of the Cedar River. And a bully of a town it was in its early days, taking possession of the county seat from the nearby burg of Frankfort by unusual force and skullduggery, as told in *The WPA Guide to Minnesota:*

*F*rankfort was declared [by county commissioners] to be the seat of county government. No official building was erected, however, and a portable tin box served as file, vault, and safe. . . . Two members of the commission were from the Austin vicinity. They reasoned that 'wherever the box was, there was the county seat.' Gaining possession of the box they rode for Austin pursued by the Frankforters in whose band rode the sheriff. . . . At the hotel in High Forest, a halfway station, they were overhauled and arrested, but not until they had bribed the bartender to hide the box in a snowbank. These events aroused the voters to the full import of the problem and in a county-wide election in 1857 Austin was named the county seat.

Austin grew on the fortunes of George A. Hormel, king of Spam, who exhorted his employees: "Originate, don't imitate." Hormel started his meat-packing business in 1891 in a grove of oak on the Cedar River, where workers cut blocks of ice in winter to refrigerate meat. From these beginnings, Hormel has grown to 24th among food companies in the Fortune 500 and employs more than 8,000 with sales in 1993 of nearly $3 billion. The **Hormel Museum,** in the Oak Park Mall on I-90 at the northwest end of town, tells the story of the company's success. Hormel's downtown home is open for tours. The **Mower County Historical Center** exhibits include the original Hormel building, log cabin, church, school, and depot, and other artifacts from Indians and pioneers. Trails at the **J. C. Hormel Nature Center,** on the former family estate, wind through a varied natural setting of woods and wetlands. *507-437-7519.*

Some 25 miles southeast of Austin is **Lake Louise State Park,** with more than 1,100 acres of woods and open fields. Here grows the nodding wild onion, a plant otherwise rare in Minnesota. Of more interest to most visitors are hiking and horseback trails along the Upper Iowa River. *507-324-5249.*

The road to Lake Louise is one of several Minnesota highways whose rights-of-way are planted with native grasses and wildflowers. Dubbed **Wildflower Waysides,** they are marked by signs of purple and gray-headed coneflowers. Another such route in the area is US 218 between Austin and Owatonna.

A snowy scene in St. Mary's Catholic Church cemetery at New Trier.

TWIN CITIES
SHARED RIVER AND HISTORY

■ HIGHLIGHTS   *page*

Fort Snelling   142
Mississippi River   148
Lock and Dam I   152
Mendota   152
Pig's Eye Lake   153

TWIN CITIES
Map page 138
Minneapolis • • St Paul
Fort Snelling

I do not know much about gods; but I think that the river
Is a strong brown god—sullen, untamed and intractable,
Patient to some degree, at first recognised as a frontier;
Useful, untrustworthy, as a conveyor of commerce;
Then only a problem confronting the builder of bridges.
The problem once solved, the brown god is almost forgotten
By the dwellers in cities . . .
— T. S. Eliot, *The Dry Salvages*

DESPITE THE EXISTENCE OF NEARLY A THOUSAND LAKES in the Twin Cities area, Minneapolis and St. Paul are, at their core, river towns, linked by the Mississippi winding through both downtowns. Because of the river, Indians settled the area centuries before white settlers arrived. Because of the river, St. Paul developed as a nexus of transportation in the Upper Midwest. Because of the river, Minneapolis became the chief flour-milling district of the country.

"St. Paul is a wonderful town. It is put together in solid blocks of honest brick and stone, and has the air of intending to stay," wrote Mark Twain in *Life on the Mississippi*.

*A*ll that I have said of the newness, briskness, swift progress, wealth, intelligence, fine and substantial architecture, and general slash and go

(previous pages) Contour planting throughout the hills of southeastern Minnesota makes for a beautifully patterned landscape.

and energy of St. Paul, will apply to his near neighbor, Minneapolis—with the addition that the latter is the bigger of the two cities.

With that nod to Minneapolis' superior size, perhaps, St. Paul's inferiority complex began. Since their earliest days on the river together, the two cities have been rivals. In fact, they never really have been satisfied with their own gifts from the Mississippi. St. Paul coveted its twin's water power. Minneapolis coveted its brother's ease of navigation. Together they developed as the Cain and Abel of the Mississippi.

When Twain saw the two towns, he remarked they were on the verge of growing together as one. Physically, that happened long ago. The two downtowns are joined by a firm web of highways, city streets, commercial districts, and residential neighborhoods. Yet they have never become one. They have never quite become comfortable with one another.

How do you explain the difference? In pioneer days, St. Paul was the last bastion of the east; Minneapolis was the gateway to the west. St. Paul was steamboats and trains; Minneapolis was flour mills and wheat traders. St. Paul is older, quieter, more cultured. Minneapolis is brighter, bigger, more vigorous.

They are opposite even in their best-known celebrations. Minneapolis has its summer Aquatennial, with a parade and a race among boats constructed entirely

A 1917 poster advertises the St. Paul Winter Carnival. (Minnesota Historical Society)

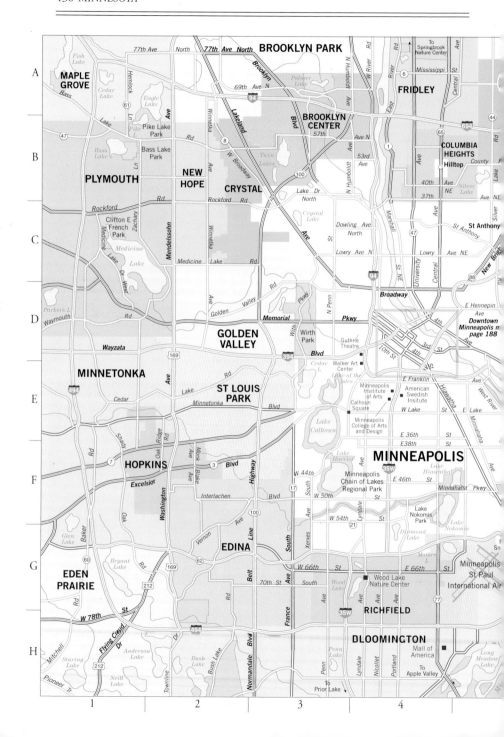

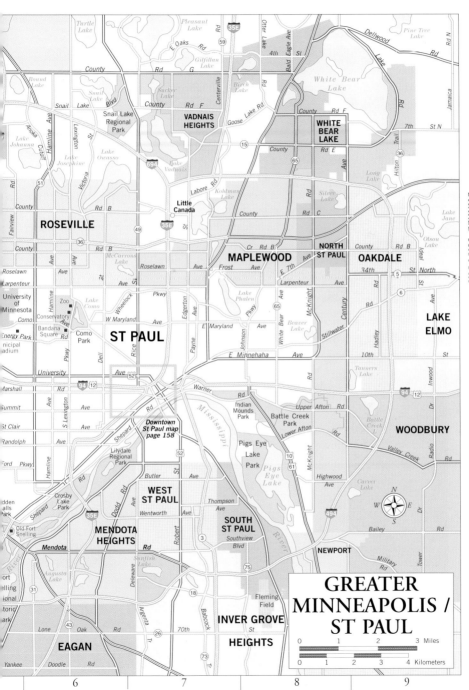

GREATER
MINNEAPOLIS /
ST PAUL

0   1   2   3 Miles

0   1   2   3   4 Kilometers

of milk cartons. St. Paul has its Winter Carnival, with a treasure hunt and a parade with "Vulcans," (devil's helpers, if you will) who dress in red and leave a black mark of charcoal on the women they kiss.

Even today, anyone from St. Paul is familiar with Minneapolis. The opposite is not true. In fact, to someone from Minneapolis, St. Paul is a foreign country, the river is a guarded border, a trip through downtown is a sure way to get lost. A Minneapolitan may summer in Grand Marais, stay at a bed-and-breakfast in Lanesboro, do business in Fargo, and fish near Walker, but he never—never—goes to St. Paul. Perhaps he's scared off by Vulcans. And it doesn't help that the street-numbering system makes no sense and that the streets follow the river on an odd bias, rather than our notions of north-south.

For 150 years, the two towns have spent much of their time defining, promoting, and coveting their differences. I have heard St. Paul described as a big town; Minneapolis, a small city. And perhaps it is best to leave it at that.

■ EARLY HISTORY OF THE TWIN CITIES

Indian place names are often concise, descriptive, and uncannily apt, capturing the essence of a place in a word or two. Thus was the thundering falls on the Missis-

This rendition of Father Hennepin at St. Anthony Falls was painted by Douglas Volk and hangs in the State Capitol. (Minnesota Historical Society)

Nicholas R. Brewer painted this view of Wabasha Street in 1908.(Minnesota Historical Society)

sippi River known as *Kakabikah* (the Severed Rock) or *Minirara* (Curling Water). Some early cartographers, such as Joseph Nicollet, recognized this gift and preserved these names, either in their original aboriginal language or in their translation to English. Father Louis Hennepin apparently recognized no such thing and named the falls, about 40 feet high, for his favorite saint.

When Hennepin saw the waterfall in 1680, it sat about 1,000 feet downstream of its present location. When Jonathan Carver visited in 1766, the falls had moved an additional 400 feet closer to its present site. In fact, St. Anthony Falls had been racing upstream ever since the close of the last ice age. Had Europeans dawdled a couple of centuries in reaching the New World, there might not be a Minneapolis because there might not have been a waterfall.

St. Anthony Falls began as so much else began in this area—with the thunderous torrent of glacial meltwater known as Glacial River Warren. As the Warren excavated the valley of its successor, the Minnesota River, the much smaller Mississippi, with a fraction of the erosive power, was left stranded high above the more powerful river. Thus was created the falls, at the confluence of the Minnesota and Mississippi.

The brand-new waterfall ran over a thin cap of hard limestone and, beneath that, St. Peter sandstone. To say "stone" is a euphemism, because the St. Peter formation is barely more solid than a beach. The churning of the falls made quick work of it, excavating a deep cave beneath the limestone cap, which collapsed and tumbled to the base of the falls. With the collapse, the falls in effect jumped upstream several yards. At the former site of the falls was created a deep gorge.

Over and over this happened, the falls persistently retreating upstream a few yards at a time. In the approximately 9,000 years from the withering of Glacial River Warren to Hennepin's visit in 1680, the falls had migrated more than eight miles, leaving behind the deep, picturesque gorge that now separates Minneapolis and St. Paul.

I have often thought that, more than any other sight from the past, I wish I could have seen the falls in the days of Hennepin and Carver, with the knowledge of what they would become. The engraving of the scene from Carver's *Travels* shows the whole Mississippi falling as a broad curtain into rapids below. A wooded island at the base of the falls and a cleft of rock in the falls itself sprout a few trees. But on both banks and far into the distance hardly any trees grow at all—only the grassy savanna groomed by Indian fires. On the west bank of the great river, above the falls, perhaps where the Whitney Hotel now stands in downtown Minneapolis, sits an encampment of Dakota teepees, faint smoke issuing from their tops. Indian canoes rest lightly on the slick water above the falls. I wish I could have seen the kind of falls this was that provided a fishing village site to Indians for hundreds, perhaps thousands, of years with power enough to build a city the size of Minneapolis on its banks.

Today, the falls bears little of its former beauty. It is girdled in concrete and steel. Had nature run its course, St. Anthony Falls would have reached the end of its limestone cap, at which point the neat structure of the falls would have tumbled into a heap of boulders and the white explorer of the era would have had to be satisfied with naming a long stretch of rapids. By building the dam, early engineers at the very least preserved the illusion of a waterfall.

■ FORT SNELLING *map page 138-139, G&H-5*

The first white outpost in the area was Fort Snelling, which commanded the confluence of the Minnesota and Mississippi Rivers. Lieutenant Zebulon Pike had negotiated the purchase of the site from Dakota Indians in 1805, though not until 1821 was the fort completed. First named Fort St. Anthony, it was later renamed in honor of the commander who supervised its construction.

The fort was never attacked. Yet it provided a strong offense in a figurative sense: Fort Snelling served as the vanguard of white civilization, with the state's first hospital, school, and library. The state's first Protestant church was organized at the fort. It served as social hall for music and dances. Indians came to the fort to receive payments owed them under the treaty by which the land was purchased. Even then, one duty of the Indian agent at the fort was to transform the Indians to the white way of life. Historian William E. Lass put a benevolent face on it: "The American government recognized the transitory nature of the fur trade and the inevitable aftermath of settlement, and it tried to prepare the Indians for the future."

Among other duties, Indian agents were assigned to protect Indian interests against white traders. Their ranks, unfortunately, were filled by the inept and corrupt. One exception was Lawrence Taliaferro, agent at Fort Snelling from 1820 to 1839. Taliaferro once wrote in his journal, "How to get rid of me at this Post seems now the main object of Tom, Dick, and Harry—so that those who may come after me can the more easily be bribed or threatened into silence and acquiesce in the plans on foot to cheat & destroy the Indians." Taliaferro fiercely resisted the venality of the day. Writes missionary Samuel Pond:

Fort Snelling is a living-history park today.

ST. PAUL, MINN

REV. LUCIAN GALTIER,

The first Catholic priest in St. Paul, arrived in 1840, and at once proceeded to select a suitable site for a church. Benj. Gervais and Vetal Guerin, offered jointly to give him enough of a ground-plot on the line of their claims, for the chapel, garden and grave-yard. It was near what is now the intersection of Third and Jackson Streets.

Father Galtier changed the name of the little settlement from "Pig's Eye" to "Saint Paul."

In 1844 he was succeeded by Rev. A. Ravoux, V.G., and in 1847 Father Ravoux enlarged the chapel. He also purchased for $100 the ground where the cathedral now stands.

The first jail was built of logs, and weather boarded, and was about as secure as if made of canvass.

Pierre Parrant or "Old Pig's Eye," a Canadian voyageur, with a bad reputation, and coarse, depraved looking features, had the honor of being the first settler of St. Paul. He was an ugly-looking fellow, with but one eye that was serviceable, the other eye was blind, marble-hued, crooked, with a sinister white ring glaring around the pupil, giving a kind of piggish expression to his low, sottish features.

His log cabin shack was erected about June 1, 1838, at the mouth of the creek which flows out of "Fountain Cave" in upper town. This shack was the first habitation, and the first business house of St. Paul.

The first year's settlers in 1838, were Pierre Parrant, Abraham Perry, Edward Phelan, Wm. Evans, Benj. Gervais, Pierre Gervais, —— Johnson.

The townsite of St. Paul was purchased from the Government, at $1.25 per acre, on or about Sept. 15, 1848.

The first deed for St. Paul property on record, is dated April 23d, 1844.

First marriage in St. Paul, J. R. Clewett and Rose Perry, April 1839.

First white child born in St. Paul, was Basil Gervais, Sept. 4, 1839; first white female child born, Rosa E. Larpenteur, in 1847.

First and only negro slave ever sold in Minnesota, was in 1847. He was religiously inclined, and talked Sioux first rate. Rev. Mr. Brunson paid $1,200 for him, secured his free papers, and he was utilized as interpreter of the gospel among the Sioux Indians.

First School, corner W. 3d and St. Peter Streets, 1847.

First School-Teacher, Miss Harriet E. Bishop, 1848.

First Sunday School, July 25, 1847.

First Protestant Service was held in Henry Jackson's house.

First Protestant clergyman who settled here, Rev. E. D. Neill, 1849.

First Death of a white man, was John Hays murdered by Edward Phelan, Sept. 1839.

First White Murderer, Edward Phelan, Sept. 1839.

First Wife Murder, July 21, 1852.

REV. LUCIAN GALTIER,
First Catholic Priest in St. Paul.

THE OLD LOG CHAPEL
Was the first church in St. Paul, erected in 1841, on the bluff, overlooking the river. It was on Bench St. (now 2d St.) between Cedar and Minnesota Streets.

FIRST JAIL IN ST. PAUL,
Erected in 1851.

Drawn from remembrance of a physiognomist.
PIERRE PARRANT, OR "OLD PIG'S EYE."
First settler in St. Paul, in 1838.

SAINT ENGRAVING CO., Engravers, St. Paul.

SAINT PA
The first log house at the right, was on the N. E. alier, as a drug store. The next log cabin on Robert Powers' livery stable was on the S. E. corner of Four where the Indian stands, was Tyson's Grocery and S tist Hill, where the park now is, just south of Noyes

SAINT PAUL
Upper Levee   Episcopal Chu
Steamboat Landing
Dr. Neill's Church.
A. L. Larpenteur's Wareho

FIRST COURT HOUSE IN ST. PAUL.
Erected in 1850-51. Located on Wabasha, between E. 4th and E. 5th Sts., where the present City Hall and Court House now stands.

OLDEST BUILDING IN T
A farm house built in 1846, thony Ave. It was inhabited by

This 1892 engraving illustrates some of the characters of early life in St. Paul. Pierre Parrant, "Old Pig's Eye," is pictured the lower left corner. (Minnesota Historical Society)

N ITS **INFANCY.**

T A. JONES.

IN 1851.

1 Robert Streets, and was occupied by Chas. Cav-
1 by Hart. Presley, as a confectionery and tobacco
cond floor, justice of peace office; Willoughby &
opposite the Pioneer Press Building; the building
Baptist Church in the distance, stands on Bap-
ng House, on Sibley Street.

N 1853.

mpson's Dwelling.   Baptist Church.   Phalen Creek.
Prince's Saw Mill.   Capitol Building.
orth and Jackson Sts.
ber's Castle.

BAN DIST. OF ST. PAUL.
ling Ave., near corner of St. An-
dier of 1812.

GEN. HENRY H. SIBLEY

Located near Port Snelling in 1834. He was the first
officer in this section of the country; the first delegate
to Congress from Minnesota Territory, in 1849, and
the first Governor of the State of Minnesota, from
May 24, 1858, to Jan'y 2, 1860. He says: "I was
successively a citizen of Michigan, Wisconsin, Iowa
and Minnesota Territories, without changing my
residence at Mendota."

The first stone dwelling in Minnesota was erected
by Gen. Sibley in 1836, and is still standing at Mendota. (See cut of said dwelling under his portrait.)

The Old House, built in 1844, located at 98 E. 4th
St., recently demolished (see cut below), and the one
removed from 100 E. 6th St. in 1890, were the two
oldest buildings in St. Paul proper.

Old Bets, the Indian Sioux Squaw, well known to
all the first settlers, as she appeared in 1850. (See
cut below). Her Sioux name was Aza-Ya-Man-ka-
wan, or "Berry Picker." She was born near Mendota in 1788, and died in May, 1863, at the age of
75 years. She was married to Ma-za-sn-gia, or
"Iron Sword." During her sickness, the Chamber of
Commerce subscribed a liberal sum for her comfort,
and she received a Christian burial.

First Suicide, Nov. 10, 1860, Wm. C. Gray, leaped
from bridge into river.

First Hotel, Old Bass Tavern, opened Aug. 1847,
by J. W Bass, N. E. Cor. 3d and Jackson
Sts. It was built of square-hewed tamarac logs; and consisted of three rooms,
its size 20x28 feet; first named "St. Paul
House," afterwards "Merchant's Hotel."

First Steamboat arrival, the "Virginia," from St. Louis, 1823.

First Ferry across the Mississippi from
here, Jan. 7, 1850.

First Bridge across river at this point,
1858.

First Grist and Saw Mill, 1844.

First Frame House built, 1844.

First Steam Saw Mill, Nov. 14, 1850.

First St. Paul Newspapers, "Minnesota Register," dated April 27, 1849; and
"Minnesota Pioneer," April 28, 1849.
This latter was the first actually printed
here.

First Daily Paper, May 1, 1854.

First Postmaster, Henry Jackson, April
7, 1846.

First Expressman, J. C. Burbank, 1851.

First Bank, 1849, "Bank of St. Croix."

First Bell, 1849.

First Fire, May 16, 1850.

First Regular Physician, Dr. J. J.
Dewey, July 15, 1847.

First Brick House, 1849.

First Water Works, 1869.

First Flag raised, Christmas, 1842.

First Regular Police Officers, May 30,
1856.

First Brick Yard, 1849.

First Steam Railroad, "Chi. & Rock
Island," 1854.

First Street Railway, July 14, 1872.

First Restaurant, Nov. 1850.

First Hardware Store, 1853.

First Electric Street Cars, Feb. 22,
1890.

First Cyclone, July 13, 1890.

GEN. HENRY H. SIBLEY.

FIRST STONE DWELLING IN MINNESOTA.
Erected by Gen. H. H. Sibley, in 1836.

OLD HOUSE BUILT IN 1844.

OLD BETS.
The Indian Sioux Squaw.

THE OLD CAPITOL.
Erected in St. Paul, in 1853. It was located upon
the same site where the present Capitol now stands.

He was a man of generous, friendly disposition, and was more popular with both whites and Indians than agents usually are. He was very gentle in his treatment of the Indians, being averse to the use of harsh means in dealing with them. . . . Some thought that he was too lenient, but the persons and property of the whites were certainly as safe during his term of office as ever after. . . . The poorer class of whites received many little favors from him and were sorry to part with him, while the Indians long deplored the departure of Mazabaksa, as they called him.

Missionary Samuel William Pond, whose diaries describe pioneer life. (Minnesota Historical Society)

Among Taliaferro's assistants was Scott Campbell, a Dakota-Scots boy, undoubtedly the son of a Dakota woman and a white trader, who had traveled west with Lewis and Clark and later worked at Fort Snelling as government interpreter. He helped to compile an early list of Dakota-English translations. "He was skillful as an interpreter, and perhaps more skillful as a mis-interpreter," writes Pond.

For those who were ignorant of [Dakota] he sometimes used his own discretion in the choice of what to say. The words of the speaker, whether Dakota or English, lost all their asperity, and often much of their meaning, in passing through his interpretation. He told what he thought the speaker should have said rather than what he did say, and frequently a good understanding seemed to have been restored, simply because there had been no understanding at all. This readiness to substitute his own language for that which he professed to translate might not be the best qualification for an interpreter, . . . but he doubtless intercepted many harsh and passionate words, which, if they had reached their destination, would have done more harm than good.

Standing at the head of steamboat navigation on the Mississippi, Fort Snelling received many prominent visitors, especially as a tour of the river, through the heart of the unsettled West, became a fashionable adventure. Among these were British novelist Frederick Marryat and Swedish author Frederika Bremer. President Zachary Taylor served as post commander early in his career.

Fort Snelling served as a prison camp in the aftermath of the U.S.–Dakota War of 1862. But as Minneapolis and St. Paul grew on either side, the fort waned in importance. Today it is operated by the Minnesota Historical Society and has been restored to its appearance in 1827. Soldier look-alikes in the uniforms of the 1820s engage visitors in the small talk of the time, run through drills, and fire the cannon. A blacksmith, trader's wife, and surgeon explain life at the fort. *South of downtown St. Paul off routes 5 and 55, directly across from the airport; 612-726-1171.*

Surrounding the historic fort is **Fort Snelling State Park,** 3,300 acres encompassing wooded uplands, savanna, bottomland forest, backwaters, and spring-fed

During a rendezvous at Fort Snelling a trader displays items that were available for trade in the fort's early days.

lakes. The tangle of trails and waterways provides canoeing, boating, fishing, biking, hiking, picnicking, and cross-country skiing. Interpretive programs and guided tours explain the geology, wildlife, and vegetation. Fort Snelling is a major wildlife refuge in the metro area, with white-tailed deer, red and gray foxes, woodchucks, badgers, and various herons, egrets, American bittern, waterfowl, and songbirds. The park is an oasis in the midst of a metropolitan area of two million. On Gun Club Lake, a backwater lake dotted with lily pads and surrounded by swamp and river bottom forest, it's easy to believe you're alone, except for the whine of jets landing at Minneapolis–St. Paul International Airport.

■ THE MISSISSIPPI RIVER TODAY

I have spent many days on the Mississippi River, closed off by the cliffs on either side of the river from the hundreds of thousands of people who live in Minneapolis and St. Paul. A fishing buddy and I call this stretch The Sewer. Admittedly, the river has an edge: Graffiti scrawled on the bridges, an occasional body floating by. The Mississippi is, after all, a catch basin of a large metropolitan area, the final conduit of a city's filth, sorrows, and sins. And the river remains a thoroughfare of transportation. In my canoe, resting as lightly on the river as a leaf, I have watched the black prows of barges surging upriver, pushing the folded volume of the river in front of them. From the vantage of a canoe, they loom frightening and huge. As they pass, the wave lifts my canoe and sets me down, and the confused turbulence thrashes the banks for several minutes.

The urban river is popular with motorboaters (too popular according to canoeists and scullers who dodge the boats and wakes). Riverboats still carry passengers. *The Delta Queen, Mississippi Queen,* and *American Queen* (largest passenger steamboat ever to float the river) still churn upstream as far as St. Paul, landing more or less where steamboats have landed for 150 years. Beautiful things they are, adorned with fretwork, flutes, and frills on a boat bigger than a football field—in Twain's words, "wedding cakes without the complications." Smaller passenger boats such as the *Jonathan Padelford* take passengers and parties on tours of less than a day on the Mississippi and lower Minnesota, including narrated trips up to Fort Snelling.

Despite the intensity of industry and use, the river's future is looking brighter. For one, it's cleaner. As early as the 1920s, the state health department had proclaimed the river at St. Paul a health hazard, even to boaters. Minneapolis, St. Paul, and South St. Paul have just completed a 10-year project to separate storm and sanitary sewers in order to clean up the storm water that flushes into the Mississippi. The metro area has also invested in improvements in the major sewage treatment plant on the river. The result: an explosion in native aquatic invertebrates, which need clean water to live. Mayflies fly so thick on some summer evenings that crews must clear their fallen bodies from bridges with snowplows. It is possible to stand at the head of the rock island just below Lock and Dam 1, sandwiched in the heart of Minneapolis and St. Paul, and catch more than a dozen species of fish with a fly rod, including channel catfish, northern pike, walleyes, and smallmouth bass.

Despite the crush of humanity on either bank, there have been days when the solitude of the moment was so great I was sure I was alone in the world. In summer, I have watched ospreys dive for fish and the black-crowned night herons descend with twilight to fish the shallows. Raccoons prowl the shorelines, and beavers swim along the banks. In winter, bald eagles hunker in the bare trees at water's edge, like white-haired old men in heavy coats.

The Mississippi will never be pristine—not in our lifetimes. Nonetheless, in

A mid-19th century view of St. Paul from Dayton's Bluff.

1988, 72 miles of the Twin Cities stretch was designated a National River and Recreation Area. The National Park Service plans to build a visitor center along the river. It's also working with local governments to beef up zoning and establish a green corridor to protect the river's banks.

The small gains made in the Twin Cities have been heartening to those of us who live here. One evening, my daughter, Kate, and I beached a canoe on an island to fish. Kate was only three at the time. I sat her on a log a few feet out into the shallow water near shore and rigged her fishing rod with a small streamer. I flicked the fly into the current and let it drift through a deep, rocky stretch. The line twitched and I set the hook. "Here, Kate, hold on," I said as I handed her the rod. Her eyes grew large as the fish pulled and leapt from the river. "Dad, I got a fish! I got a fish!" Paddling back, we saw three beavers and a raccoon. It was an evening I want never to forget, though Kate was too young to long remember. I hope when she gets old enough to treasure such evenings, perhaps with children of her own, the river will be an even better place. With luck, she'll never call it The Sewer.

Crew members from the Padelford Packet Boat Company pose in St. Paul (above). Their paddle-wheel steamer takes visitors for tours up and down the river (right).

PLACES TO VISIT ON THE MISSISSIPPI RIVER

Downstream, at **Lock and Dam 1** on the Minneapolis side of the river, an observation area allows visitors a good vantage of the barges, towboats, and pleasure craft locking through from one side of the dam to the other. Drive or walk to the lock by way of West River Road.

Just downstream, at the confluence of the Mississippi and Minnesota, **Fort Snelling** still commands the valleys of the two rivers. In the same area, on the St. Paul side of the river, five miles of hiking and biking trails wind through the wooded river bottoms of **Hidden Falls–Crosby Farm Regional Park**, where there is also a marina and nature center. The name derives from a falls that forms in a small ravine after heavy rains. *Crosby Farm, 2600 Mississippi River Boulevard, South, Hidden Falls, 1313 Hidden Falls Drive; 651-266-6400.*

Across the broad Minnesota River Valley from the fort sits the small town of **Mendota,** the first permanent non-Indian settlement in Minnesota. There you'll find the house of **Henry H. Sibley,** fur trader and first governor of the state. The house, built of native limestone in 1835, was the first stone house in the state. Also on the grounds of this historic site is the 1837 Greek Revival house of fur trader **Jean Baptiste Faribault** (whose son, Alexander, is the town's namesake). The Faribault house contains the collec-

tion of Episcopal bishop Henry Whipple, a friend of the Dakota who gathered more than 20,000 artifacts, including ceremonial pipes, manuscripts, and quilts. *1357 Sibley Memorial Highway (Highway 13) in Mendota; 651-452-1596.*

Nearby the Sibley historic site is **St. Peter's Church,** built in 1853, whose spire towers over the Minnesota and Mississippi valleys.

Farther downstream, about two miles southwest of downtown St. Paul, **Lilydale Regional Park** lies on the south side of the river on land once occupied by the flood-prone houses of Lilydale. Natural caves in the bluffs were enlarged and used to store beer and cheese and grow mushrooms. Clay was mined in the old Twin City Brick Quarry. Today kids pick through the exposed Decorah Shale for Ordovician marine fossils. *Lilydale Road and Highway 13; 651-266-6400.*

Downstream of St. Paul's downtown at Earl and Mounds Boulevard, **Indian Mounds Park** occupies 25 acres on a tall cliff on the north side of the river. The site is exceptional for two features: first, the stunning overlook of St. Paul upstream and the river valley downstream; second, the aspect for which it is named —a half-dozen prehistoric Indian burial mounds. They are all that remain of 18 that existed when the city was settled in 1856.

More Indian culture survives in the name of **Battle Creek Park,** along US 10 and 61, where the Mississippi curves south. The creek was named for an 1842 skirmish between the Dakota and Ojibwa. Between the highway and the river lies **Pig's Eye Lake,** named for Pierre Parrant, the preeminent city father and pernicious saloon owner *(see page 156).*

Despite the railroad tracks and industry that flank the lake, it harbors one of the largest heron rookeries in the area.

The river runs southward, flanked by other backwaters and natural areas such as **Spring Lake Park Reserve,** which overlooks Spring Lake, a backwater lake on the Mississippi, about 10 miles downstream from St. Paul.

The Sibley House in Mendota is one of the state's earliest manors. (Minnesota Historical Society)

(following pages) View of downtown St. Paul with barges plying the Mississippi River.

Twin Cities: Shared History

S T .   P   A   U   L

■ HIGHLIGHTS

	page
Minnesota History Center	162
Landmark Center	164
Waterfront	166
Summit Avenue	170
Lake Como and Como Avenue	175
University of Minnesota	175

ST PAUL
Map page 158
• St Paul

ST. PAUL BEGAN AS A SMALL BAND OF SQUATTERS huddled on Fort Snelling military land. Many were French Canadian drifters and refugees from Selkirk's Canadian Red River settlement. Evicted by the Army, they settled downstream on the north side of the Mississippi. One was French Canadian trader Pierre Parrant, who set up a saloon at Fountain Cave, near the steamboat landing. According to J. Fletcher Williams's history of St. Paul, Parrant was "intemperate and licentious... [a] coarse, ill-looking, low-browed fellow." He saw in only one eye; the other was "blind, marble-hued, crooked, with a sinister white ring glaring around the pupil," which lent "a kind of piggish expression to his sodden, low features." He became known as "Pig's Eye," and so did the settlement that grew around his bar, which came to be known as Pig's Eye Pandemonium. In fact, mail arrived by steamboat, addressed to Pig's Eye.

If only the name had stuck! Today, I could address my letters from Pig's Eye. Minnesota would have the most unusually named capital in the nation. Who can imagine what the state seal or license plate might have become? Instead, when Father Lucian Galtier built a church of pine logs, also near the steamboat landing, he christened it St. Paul. The name gradually took over the settlement. Wrote one local rhymester:

> *P*ig's Eye, converted thou shalt be, like SAUL;
> Arise, and be, henceforth, SAINT PAUL!

Once again the name of a saint obliterated a perfectly good and natural place name.

As the town grew, Pig's Eye himself, perhaps feeling crowded by civilization, moved downstream several miles to a backwater still known as Pig's Eye Lake. One writer of the day, recalling the day Parrant left St. Paul, reported, "Very few cared to know why he went, and some were glad that he had really gone."

Still, it wasn't the name that distinguished St. Paul. No, it was the cleft in the river bluffs and deep river channel that allowed steamboats to land. Upstream lay 15 miles of rapids and shoals and steep cliffs, and then the Falls of St. Anthony. St. Paul represented the farthest upstream a sizable river boat could reliably navigate and unload. As the steamboat trade grew, so too did St. Paul. Riverboats arrived only sporadically until the Galena Packet Company started weekly trips in 1847. On a rising tide of boat traffic, St. Paul became the busiest river port in the area. By the late 1850s, up to two dozen steamboats would jockey for position at the lower of the two landings that developed in town. Days were filled with the bustle of boats and steam, carriages, carts, and livestock, and the shuffle of cargo loading and unloading and passengers debarking and boarding.

In warm weather, that is. In the depths of winter, boat traffic dwindled and then stopped, choked by river ice. The yearly isolation provided a strong incentive to join this port to the rest of the Midwest by rail. St. Paul became the pulse of the river, throbbing with the steam of locomotives, the screech of steel wheels. The heavy smoke from the engines rolled over the river flats below town. The railroads

ARRIVING IN ST. PAUL

MAY 25TH, 1855

*O*n a beautiful Sabbath morning we rounded the bend immediately below St Paul and the city burst upon our view the white steeples of the churches towering aloft far above the surrounding Houses adds greatly to the appearance of the place after firing our swivel as steamboats Generaly do we rounded to and went ashore I have been in some *few towns* in my journey through life but a more motley Crowd than stood on the landing at St Paul I have never saw in any town of its size Irishmen, Dutch, Californians, nigers omnibus drivers, Boatmen, speculators Dandys, Gamblers Winnabages & Soux Indians half Breed, Frenchmen, & Hosts of others too numerous to minten as we passed up to the American house . . . the Bells were ringing for divine servic and the streets were thronged with as well dressed people as You would see in any of our large towns the fact is there are numbers here from New York when we landed at the American I saw one specimen of this Class Genus homo who was looking at the scenery through a large opera Glass and remarked to a bystander that it was *demed Foine* but wild.

—From *Selections from Minnesota History,* 1965

made St. Paul the transportation nexus of the Upper Midwest. They were carved deeply, indelibly into the bluffs along the river, a fixed architecture of industry that even today keeps most citizens from the bank of the river that gave this city life.

■ DOWNTOWN ST. PAUL

As trains diminished in importance after World War II, St. Paul lost a bit of its bustle and not just a few of its jobs.

Not long ago, big-shot CBS newsguy Morley Safer called St. Paul "one of the most boring cities in the United States." A lot of us took offense. We shouldn't have. It's true. Life is pretty quiet here. One day I dropped a friend from Manhattan in downtown St. Paul for an afternoon. "There must be something wrong," she reported at the end of the day. "There are no people. It must be poison gas."

Don't expect much nightlife in downtown St. Paul. The hibernation quotient after 6:00 P.M. is legendary. Instead, visit some of the historic buildings and museums during the day or early evening. Take in a concert or show. Then join your friends for drinks in the convivial bars in Ramsey Hill—places such as W. A. Frost, Sweeney's, or Chang O'Hara's. Or do as we do: When it's dark, go to bed.

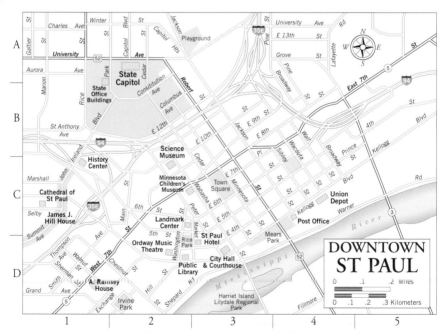

Examples of old and new architecture can be found in St. Paul's downtown area.

◆ MINNESOTA STATE CAPITOL *map page 158, A&B-1&2*

The State Capitol (University Avenue and John Ireland Boulevard) dominates the old river terrace overlooking downtown. A publication of the Smithsonian Institution, in a rather lukewarm compliment, called it a "monumental Beaux-Arts Classical structure typical of late-19th-century statehouses but nonetheless a masterpiece of that genre." Completed in 1905, it was designed by St. Paul architect Cass Gilbert (who designed the Woolworth Building in New York City, one of the nation's first skyscrapers). Gilbert modeled the building on older buildings, such as the U.S. Capitol, as well as classic Italian and Greek buildings. The dome, which outwardly bears resemblance to the U.S. Capitol, was copied from Michelangelo's dome for St. Peter's Basilica in Rome. The building features European marble combined with native granite, limestone, and sandstone. Interior details include carvings, sculptures, and paintings of native and domestic animals and plants, such as loons and the showy lady's-slipper. At the base of the dome, a golden statue of a chariot and four horses overlooks the long stairway to the main entrance and is called *The Progress of the State.*

The derivative capital and its shiny statue weren't universally approved. Hanford L. Gordon, Minnesota pioneer and cowboy laureate, wrote the editor of the *St. Paul Pioneer Press:*

> *Th*ose Roman horses and the chariot don't represent Minnesota, not one corner of it from Winona to Pembina. . . . Take a sledge hammer and smash them Roman broncos and that chariot! Clean 'em out and put a grand heroic statue of Alexander Ramsey in their stead. . . . [Ramsey was the] bedrock of it all—first governor of the territory, father of the state, grand old man, full of Scotch grit and common sense and full of Dutch sauerkraut and honesty.

Gilbert, said the *Duluth News-Tribune,* "forgot this was Minnesota in North America and not Italy. The whole marble excrescence has no proper place in the land of hard, brilliant sunlight and winter snows and its brass colored horses are no more of an unnatural effrontery than is the rest."

Gilbert originally envisioned a grand mall flowing from the Capitol down the gentle slope toward downtown. Over the years, roads have crisscrossed the mall. Some have been removed, but unfortunately Interstate 94 now separates the Capitol complex from downtown and the St. Paul Cathedral. The mall does make a

The controversial gold-leaf charioteer perched upon the state capitol represents prosperity, the horses being nature and the woman civilization.

pleasant site for the Taste of Minnesota festival, held for several days around the Fourth of July. At the far end of the mall, opposite the Capitol, is the Minnesota Vietnam Veterans' Memorial, a granite wall inscribed with the names of the 1,200 Minnesotans who died in that war.

Within sight of the Capitol just to the south is the **Minnesota History Center**. The home of the Minnesota Historical Society, it is a delightful architectural contradiction. Built of layered native Rockville granite and Winona limestone (completed in 1992), it seems at once massive and ethereal. The building itself is huge—sufficient, as one friend suggested, to store the history of the next millennium. On the first level are the Café Minnesota, museum stores, an auditorium, and the great hall, where the floor is embedded with Minnesota-themed images—a tepee, a grain elevator, a walleye. The State History Research Center occupies the second floor; the third is devoted to museum exhibits about the land and people of Minnesota. *345 West Kellogg Boulevard at John Ireland Boulevard; 651-296-6126.*

Skyways, Minnesotans' adaptive response to harsh winters, run at second-story level between many downtown buildings. In fact, St. Paul claims to have the longest public skyway system—five miles—in the world. Take that, Morley Safer! (In truth, it is similar in length to the Minneapolis skyway system.)

The Minnesota Children's Museum is a great place to keep kids up to age 10 entertained with hands-on exhibits. The museum store sells puzzles, maps, games, and books. In Habitot Gallery, infants, toddlers, and preschoolers explore a make-believe pond, prairie, and forest. In World Works, kids can shred and pulp office paper and recycle it. *10 West Seventh Street at Wabasha; 651-225-6000.*

West a block, on Seventh Street, is **Assumption Catholic Church,** the oldest church extant in the city, built in 1873. **Mickey's Diner,** a city landmark on Seventh Street and St. Peter, was built in 1938. *651-222-5633.* **Town Square** at Seventh Street and Minnesota provides shopping. One highlight is Town Square Park, an indoor retreat with waterfalls, pools, and greenery.

◆ AROUND RICE PARK *map page 158, C&D-2&3*

At the intersection of Fifth Street and Market sits **Rice Park,** established as a public square in 1849 at the very dawn of the city. Today it serves as the cornerstone of one of St. Paul's most attractive locations. To the north is **Landmark Center,** *75 West Fifth Street,* the restored Richardsonian Romanesque Federal Courts Building, built from 1894 to 1904 and faced in granite from central Minnesota. Many Prohibition-era gangsters were tried there. In fact, St. Paul was a safe haven for

Downtown St. Paul in the 1920s. (Underwood Photo Archives, San Francisco)

The impressive Minnesota History Center houses a museum, library, genealogy collection, and restaurant.

mobsters during the 1920s and 1930s. Police laid off as long as criminals committed their crimes elsewhere. But as more crooks poured into town, their "good behavior" didn't last. Speakeasies abounded. Prominent citizens were kidnapped. Among the city's denizens were Ma Barker, Alvin "Creepy" Karpis, and Lester "Babyface Nelson" Gillis. Lincoln Court Apartments were the scene of a gunfight between John Dillinger and the FBI in 1934. For tours with a gangster slant, call *Down in History Tours; 651-292-1220, or Landmark Tours; 651-292-3230.*

Landmark Center houses the **Minnesota Museum of American Art,** *651-292-4355,* the **Ramsey County Historical Society,** *651-222-0701,* and the **Schubert Club Musical Instrument Museum,** with a collection of keyboards, phonographs, and instruments dating to the 1600s. *651-292-3268.*

To the west of Rice Park sits the **Ordway Center for the Performing Arts,** home of the St. Paul Chamber Orchestra, *651-292-3248,* and the Minnesota Opera, *612-333-6669.* Completed in 1985, the Ordway, with its hardwood, copper, and brick, exudes warmth and elegance. *Box office: 651-224-4222; www. ordway.org.* Next door to the Ordway (toward the river) is the exclusive **Minnesota Club,** an Italian Renaissance building erected in 1914.

To the south of Rice Park is the St. Paul **Public Library** and **James J. Hill Reference Library**, in a 1916 Italian Renaissance building. To the east of the park is the
St. Paul **Hotel**, one of the city's finest, built in 1910 *(see pages 330, 331, and 333)*.
Inside is the St. Paul Grill, which overlooks the park. It is an especially beautiful
scene in winter, with thelights and sculptures of the St. Paul Winter Carnival.

◆ LOWERTOWN   *map page 158, D-3&4*

Across downtown, **Mears Park** (which like Rice Park dates from 1849) and **Galtier Plaza** anchor the historic warehouse district known as Lowertown, so named
because it developed around the lower of the two steamboat landings. Bands play
Mears Park on many summer weekends. Because of city incentives to attract residents to downtown, many artists now live in Lowertown.

The **City Hall and Courthouse** building, dedicated in 1932, has a stunning
black marble lobby that leads to a commanding 36-foot-tall statue by Swedish
sculptor Carl Milles, one of the largest carved onyx statues in the world. Known
until recently as the *Indian God of Peace,* the statue was re-christened the *Vision of
Peace,* in deference to Indian groups who argued that the name suggested Indians

*The Landmark Center, built of Minnesota pink granite, was once the Federal Court building
where gangsters of the Prohibition era went to trial. Rice Park is in the foreground.*

ST. PAUL

ST. PAUL

King Boreas IV is crowned king at his ice palace during a 1930s St. Paul Winter Carnival. (Underwood Photo Archives, San Francisco)

were polytheists and idolaters. Popularly, it's known as Onyx John. Its $75,000 cost was a Depression-era controversy, but the statue has remained one of the most enduring symbols of this river town. *15 West Kellogg Boulevard.*

The Science Museum of Minnesota recently moved to eight acres of indoor exhibit space along the waterfront. New exhibits include the Galley, and a larger Dinosaur and Fossils Gallery. The Mississippi River Gallery explores the secrets of the river outside. The facility even has a 17-foot tornado on display. A consistently popular attrraction is the Omnitheater, with wraparound images and thundering sound. *120 West Kellogg Boulevard; 651-221-9444.*

Union Depot, a neoclassical building finished in 1924, recalls St. Paul's railroad heyday, when a dozen major lines ran through the city and a fourth of the workers in St. Paul worked for them. It has been renovated for restaurant and office space. *Fourth and Sibley.* Get fresh produce at the St. Paul's waterfront **Farmers Market.** at Fifth and Wall. Along the riverfront **Kellogg Park** provides a pleasant promenade along the Mississippi.

◆ WEST SIDE   *map page 158, D-3&4*

Across the river from downtown is **Harriet Island.** The island was named for Harriet Bishop, the state's first public school teacher, who set up a classroom in a one-time blacksmith's shop that overlooked the island. Today, Harriet is an island in name only. The channel that ran between the island and the bank was filled in. The city's houseboat community docks at the marina here. So does the *Minnesota Centennial Showboat,* which began life in 1899 as the *Gen. John Newton,* a freight and mail packet. Today the showboat is a floating stage for University of Minnesota theater students who perform melodramas, comedies, and light opera for an audience on shore. Also moored at the island are the Covington Inn and No Wake Cafe, a popular bed-and-breakfast and cafe built on a barge *(see pages 330 and 331).*

About a mile south of the river lies **Concord Street,** the artery of St. Paul's West Side, the city's large Hispanic community. The spiritual heart of the community may be Our Lady of Guadalupe Church, but the commercial heart is the small Mexican markets and delightful hole-in-the wall restaurants scattered along and near Concord, where English is often a second language.

If you're on the West Side at night, try to find Smith Avenue and come back into downtown by way of the **High Bridge** over the Mississippi. (This is easier said than done.) The drive toward the bridge on Smith provides a startling and delightful view of the Capitol. During the day, **Cherokee Park,** along the river just west of Smith, provides a sweeping view of St. Paul and the river.

◆ FORT ROAD   *map page 158, D-1&2*

On West Seventh Street (also known as Fort Road because it leads to Fort Snelling), near downtown, lies **Irvine Park,** one of the oldest residential areas of the city. Many houses and row houses around and near the park have been kept in good condition or restored. One of the most prominent houses is the **Ramsey House,** home of the first territorial governor, second state governor and two-term senator. The Second Empire–style house was finished in 1872. The home, with period furnishings, is now a Minnesota Historical site and is open for tours. *265 South Exchange Street; 651-296-8760.*

Across the street is **Forepaugh's,** former home of dry goods entrepreneur Joseph Lybrandt Forepaugh and his wife, Mary, and now one of St. Paul's best restaurants. It specializes in French cuisine. The house was built in 1870, was split into apartments as the rest of the neighborhood declined after the turn of the century, and was refurbished and decorated with period furnishings at great expense during the

ST. PAUL

mid-1970s. When I last ate here, the waitress told me that a maid with whom Forepaugh dallied hanged herself, and now her ghost haunts the upper floors. Forepaugh himself fared little better. He sold the house, built a new mansion on Summit Avenue, and committed suicide in 1892. *(See page 329.)*

Early on, St. Paul became the brewing center of the state, owing to a large German population and the numerous cool springs and caves at the base of the limestone and sandstone cliffs. At one time, at least 14 breweries nestled in St. Paul's river bluffs. **Minnesota Brewing Company** brews Grain Belt Premium, Landmark, and—best name if not the best beer—Pig's Eye. The company provides daily tours. *882 West Seventh Street; 651-228-9173.*

◆ UNIVERSITY AVENUE *map page 158, A-1*

Running from the Capitol due west to Minneapolis is University Avenue. The street, one of St. Paul's ugliest, is flanked by car dealerships, old commercial buildings, bars, and some X-rated flick houses. Its virtues are the many Asian markets and businesses, especially Vietnamese restaurants, many of them very good and none pretentious. Use some caution in this neighborhood at night.

ST. PAUL

(above) A young Vietnamese boy sells vegetables at the St. Paul market.
(left) Kegs of beer are plugged at the Minnesota Brewing Company plant.

■ HISTORIC SUMMIT AVENUE   *map page 158, C/D-1*

In 1855 Edward Duffield Neill, pastor of House of Hope Presbyterian Church, built his sturdy limestone villa by the muddy path that ran along the Mississippi River bluff upstream from town. In doing so, he started a game of fashionable one-upmanship that would create one of the most enduring boulevards of Victorian architecture in the country. His was the first house along St. Paul's sumptuous Summit Avenue. The homes along tree-lined Summit and nearby residential streets were once the mansions of the city's elite, monuments to the Gilded Age. Stretching from the Cathedral of St. Paul westward eventually to the Mississippi River, Summit was the place to see and be seen, on flashy trotters and riding horses pulling surreys and broughams. In fact, Neill's house, as fashionable as it was, would not survive. It was razed in 1886 to make room for the grim, grandiose mansion of James J. Hill.

During the mid-20th century, the neighborhood fell on hard times. "During the postwar decades, Summit Avenue was in great danger of disappearing, as have so many other fashionable boulevards when their moment of glory has passed,"

James J. Hill poses with the engineer and fireman of one of his trains in 1907. (Minnesota Historical Society)

THE RICH *ARE* DIFFERENT

My grandmother, when she first came to St. Paul, got a job on the hill. To work "on the hill" was St. Paul lingo, meaning you were a maid or some kind of domestic help in one of the mansions along Summit Avenue or in the Crocus Hill area nearby. The hill was not just a geographical area; it was a designation of caste.

I always took Fitzgerald's side in the exchange he and Hemingway are supposed to have had about wealth. He was the hometown boy. But beyond my loyalty, I felt his romantic cry that "the rich are different from you and me"—a pure St. Paul cry—was more to the point than the answer Hemingway gave himself. *Of course* "the rich have money"—but it doesn't end there. . . .

The rich get to live differently. They are therefore different. Fitzgerald's line is less chumpy than Hemingway has made us think. It speaks the case for many people and explains in part why there is such a thing as a celebrity in our culture. His unguarded cry is true, even if he was "romantic about the rich," as people say. His statement speaks more truly than Hemingway who merely got the last word in a conversation. . . .

—Patricia Hampl, *A Romantic Education,* 1981

wrote historian Ernest R. Sandeen. Many of the homes were split into apartments and were left to deteriorate. The neighborhood underwent a revival in the last 30 years, however, and has recaptured much of its former style. The east (the oldest and grandest) end of the avenue was designated a historic district in the 1970s. In the 1990s, the remaining stretch clear to the Mississippi was designated as well. The avenue and neighborhoods on its flanks are a great place to tour by car, bike, or on foot.

◆ SUMMIT AVENUE TOUR

The Cathedral of St. Paul, at the east end of Summit, looks to the Capitol and the downtown, separated from each by a gulf of freeways and entry ramps, as if contemplating the separation of church from state and all things secular. The Cathedral sprung from the vision of Archbishop John Ireland. E. L. Masqueray designed it. Completed in 1915, the Cathedral was clad with St. Cloud granite. Its copper dome soars to more than 300 feet. Like the dome of the Capitol across the way, it suggests Michelangelo's St. Peter's Cathedral in Rome. The space inside is huge: the building can seat 3,000. Neither Ireland nor Masqueray lived to see completion of its interior in 1953.

West and across Summit is the **James J. Hill House,** built in 1891 by the transportation baron who built the Great Northern Railway to the West Coast. The largest and one of the most depressingly impressive private residences in the Midwest, this looming, Richardsonian Romanesque structure is clad in black-stained red sandstone. Its interior is decorated with carved woodwork, stained glass, tiled fireplaces, cut-glass chandeliers, and a skylight lighting the art gallery. Said Hill to the architects, "I want very little stained or leaded glass, but I want it good." Showing the same determination to control the work on this project as he did on many in his life and business, Hill fired the architects part way through the project and hired a new firm to finish the house. When complete, the 36,000-square-foot mansion had 22 fireplaces and its own barn, power plant, and mushroom cave. It cost nearly $1 million to build in an era when stonecutters earned $3.50 a day and wood carvers up to $1 an hour. The fuel bill for January 1894 was $449, when coal cost $4 a ton. When he moved his family, he razed the former house, a large, beautiful and still-new Italianate three-story in Lowertown. He told his daughter Clara that he feared the neighborhood was deteriorating, and "could not bear to drive by here, day after day, and see milk bottles in the windows." Hill lived in his mansion till he died in 1916. Hill's daughters bequeathed the building to the archdiocese. For the next 53 years, the mansion served as school convent, college, and conference center. In 1978 the Minnesota Historical Society acquired the building. Today, the society holds art exhibits, concerts, and guided tours there. *240 Summit Avenue; 651-297-2555.*

The private house at 312 Summit, built in 1858, is the oldest house still standing along the avenue. A little farther west, at 432 Summit, is perhaps the most striking and beautiful house along the avenue, the Italianate **Livingston-Burbank-Griggs** villa, built in 1862 of gray limestone by Vermonter James Burbank, who made his money in river shipping and a stagecoach line. Rooms were finished with whole interiors imported from France and Italy.

Summit might be known as authors' row. Nobel Prize–winning author Sinclair Lewis lived briefly at 516 Summit. But the writer most closely identified with the avenue is F. Scott Fitzgerald. He grew up near Summit, at 481 Laurel (private). In the summer of 1919, as he rewrote *This Side of Paradise,* the book that would launch his career, the 22-year-old Fitzgerald rented an apartment in the brownstone row house at 599 Summit. The author described the brownstone as "a house below the average on a street above the average." Yet he could refer to the avenue as "a museum of American architectural failures." Fitzgerald, never accepted by Summit Avenue gentry, remained forever ambivalent about the wealth around him.

The Cathedral of St. Paul is modeled after St. Peter's Basilica in Rome.

◆ NORTH AND SOUTH OF SUMMIT AVENUE

Generally speaking, to the north of Summit is **Ramsey Hill** and to the south is Crocus Hill. **Ramsey** is older, with a mix of Queen Anne and other Victorian-style homes, many beautifully restored; Crocus is slightly newer, though perhaps more exclusive. The heart of Ramsey Hill is at Western and Selby where stylish bars and restaurants like **W. A. Frost & Co.** *(see page 331)* now occupy renovated buildings. (A young Fitzgerald used to pop in to the old Frost Co. pharmacy for smokes and Cokes.) One essential oddity: the **St. Paul Curling Club,** *470 Selby Avenue; 651-224-7408.* The Scottish game of curling combines elements of many sports in an absurd whole: players appear to be playing shuffleboard on ice with slightly squat bowling balls with handles (called "stones"). With brooms they sweep the ice in the path of each stone to cause the stone to curve or to help speed it to its target.

Back on Summit, just east of Lexington Avenue, is the three-story English Tudor **Governor's Residence.** Built in 1910 as a private residence for lawyer and lumber baron Horace Hills Irvine, it was offered to the state in 1965. On the grounds is Paul Granlund's Garden Memorial to Vietnam vets. *1006 Summit.*

◆ GRAND AVENUE

Running parallel to Summit, one block south, is Grand Avenue, an insouciant mix of houses, stores, coffee shops, restaurants, bars, and other businesses. Take a stroll along Grand, between Dale Street and Lexington Avenue. Take your pick for dining: Mexican at La Cucaracha, Southern-style at Dixie's, Japanese at Saji-Ya, Asian at Lotus, Mediterranean at Barbary Fig. Perhaps the best dessert in town is at Cafe Latté. In June, a crowd of hundreds of thousands gathers along the avenue to eat, drink, watch a parade, and listen to live music during Grand Old Days.

St. Paul remains a city of neighborhoods, many still vigorous despite the atrophy of retail space downtown. My own house is in **Merriam Park,** a commuter community built along the rail line between Minneapolis and St. Paul. John L. Merriam platted the land in 1881 to design a "suburban residence town" equidistant between the two downtowns. Houses sprung up shortly after. Two of the earliest were the Merriam Park "twins"—modest turreted Victorians. The first house I owned, the place my daughter lived as a baby, was right next door, built solid as an oak stump in 1900. The house I live in right now is across the alley, a big duplex built in 1911 with hardwood floors, leaded-glass windows, and two porches in front. In the summer I sit on the porch in the evening, only a mile from the Mississippi, to smoke a cigar and watch St. Paul stream by on Marshall Avenue. Don't bother to come here. It's nothing special—just to those of us who live here.

■ COMO AVENUE AREA *map page 139, D-6*

Como Park at Lexington Parkway and Como Avenue is a modest yet locally popular park, surrounding 70-acre Lake Como. The **Conservatory** embraces a sunken garden and indoor pond, and other floral displays. Also on the grounds are the Spanish Mission Revival pavilion and the Como Ordway Memorial Japanese Garden. Always popular with children is the zoo (free admission), with primates, big cats, and other native and exotic animals. Concerts and plays are scheduled regularly through summer at the pavilion along the lake. More than two miles of hiking and biking (including skating) trails circle the lake.

Just south of Como Park is **Bandana Square,** with specialty shops and restaurants in a mall made up of turn-of-the-century railroad buildings. Among the many eateries here is the Dakota Bar & Grill—more than a great restaurant, it's probably the best jazz club in town. Bandana is also home to the Bandana/Twin City Railroad Club, with more than 3,000 square feet of model railroad displays.

◆ UNIVERSITY OF MINNESOTA, ST. PAUL *map page 139, D-5&6*

The **St. Paul campus** of the **University of Minnesota** sits at Cleveland and Como Avenues (northwest of downtown). Known as the "Ag Campus," or "Moo U" when I attended many years ago, it is home of many of the university's biological and agricultural science schools. Children enjoy tours of the animal barns. Also on campus is the **Gabbert Raptor Center,** a clinic where injured eagles, hawks, and owls are nursed to health and, if possible, returned to the wild. The center provides tours and educational programs for children and adults.

At the north end of campus is the **Gibbs Farm Museum,** a Ramsey County Historical Society site depicting life on a farm at the turn of the century with a refurbished farmhouse, two barns, and a one-room schoolhouse. The site was first farmed by Heman Gibbs in 1849. *2097 West Larpenteur Avenue; 651-646-8629.*

Occupying the southeast corner of campus is the state fairgrounds, where the **Minnesota State Fair** is held for 12 days each summer. It's a hugely popular event and one of the best state fairs in the country.

ST. PAUL

◆ ST. PAUL SAINTS *map page 139, D-6*

While the Twins play in the Metrodome and ostensibly belong to the whole state, the minor-league **Saints** are uniquely St. Paul. They aren't the only minor league baseball team in the state, but they are the most successful and wacky, promoted with gimmicks that have included mascot pig with wings (a natural posterboy for Pig's Eye beer), haircuts and massage therapy for spectators, and rubber- suit sumo wrestling between innings. If only major-league baseball could be as much fun. The Saints play at Municipal Stadium, *1771 Energy Park Drive; 651-644-6659.*

■ ST. PAUL SUBURBS *map page 139*

Lake Elmo Park Reserve, about a mile northeast of I-94 and I-694, includes 2,000 acres of woods and wetlands, the largest tract of public land in Washington County. The park contains nearly 20 miles of trails, including bridle paths.

(Above) The minor-league St. Paul Saints baseball team is as big an attraction as their major league counterparts. (Right) Large sand castles are one of the favorite attractions at the Minnesota State Fair, held annually in late August.

Aviation buffs will find two attractions at **Fleming Field** in South St. Paul: the anachronistically named Confederate Air Force, a collection of working vintage military aircraft, and the U.S. Fighter Squadron. To reach Fleming Field from St. Paul take MN 52 (the Lafayette Bridge) south to I-494, exit on Upper 55th, and then drive east on Henry until you see the hangars. *651-455-6942.*

(above) Betty Olson hugs her Brown Swiss cow at the fair.

A horsemanship show gets underway at the fairgrounds (opposite, top). Butter sculptures are another of the attractions spread throughout the fair (opposite, bottom).

M I N N E A P O L I S

■ HIGHLIGHTS   *page*

St. Anthony Falls   182
Nicollet Mall   188
Walker Art Center   190
Minnehaha Falls   195
University of Minnesota   196
Hennepin Parks   199
Lake Minnetonka   199

MINNEAPOLIS
Map page 188

Minneapolis •

IF ST. PAUL IS THE RIVER AND ROMANESQUE SANDSTONE MANSIONS, Minneapolis is lakes and glass and steel. It has, for better or for worse, what St. Paul does not: a vigorous downtown with a vibrant retail district and big-league sports. It is that rarity in Minnesota: a city with nightlife.

The Minneapolis skyline.

MINNEAPOLIS

Skyways link most downtown buildings, providing shelter from the bitter winter weather.

Minneapolis is a coinage of the Dakota word for water and the Greek for city. In addition to the Mississippi, which runs through its core, 22 lakes lie within the city's borders. In particular, the public parks that surround the lakes in the southwest corner of the city almost define Minneapolis. In all, there are more than 150 parks in town.

St. Paul's skyline evokes the past; that of Minneapolis suggests the modern. It is the largest and most beautiful skyline in the state. At times, especially as it reflects the afternoon sun, it is positively buoyant. The multifaceted crystal of the 57-story IDS Center, the tallest building in town, dominates the skyline. Nearly as tall is the Norwest Bank building. Clad in sandstone and lit at night, it seems at once Art Deco yet thoroughly contemporary. The First Bank building is modern glass and stone with an illuminated "halo."

The city's fault lies in that at times it tries too hard to impress, as it did a few years ago with its "Minne-apple" campaign, a self-conscious imitation of the Big Apple. In that, we reveal our Midwestern insecurity.

■ ST. ANTHONY FALLS   *map page 188, C-3*

St. Paul may have sat at the head of navigation, but upstream roared St. Anthony Falls, and its power to turn the mill wheels of an advancing civilization would not be denied.

Soldiers from Fort Snelling (initially called Fort St. Anthony) built a sawmill on the west bank of the falls in 1821 and the first flour mill nearby in 1823. Franklin Steele built a cabin at the falls in 1838. A decade later he built a dam of timber and rock stretching across the eastern half of the channel, thereby diverting water for power to saw logs. Soon Steele owned five sawmills on the east bank. Another industrious party on the west bank constructed a dam across that half of the river, raising the height of the falls to 48 feet and channeling the water through a 1,000-foot canal into tailrace tunnels, turning millwheels and, later, turbines.

Steele's settlement on the east bank was called St. Anthony. The village across the river was known as Minneapolis. Between them, the river carried pines from northern pineries and powered sawmills and flour mills for the wheat arriving from southern and western Minnesota. In low water, in fact, the falls nearly dried up, so great were the demands for its hydropower.

Still, there was water enough to undercut the limestone lip of the falls and cause the upstream creep that had moved the falls for thousands of years. Each collapse threatened the mills along the shores. The federal government twice tried to shore

Peter Gui Clausen's painting illustrates the reconstruction of St. Anthony Falls in 1869.
(Minnesota Historical Society)

An anonymous lithograph done in 1890 of the Washburn Crosby County Merchant Mills.
(Minnesota Historical Society)

up the face with a timber "apron," but both were ripped out by floodwaters. In 1868 water broke through the thinning limestone cap rock and tore through a tunnel that W. W. Eastman was digging beneath the riverbed above the falls to deliver water from Nicollet Island to sawmills on Hennepin Island. The river roared into the tunnel, forming a ferocious whirlpool. Fearing the whole falls would collapse in a pile of rubble, townspeople dumped loads of rock, logs, and debris into the vortex to block the tunnel. No use. The tunnel collapsed, taking with it several mills on Hennepin Island. Other fractures crept through the limestone cap rock until the Corps of Engineers blocked the tunnel with a dike. Not until the late 1870s was the corps successful in building a timber apron across the face of the falls.

The decade from the late 1860s to the late 1870s might be known as the age of disaster. Not only did the falls collapse, but fire destroyed the east side of the dam and east bank sawmills. The financial panic of 1873 injured all businesses. An explosion and fire in 1878 destroyed much of the west bank milling district, killing 18. In one night a third of the city's milling capacity was lost. Engineers were out the night of the fire making plans to rebuild the mills.

But, as though prosperity were born of disaster, the next 50 years, until the Depression, were to be the golden age of Minneapolis milling. Companies around St. Anthony Falls pioneered the move from millstone technology to roller technology, which could make efficient use of the spring wheat grown in the upper Midwest. As a result, Minneapolis (which absorbed St. Anthony in 1872) became the biggest milling center in the United States. Water from St. Anthony Falls turned up to 95 water wheels or turbines. As many as 80 trains a day rolled across James J. Hill's Stone Arch Bridge, carrying grain to mills, and manufactured and household goods to farms out west.

Remnants of early milling days are clearly visible today. Take a tour of the St. Anthony Heritage Zone with the Minnesota Historical Society which has an office on the east bank next to the falls. *Tours mid-April through October, 125 Main Street Southeast; 612-627-5433; www.mnhs.org.*

These days the falls are well contained by concrete and stone block, a series of dams falling about 40 feet, not the wild tumult over limestone of ages past. Some of the oldest buildings in Minneapolis sit on the east bank, the site of old St. Anthony. Upton Block, the oldest brick building still standing in the city, dates from 1855. Prostitutes populated the upstairs of these buildings in the early 1900s. During the 1950s, the buildings of southeast Main Street fell into disrepair; many were abandoned. Revitalization began in the 1970s. One of the first structures to be renovated was Pracna on Main, the 1890 building once occupied by Frank Pracna's saloon. Today a string of spiffy bars, restaurants, theaters, and stores occupies the riverfront. Horse-drawn carriages rattle over the cobblestones.

◆ BANKS, BRIDGES, AND ISLANDS *map page 188, C&D-3&4*

Our Lady of Lourdes Church, just up the hill from Main Street, was built in 1857 by Universalists and purchased 20 years later by French Catholics. It is the oldest continually used church in Minneapolis. Nearby, at Central and University avenues on a public park called Chute Square, sits the **Ard Godfrey House,** built in 1849 by a Maine millwright who worked at the dam and mills. It is the oldest house on the east bank and still contains original furnishings.

The **Pillsbury "A" Mill,** built in 1881 of limestone from the river bluffs, was once the largest flour mill in the world and for its time one of the most technologically advanced. The mill was first on the falls to have electric lights. Water powered the mill into the 1950s. It still operates, powered now by electricity.

Our Lady of Lourdes Church.

An iron bridge carries pedestrians to **Nicollet Island**. (The island has road access as well.) The lovely, sandstone **Nicollet Island Inn** *(see page 323)* used to be Island Sash and Door, making use of lumber milled on island. The building is a reminder of the days in the late 1800s when booms stretched across the river to hold floating saw logs and Minneapolis sawed more lumber than any milling center in the United States. Today, you can sit in its restaurant and (in the summertime) look out at lush greenery and the flowing Mississippi River. Houses sit on the northern half of the island. Set in the heart of Minnesota's biggest city and owning one of the most spectacular views of the nighttime skyline, the century-old homes nonetheless seem isolated and rural.

On the west bank of the river, more than two dozen mills once sat alongside a canal that ran parallel to the river and delivered water for power. Still standing today are the Crown Roller Mill with its mansard roof and the dilapidated Washburn-Crosby Mill (owned by the forerunner of General Mills), which has suffered a series of fires, including the disastrous explosion in 1878. The old Sarasota Mill has been converted to offices, and the Standard Mill is now the Whitney Hotel. *(See page 323.)*

"They told me not to build another brick lump. . . ." said Frank O. Gehry, architect of the Frederick Weisman Art Museum at the University of Minnesota.

Built in 1883, the **Stone Arch Bridge** still stands astride the river. James Hill had designed it as a monument for the ages, and also to provide a grand entrance to Minneapolis. It sweeps in a gentle arc 2,100 feet long as it crosses the Mississippi a few hundred yards below the falls. It was built with 23 arches from limestone mined in Mankato on the Minnesota River. At one point, Hill threw a fit over the quality of stone for his bridge. In his inimitable way, he bought the quarry so he could directly supervise the operations. Train traffic quit running with the closing of the downtown depot in 1981, and now the bridge has been resurfaced for pedestrians, skaters, bikers, and trolleys—a monument to the future of a livable city. From the bridge you can see, in addition to a striking view of town, the ruins of several tiny and very old mills. In the river below is a small pile of riprap, all that remains of Spirit Island—a feature Hennepin noted and where Dakota Indians left offerings.

As you cross the bridge back to the east bank, you can follow steps down to river level and enter the magic retreat of **Lucy Wilder Morris Park**, a pocket park hidden below the bluff line. Follow walkways and trails beneath the canopy of hardwoods, in the cool shadow of the limestone cliffs. Along the way are old channels and tailraces, where spent water from the mills would surge again into the

A lot of old brick lumps in the guise of abandoned factories and mills still dot the landscape of the Twin Cities.

river. Near rusted steel girders are trees that beavers recently gnawed. One unremarkable limestone abutment is perhaps all that remains of the original face of the falls. A village site for hundred of generations, the falls underwent a remarkable transformation in only one. But even now, a sense of wildness and seclusion pervades this little park: what man changes, nature reclaims.

■ DOWNTOWN MINNEAPOLIS   *map page 188, B&C-1&2*

The Nicollet Mall forms a mile-long hallway to the downtown. Open only to pedestrians, buses, and cabs, Nicollet is lined by sidewalks, fountains, trees, and public sculpture. It is never far from the city's five-mile-long skyway system of 60 elevated walkways. One of the toniest retail centers is **Gaviidae Common**, with Neiman Marcus, Saks Fifth Avenue, and Dayton's. Near the south end of the mall is **Orchestra Hall**, home of the Minnesota Orchestra. The hall is high-tech and contemporary, with excellent acoustics. *1111 Nicollet Mall; 800-292-4141.*

Named for one of the state's most popular and prominent Democrats, **The Hubert H. Humphrey Metrodome** is home to the Minnesota Twins baseball club,

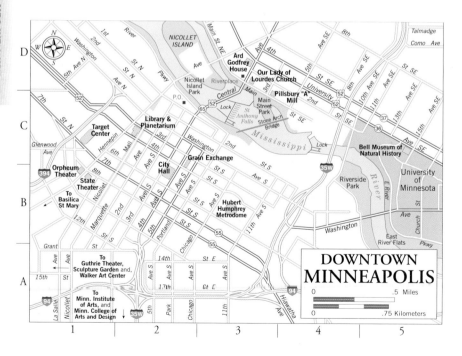

Traders check the quality of grains at the Minneapolis Grain Exchange. Billions of dollars are traded here each year, and the city is home of Cargill, perhaps the world's largest grain trading corporation.

MINNEAPOLIS

the Minnesota Vikings football team, and University of Minnesota's Minnesota Gophers football squad. In winter, the concourses of the dome are set up for in-line skating. *900 South Fifth Street; Minnesota Twins; 800-33-TWINS, Minnesota Vikings; 612-333-8828, University of Minnesota Gophers; 612-626-7828.*

The **Minneapolis Grain Exchange,** the home of the cash grain and futures market, is open for free tours from the visitor's balcony, reservations required. *400 South Fourth Street South; 612-321-7101.*

The Richardsonian Romanesque **Minneapolis City Hall,** dominated by its four-faced clock tower, was built around the turn of the century. The looming statue, *Mississippi, Father of Waters,* was carved from the largest block of marble to come from the quarries near Carrara, Italy. In the early days, when space was abundant and government small, second-floor space was leased to a chicken hatchery and basement space for a horse stable and blacksmith shop. Over time, city and county offices outgrew the building, subdividing impressive ceremonial spaces. (In recent years most county offices have moved across the street to the 24-story twin towers of the much newer Hennepin County Government Center.) *Fifth Street and Third Avenue South.*

Renowned cellist Yo-Yo Ma performs with the Minnesota Orchestra at Orchestra Hall.

◆ HENNEPIN AVENUE   *map page 188*

Once a run-down street of strip bars and trouble spots, Hennepin Avenue has undergone a revival and is now one of the city's entertainment and restaurant thoroughfares. The **Minneapolis Public Library and Planetarium** sits at the north end of the avenue. Near the corner of Ninth Street, the **The Historic State Theatre** and **Orpheum Theatre** offer plays, concerts, and musicals. *For both theaters, call 612-339-7007.* Near Loring Park at Hennepin and 16th Street is the **Basilica of St. Mary,** patterned after the Basilica of St. John Lateran in Rome.

Across Hennepin Avenue is the **Warehouse District.** These days it is the city's nighttime entertainment center, with retail stores, bars, trendy restaurants, and clubs with some of the best bands coming to town. **Target Center** is home of the Minnesota Timberwolves basketball team. *612-337-DUNK.*

The **Walker Art Center, Guthrie Theater,** and **Minneapolis Sculpture Garden** form a nexus of art and culture just southwest of Loring Park. The Walker's permanent collection of 20th-century paintings, photographs, sculpture, and changing exhibits is considered one of the foremost contemporary collections in the country. The Walker also sponsors lectures, classes, and films. The Guthrie is the preeminent theater of the Twin Cities. With seating for 1,300 in a 180-degree arc around a thrust stage, it brings to life works by writers as diverse as Shakespeare and Rodgers and Hart. The Sculpture Garden, the largest of its kind in the country, covers 10 acres and is filled with more than 40 sculptures by internationally recognized sculptors from around the world. The giant spoon and cherry by Claes Oldenburg and Coosje van Bruggen has become a Minneapolis trademark. *Walker Art Center, 725 Vineland Place, 612-375-7622. Guthrie Theater, 612-377-2224.*

The **Washburn–Fair Oaks Historic District** lies farther to the southeast, a neighborhood of 19th-century mansions, including the 1888 Romanesque Revival McKnight-Newel House, *1818 La Salle Avenue,* the 1912 Jacobean Charles Pillsbury House, *106 22nd Street East,* and a hybrid of Gothic and Richardsonian Romanesque styles, the 1903 Alfred Pillsbury house, *116 22nd Street East.*

■ SOUTH MINNEAPOLIS   *map page 139, E-4*

The area south of downtown developed as the ritziest and most cultured of Minneapolis' neighborhoods. That is especially true of the residential areas around the

The Spoonbridge sculpture at the Minneapolis Sculpture Garden. The Basilica of St. Mary is in the background.

A gallery in the Minneapolis Institute of Art.

chain of lakes in the south and southwestern parts of town. The south-central area— generally between Franklin and Lake Streets, and Nicollet and Cedar— once one of the most prestigious residential areas of Minneapolis has deteriorated in recent years.

The **Minneapolis Institute of Arts**, an oasis of culture in a declining neighborhood, is one of the finest art museums in the Upper Midwest. Most impressive are the new Asian galleries, which span nearly 5,000 years and contain many of the institute's 6,000 works in its impressive collection from China, Japan, Korea, Southeast Asia, India, and the Middle East. Among the objects are bronzes, ancient jades, textiles, calligraphy, and furniture. Other strong points are American and English silver work and 18th-century French and Italian furniture. The works of many American painters and photographers are displayed as well. *2400 Third Avenue South; 612-870-3046.* Attached to the Institute of Arts is the highly regarded **Children's Theater,** where productions run September to mid-June; *box office: 612-874-0400.* Next door is the Minneapolis College of Art and Design, a four-year school. *2501 Stevens Avenue South.*

A few blocks east, the **American Swedish Institute** maintains a collection of

A mass being said at the Basilica of St. Mary's.

Swedish art, including more than 600 examples of Swedish glass. The institute is housed in a Romanesque mansion built in the first years of the 20th century by Swedish immigrant Swan Turnblad, one of 40,000 Swedes to come to the Twin Cities by 1910, making the metro area the largest Swedish settlement in America after Chicago. The diminutive one-time typesetter—he was only five feet, four inches—parlayed his wages into a fortune as the successful publisher of the *Svenska Americanska Posten* newspaper. Turnblad's residence was as large as he was small. It has 33 rooms, a two-story grand hall entry, wall panels of oak, walnut, and exotic woods, porcelain tile stoves, and sculpted ceilings. More than 80 carved cherubs decorate the Music Room. A carved oak and mahogany table can seat 24. Yet the home was not unlike many mansions that once lined Park Avenue. Unlike Summit Avenue in St. Paul, Park Avenue never recovered from the deterioration of most of its houses during the middle of the 20th century. Four years before Turnblad died he gave the newspaper and the mansion to the American Institute of Swedish Arts, Literature and Science (later shortened to its present name). The institute sponsors folk art classes. Genealogists search the institute's archives. There are also a museum shop, bookstore, and coffee shop. *2600 Park Avenue South; 612-871-4907.*

A bit to the west, near the city's well-known chain of lakes, is **Uptown.** This center of boisterous street life (by Midwestern standards) sprung from the development of Calhoun Square and other buildings and businesses at the intersection of Lake Street and Hennepin Avenue. Prosperity has radiated outward. Now, many stores, restaurants, theaters, and nightclubs along Lake, Hennepin, and Lyndale Avenue draw crowds on the weekends.

■ PARKS AND NATURAL AREAS   *map page 139, D, E&F-3,4&5*

Nineteenth-century city planners had the foresight to design a top-notch park system and a network of parkways into the burgeoning schematic of Minneapolis. The 55 miles of parkways, known officially as the **Grand Round,** run through the city, connecting many of the public parks, which number about 170. In all, Minneapolis owns about 6,000 acres of parkland, of which 1,400 acres are water. The parks include nearly 80 miles of biking (and skating) and walking trails. Bordering many of these parkways and parklands are attractive residential neighborhoods, with houses dating from the early 1900s.

The bandshell along Lake Harriet entertains weekend visitors and boaters.

The park and parkway system finds its most successful expression in the chain of waterways on the western and southern edges of the city, from Wirth Lake to Cedar Lake, Lake of the Isles, Lake Calhoun, Lake Harriet, along Minnehaha Creek, to Lake Nokomis, Lake Hiawatha, and finally, Minnehaha Falls. The watercourses are circled by tarred paths and filled on pleasant summer evenings with walkers, runners, skaters, and cyclists. The lakes, where gas-powered motors are banned, are popular with sailors and canoeists. The larger of the lakes provide tremendous fishing for largemouth bass. Harriet in particular harbors large muskies.

Wirth Park, *south of Minnesota 55 on Theodore Wirth Parkway,* is the city's largest park at more than 700 acres, which includes a golf course. Of special interest is the **Eloise Butler Wildflower Garden and Bird Sanctuary,** located in a glen with a bog which replicates the tamarack, fir, cedar, and pine bogs of the far north. Other natural areas bloom with prairie and woodland flowers.

On the shore of **Lake Harriet** is a band shell, where concerts are scheduled through the summer. On the northeast shore, **Lyndale Park Gardens** embraces vast garden plots of roses, exotic and native trees, perennials, and fountains. The **Thomas Sadler Roberts Bird Sanctuary,** 13 acres of wetlands and woods, occupies a strip of land between Lake Harriet and Lakewood Cemetery, on the north edge of the lake.

Minnehaha Creek cascades more than 50 feet into an amphitheater of limestone and sandstone near the creek's confluence with the Mississippi River. **Minnehaha Falls**—the name means, literally, "laughing water"—achieved international recognition from Longfellow's 1855 poem, *The Song of Hiawatha:*

> *W*here the Falls of Minnehaha
> Flash and Gleam among the oak-trees,
> Laugh and leap into the valley.

Minnehaha Falls was formed when St. Anthony Falls, slowly backing up the valley of the Mississippi, left Minnehaha Creek hanging far above the level of the larger river. During the thousands of years that followed, St. Anthony Falls retreated an additional seven miles. Minnehaha, with far less erosive power, migrated only a couple of hundred yards. A statue of Hiawatha and Minnehaha stands in the park surrounding the falls. Also on display is the John H. Stevens house, *4901 Minnehaha Avenue,* built in 1849 near St. Anthony Falls by the founder of Minneapolis. In those days Minneapolis was still very much an Indian settlement. Wrote Stevens: "We have often gone to bed at night, within our homestead, waked up in the morning and seen that while all were asleep, the wigwams of either the Sioux, Chippewa or Winnebago, had gone up." The house was later moved to the park.

■ UNIVERSITY OF MINNESOTA *map page 188, B&C-5*

With 45,000 students and 250 fields of study, the main campus of the University of Minnesota in Minneapolis is one of the largest in the United States. The mall at the heart of the campus is classically balanced. **Northrup Auditorium**, at the head of the mall, provides a venue for concerts and dance. The **University Theatre** in Rarig Center provides a stage for student productions of comedies, musicals, dramas in a four-theater complex. The stainless steel exterior of the **Weisman Art Museum**, designed by architect Frank Gehry, is striking—though some would say laughable and pretentious, the Tin Man recycled. *333 East River Road; 612-625-9494.*

The **Bell Museum of Natural History** is in many ways an old-style museum with stuffed animals set in natural-looking dioramas. The backdrops to the dioramas are the real art. Many were painted by eminent wildlife artist Francis Lee Jacques. *University Avenue at 17th Avenue Southeast; 612-624-7083.*

The commercial communities around the university provide an entertaining place to dine, drink, and shop in a bohemian atmosphere. The **West Bank**, *at Cedar and Riverside Avenues,* is the largest, with a wide variety of stores and bars, many with live music. On the opposite side of the river are **Stadium Village**, *around Washington Avenue and Oak Street,* and **Dinkytown**, *Fourth Street and 14th Avenue.*

■ MINNEAPOLIS SUBURBS *maps pages 59 &139*

◆ SOUTH

Though clearly visible from I-35, the **Wood Lake Nature Center** provides a quick retreat to nature. More than three miles of trails and boardwalks wind through forest and wetlands, allowing excellent access to areas for watching birds and woodland mammals. An interpretive center and wildlife viewing blinds are on site. *Just south of Minneapolis in Richfield, 6710 Lakeshore Drive; 612-861-9365.*

Visit the **Minnesota Zoo** in Apple Valley to see animals in replications of their natural habitats. Five trails wind through exhibits with more than 2,700 animals and 800 plant species. The Minnesota Trail and Northern Trail wind through

The Mall of America brings thousands of visitors to the Twin Cities.

exhibits of animals of the northern hemisphere, including many native to Minnesota, such as gray wolves, bison, and mountain lions, but also Siberian tigers and Asian wild horses. Other wildlife on display at the zoo includes gibbons, the rare Southeast Asian sun bear, a coral reef exhibit of sharks and tropical fish, and dolphins. A monorail tour provides an overview, literally and figuratively, of the zoo grounds. Some of the summer's best concerts take place in the 1,500-seat amphitheater. *20 miles south of Minneapolis via I-35W to MN 77; 952-432-9000.*

The motto of the **Mall of America**, in nearby Bloomington, might be "Build it and they will come." Many of us were skeptical that anyone would want to visit the largest mall in the nation more than once, but experience has proved us wrong. Since the mall opened in 1992, it has become not only a favorite with area shoppers, but also the most popular tourist draw in the state, with 40 million visitors annually. What would Morley Safer say to that? The mall's 4.2 million square feet include the seven-acre Knott's Camp Snoopy, the largest U.S. indoor theme park, with 23 rides; department stores, including Nordstrom, Macy's, Bloomingdales, and Sears; more than 400 specialty stores; and bars, restaurants, and nightclubs, including theme bars such as Planet Hollywood and the Rain Forest Cafe. Under-Water World is an inside-out mega aquarium. Visitors walk down an acrylic tunnel surrounded by more than a million gallons of water. The aquarium depicts a progression of habitats with appropriate species: a trout stream, a Minnesota lake, the Mississippi River, the Gulf of Mexico, and finally a reef off the coast of Belize, with colorful tropical fish, including sharks and stingrays. *The mall is south of downtown off MN 494 east, 2C 77S exit; 952-883-8800.*

◆ SOUTHWEST AND WEST

Planes of Fame is the home base for working World War II fighters, bombers, and trainers at **Flying Cloud Airport** in Eden Prairie, one of North America's largest collections of working World War II military aircraft. Among the planes are a B-17 Flying Fortress, B-25 Mitchell, P-38 Lightning, F4U Corsair, British MK XIV Spitfire, and Russian Yak-11.

More than five miles of trails and boardwalks wind through the rolling, pastoral setting of the **Minnesota Landscape Arboretum** in Chanhassen. Or take Three-Mile Drive through plantings of shrubs, conifers, deciduous trees, and fruit trees. You can hike, drive or take a guided tram tour. The arboretum was established by the University of Minnesota to test domestic landscaping plants. Today, the plantings in the woodland, wetland, and prairie settings at the arboretum total about a fourth of the plant species found in the state. Birds and wildlife are common. Also on the grounds are a horticultural library and picnic area.

Wander through bottomland forest and riverine wetlands of the **Minnesota Valley National Wildlife Refuge** to see a variety of birds and mammals, including white-tailed deer, fox, waterfowl, and shorebirds. The refuge, consisting of several thousand acres, stretches more than 30 miles along the Minnesota River, from Jordan nearly to the river's confluence with the Mississippi. Hiking and ski trails crisscross much of the refuge. In the Louisville Swamp Unit two homesteads made of stone in the 1860s still stand. Mazomani and his band of Dakota lived in the area during the early days of white settlement. An expansive and stunning visitor center overlooks the valley, just off I-494

Minnesota Valley State Recreation Area provides hiking, camping, canoeing, horseback riding, and fishing at several sites between Shakopee and Le Sueur.

Along the Minnesota River just east of Shakopee on MN 101 is **Valleyfair Family Amusement Park**, with more than 40 rides, including four roller coasters (one is among the country's largest) and three water rides. The price of admission covers all rides and attractions. *952-445-6500.*

At **Murphy's Landing**, nearby in Shakopee, you can step into an 87-acre outdoor museum and enter the world of the frontier in the mid-1800s. Among the exhibits are a fur trader's log cabin, farmstead, and one-room schoolhouse. On-site interpreters will greet you in 19th-century costumes. Also in Shakopee are **Mystic Lake Casino** and **Canterbury Downs,** home of Minnesota's on-again-off-again attempts to make a go of parimutuel betting.

◆ WEST

Scattered throughout the western Twin Cities suburbs are 14 **Hennepin Parks** facilities totaling more than 25,000 acres. The largest of these are the extensive "park reserves," such as **Baker, Carver, Crow-Hassan, Elm Creek, Hyland, Lake Rebecca,** and **Murphy-Hanrehan.** These predominantly natural areas encompass the savannas, woodlands, wetlands, streams, and lakes characteristic of the area before settlement. Uses vary somewhat from park to park, but include hiking, biking, mountain biking, horseback riding, cross-country skiing, and snowmobiling. Hennepin Parks provide many educational activities throughout the year at their nature centers and visitor centers. Several parks in the system are home to the majestic trumpeter swan.

With its many bays, islands, and 125 miles of shoreline, **Lake Minnetonka** is a mecca for sailboats and powerboats. It is perhaps the best all-around fishing lake in southern Minnesota. Check out Lord Fletcher's on the Lake for dinner with a view over the water. *(See page 321.)* The "streetcar boat" *Minnehaha,* which shuttled people across the lake from 1906 to 1926 before being scuttled, has been resurrected, restored, and put back into service for tours of the lake. The bustling lakeside community of **Wayzata** was just a small village when railroad baron James J. Hill ran track for his Great Northern straight through town, dividing much of the town from the lake. Townspeople protested. Hill, in a snit, moved the track a mile from the town site and declared Wayzatans would have to "walk a mile for the next 20 years." Hill and villagers were able to come to agreement, and in 1906, Hill moved the tracks back into town. Today, the **Wayzata Depot** is a national historic landmark and center of many community celebrations.

Three miles north of the lake is **Wolsfeld Woods Scientific and Natural Area.** Though only 185 acres, it is one of the state's best remaining examples of the Big Woods, a hardwood forest that once covered much of south-central Minnesota.

◆ NORTH   *map page 139*

Undoubtedly you've bandied about expressions such as "bandy-legged," but unless you're from Scandinavia, Russia, or Minnesota, you've probably never seen a bandy game. The **John Rose Minnesota Oval** in Roseville, in addition to speed-skating and family skating events, hosts the only major bandy tournaments and leagues in the United States. It's a shame bandy isn't more popular. The problem lies in maintaining a sheet of ice the size of a football field in anything balmier than Minnesota's superboreal winters. The players, 11 on each side, wear skates and chase a small plastic ball with short clubs that look like field hockey sticks. Otherwise, the rules are much the same as soccer's. No one has more fun than the goalie, who hops around on skates, guarding a goal nearly as large as a soccer goal, trying to catch a ball that may reach speeds of 120 miles an hour, with his hands. As one goalie told me: "You tape your fingers up real heavy. That way they don't break." *2661 Civic Center Drive, Roseville; 651-415-2160 and hotline: 651-415-2170.*

The oak woodlands, prairie, and wetlands of 127-acre **Springbrook Nature Center** in Fridley provide respite from the rapid development of business, homes, and highways all around. It's a good place to watch birds and woodland wildlife. There's an interpretive center on site. *100 85th Avenue; 612-572-3588.*

Bunker Hills Regional Park in Anoka County comprises 1,500 acres of rolling sandy hills, small lakes and marshes that make up a region known as the Anoka

Sandplain. Five miles of trails are available for hiking and skiing. Waterfowl congregate at 61-acre Bunker Lake. *550 Bunker Lake Boulevard; 612-757-3920.*

The **Oliver H. Kelley Farm** is a living-history farm near the banks of the Mississippi, on US 10, two miles southeast of Elk River. Kelley, who began his farm here in 1849, was a "book farmer"—a progressive who relied on the latest technology, which he learned about in journals. Starting out in grain and livestock, he shifted to growing vegetables for the burgeoning Twin Cities market just to the south. Today, farmers in period clothing plow with oxen and till with a horse-drawn harrow. Managed by the Minnesota Historical Society, this site also preserves historic varieties of vegetables and grains to protect genetic diversity of our food crops. *612-441-6896.* **The Brooklyn Park Historical Farm** provides another living example of farm life early in the 20th century. *4345 101st Avenue North, Brooklyn Park; 612-493-4604.*

As settlers moved from the woodlands to the prairies, they happened upon a transitional landscape that must have struck them as a picture of heaven: long, grassy expanses easy to plow; scattered oaks to provide shade, timber, and firewood. These areas, called oak barrens or savannas, have almost completely disappeared in recent decades, either developed or grown up into woods as settlers suppressed wildfire. Two areas that have retained this charm of shaggy parkland are the 86-acre **Helen Allison Savanna and Cedar Creek Natural History Area.** Owned by the University of Minnesota, they consist of rolling landscapes of sandy soil and dunes and pockets of wetlands, presided over by scattered pin and bur oaks. In the open, grass and other prairie plants dominate. Cedar Creek is a University research area, where work continues on plant evolution and prairie ecology. Tours are provided. *From I-694, take MN 65 north 22 miles. Turn right on Anoka County 24. After one mile, turn right onto Anoka County 26 and proceed 3.5 miles. The Helen Allison area is to the right of the highway, just before the intersection with Anoka County 15. Park on Anoka County 15 about a quarter mile south of the intersection..Cedar Creek lies two miles north of Helen Allison on County 24.; 612-434-5131.*

At more than 23,000 acres, **Carlos Avery State Wildlife Management Area** forms the largest block of public land in the Twin Cities area. Some of the area is managed as wildlife sanctuary, but much is meant for recreation such as hunting. Forest, fields, and diked wetlands harbor white-tailed deer, beaver, mink, waterfowl, shorebirds, and eagles and other raptors. Perhaps the most spectacular visitors are migrating sandhill cranes.

ST. CROIX RIVER

■ HIGHLIGHTS	page
Stillwater	207
Scandia	210
Taylors Falls	211
North West Furpost	215
St. Croix State Park	221
Kettle River canoeing	221

BETWEEN FORESTED BLUFFS and occasional rock outcrops, the clear waters of the St. Croix River glide majestically and, for the most part, placidly along Minnesota's eastern border. The river, according to 19th-century Swedish author Fredrika Bremer, is "one of God's beauteous spots of earth." Indeed, even those of us who have spent out lives driving through the river valley and canoeing its broad waters are suddenly struck by the beauty of the St. Croix, as if seeing the river for the very first time.

The St. Croix (together with the Bois Brule in Wisconsin) served as a highway for Indians, voyageurs, and explorers traveling between the Mississippi and Lake Superior. The St. Croix probably took its present name from a French trader named Sainte-Croix or Sieur de la Croix.

The St. Croix Valley was the site of many battles between Dakota Indians, who occupied most of Minnesota in the early days of white exploration, and the Ojibwa, who streamed into the region along both the north and south shores of Lake Superior and wrested control of eastern and northern Minnesota from the Dakota during the 1700s.

In the Battle of Point Prescott, at the confluence of the St. Croix and Mississippi rivers, a large war party of Ojibwas surprised a complacent and wholly unprepared encampment of several Dakota bands. According to accounts told to Ojibwa historian William W. Warren, the Ojibwa took more than 300 Dakota scalps, and many more Dakota died in trying to flee across the wide St. Croix.

Looking north up the St. Croix River in 1912. The log booms of Atwood's Mill are visible in the foreground. (John Runk, Minnesota Historical Society)

ST. CROIX RIVER

In the late 1700s, a war party of Ojibwas met a force of Fox and Dakotas on the portage around the long pitch of rapids at what is now Taylors Falls. The two parties battled in the rocky gorge for much of the day until Ojibwa reinforcements arrived by canoe from upriver. The Fox and Dakota warriors, trapped by the superior force in the narrow canyon, died in such numbers, according to James Taylor Dunn, that the gorge became known as the Valley of Bones.

■ ST. CROIX RIVER LOGGING

Despite its rather southern latitude, much of this land was once covered by pine forests, as though Minnesota's boreal forest of pine, spruce, fir, and birch reached down a finger from the north and nearly touched what would become the Twin Cities.

Eastern loggers, having cut much of the old-growth pine forests in Maine and New England, and making great progress toward that end in Michigan, covetously eyed the bountiful pine forests in the so-called St. Croix Delta, where great white pines rose 100 feet or more and stood five feet across at the base. Lying between the St. Croix and upper reaches of the Mississippi (including the Rum River Valley), the delta belonged to the Ojibwa Indians—until 1837, that is, when the federal government negotiated a treaty for rights to these virgin pineries.

With the ratification of the treaty, loggers raced into the woods, even though the land was still held by the federal government and would not be sold for another decade. Joseph R. Brown—the same Joseph Brown who later would figure so

prominently in the history of the Minnesota River Valley and its Dakota Indian inhabitants—began logging and trading with the Ojibwa at the site of Taylors Falls in 1837. A small mill opened in Marine on St. Croix in 1839. Franklin Steele—the same Pennsylvanian who would claim the water power at St. Anthony Falls in the early history of Minneapolis—opened his mill in 1842 at what would become Taylors Falls. The first lumber mill in Stillwater began operating in 1844. That city soon would become the king of St. Croix mill towns.

Loggers needed a way to sort the flood of timber carried on the currents of the St. Croix from these northern forests. The solution was a logging "boom," a barrier of floating logs stretched across the river to catch logs for sorting. In 1851 investors organized the St. Croix Boom Company and began operating opposite the Wisconsin town of Osceola. The river there proved too narrow, so in 1856 the operation moved downstream to a site two miles above Stillwater. Up to 600 men worked the boom to sort the logs by the owners' brands and raft them down river to mills in Stillwater and Winona (on the Mississippi). Until about 1860, some 60 million board feet of logs moved through the boom yearly. By 1880, the flow averaged 200 million board feet; by 1888, 300 million. Old photographs show the river to be a corduroy of logs. Pioneer newspaper editor James Goodhue wrote, "Centuries will hardly exhaust the pineries above us." But exhaust them we did—in a mere half century. Shipments peaked in 1890. The boom folded operations in 1914. The following year, with the exhaustion of the northern pineries, the last raft of lumber left town downstream, behind the *Ottumwa Belle.*

Today, the site is marked by a Minnesota Historical Society plaque. The river stretches broad and flat, bank to bank, and down toward Stillwater. I imagine the river filled with logs. Didn't these people wonder what might come after the logging? I wonder and I look at the placid river. Did they ever reflect for a moment on the loss of the old-growth forests that once covered much of the watershed and anticipate that we might miss the sight of these majestic trees—or at the very least, miss the logging industry they supported? Perhaps not, if we are to believe that the words of Horace Greeley were representative of the times. "This region," said Greeley in 1865, "will breathe freer when its last pine log is cut, run, sawed, rafted, and sold." His words seem oddly belligerent. What they represent, however, is the chauvinistic belief in progress, that the plow follows the ax, that with farming comes civilization, and that with the disappearance of the forest, the Indian too will disappear, and so will the ignorance, savagery, and paganism he represents.

■ WILD AND SCENIC RIVER

Despite its use as a highway for logs and boats, much of the St. Croix Valley has remained sparsely developed. Water quality has remained good. The banks of the river have remained wild, and the upper stretch of the St. Croix is a sublimely beautiful stream in which to dip a canoe paddle. With many public parks and forests along both shores, it is possible to put in on the upper reaches of the stream and paddle for several days, camping out in wooded sites, lounging and swimming on sandbars, fishing for smallmouth bass, northern pike, muskies, and walleyes, and gliding over gentle riffles, with only a scattered few rapids large enough to warrant your attention.

In recognition of its beauty and to help protect its banks from development, the upper St. Croix, from Gordon Dam in northern Wisconsin to Taylors Falls on the border between Minnesota and Wisconsin, was named one of the nation's first federal Wild and Scenic Rivers in 1968. The river downstream from Taylors Falls, more the domain of powerboats than of canoes, was added four years later. (Headquarters for the St. Croix National Scenic and Recreational Riverway are in St. Croix Falls, Wisconsin.)

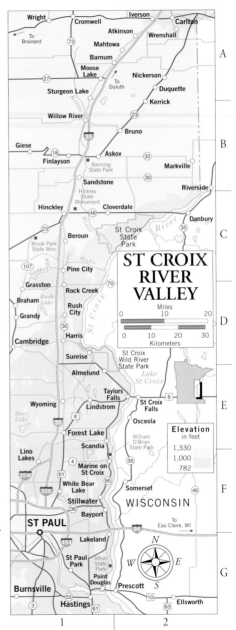

Ecologically speaking, the St. Croix is healthier than probably all other comparably sized streams in the state. One measure is the great number of native mussel species that live in the lower reaches (many of which have disappeared from rivers such as the Mississippi). Today, most of the pine are gone, logged during the 1800s. But the land made for marginal farms, and much has remained sparsely settled. Testimony to the wildness of the watershed is this fact: Packs of gray wolves occasionally roam as far south as Hinckley—barely more than an hour's drive north of the Twin Cities.

■ UP THE RIVER

A healthy river, beautiful scenery, historic towns, and an abundance of public land invite travelers to the St. Croix Valley throughout the year. Start at **Point Douglas**, the triangle of land across from Prescott, Wisconsin, where the St. Croix joins the Mississippi. Looking over this same region in 1852, Alexander Ramsey, first governor of the territory, referred to "the opulent valley of the St. Croix." Opulent it

ST. CROIX RIVER

SIGNS OF SPRING

Looking forward to spring plays the same part in morale-building in the north as rumors do in an army camp. The very thought of it is something to live for when the days are bitter and winter is stretching out a little longer than it should. When March comes in, no matter how cold and blustery it is, the time is ripe for signs.

It was [on the sunny side of the house] that I got my first real whiff of spring: the smell of warming trees, pines, and balsams and resins beginning to soften on the south slopes. I stood there and sniffed like a hound on the loose, winnowing through my starved nostrils the whole composite picture of coming events.

Beside me was a balsam, and I took a handful of the needles and rubbed them in the palm of my hand. . . . I saw the squirrel sunning himself on a branch just above me. Its eyes were closed, but I knew it was aware of my slightest move, for when I shifted my position the white-edged rims opened wide. It stretched itself luxuriously, quivered in a sort of squirrelly ecstasy, loosened up as though it was undoing all the kinks and knots of its muscles.

—Sigurd F. Olson, *The Singing Wilderness,* 1956

remains, though a bit more peopled and developed, with towns and houses and roads and orchards.

An early military road ran from Point Douglas along the Minnesota side of the St. Croix River north beyond Taylors Falls. As you travel country highways up the Minnesota side of the river, you will cross and follow this old route.

A mile north of Point Douglas is **Carpenter St. Croix Valley Nature Center.** It has more than 15 miles of hiking trails and a mile of shoreline along the St. Croix. Various public programs and activities are scheduled according to season. *12805 St. Croix Trail, Denmark Township; 651-437-4359.*

Farther up the river, between Washington County 21 and the river, is **Afton State Park,** 1,700 acres of woodlands, savanna, and prairie, with camping and 20 miles of hiking trails. In winter, the trails, which roll and wind through the uplands and then plunge off the bluffs down to river level, form one of the most challenging networks of cross-country ski trails in the area. *651-436-5391.*

North of the park is the quaint and secluded village of Afton, whose name was inspired by Robert Burns' poem, *Flow Gently, Sweet Afton.* The 19th-century clapboard buildings that stand in the historic quarter known as The Village derive from the New Englanders who platted the community in 1855. The Afton House Inn can set up charter boat tours of the river. *651-436-8883.*

Farther north on Minnesota 95 is **Bayport,** which is dominated by two huge concerns. The first is the state's maximum security prison, a classic "big house" built in 1914. The second is Andersen Corporation, long-time makers of a well-known brand of windows. Plant tours are available. *651-439-5150.*

■ STILLWATER *map page 205, F-1*

Nestled in the bluffs at the head of Lake St. Croix (a natural widening of the river), Stillwater (pop. 13,900) is as bright and cheery a river town as you can imagine. Founded in 1843, it is one of Minnesota's oldest towns. A sign proclaims it the "Birthplace of Minnesota," not only for its early date of incorporation, but also for the territorial convention held there in 1848, which led to the formation of the Minnesota Territory the following year. The convention site at Main and Myrtle Streets is marked by a plaque.

Stillwater has been spiffed up in recent years and the red carpet is rolled out to tourists who flood the streets in summer and fall, when hardwoods in the valley explode with color. Crafts shops, boutique malls, restaurants, bars, and antique shops have filled many of the town's old buildings. (Parking here can be a problem.)

ST. CROIX RIVER

Many buildings date to the logging era. The most notable, perhaps, is the 1867 **Washington County Courthouse**, *101 West Pine Street*, a brick and stone building with Greek Revival and Italianate characteristics. It is one of Minnesota's oldest public buildings. The **Washington County Historical Museum**, *602 North Main Street; 651-439-5956*, occupies a 14-room stone building that served as the state prison warden's house when it was built in 1853. The museum holds Indian artifacts, tools of the logging trade, and displays related to the early days of the prison. Other old buildings, all still private, are the 1882 Excelsior Block, *120 North Main*, the 1891 John Karst Building, *125 South Main Street*, and the 1890s Staples Block, *119 South Main*. The chamber of commerce distributes a booklet with a walking tour of the historic public, commercial, and residential buildings downtown. *221 East Myrtle; 651-439-4001; www.ilovestillwater.com.*

Northern Vineyards Winery, operated by the Minnesota Winegrowers Cooperative, has taken over the old Staples Mill. *223 Main Street North; 651-430-1032.* The historic, well-known, and rather pricey **Lowell Inn** and restaurant occupies a large colonial building at *102 North Second Street; 651-439-1100. (See page 327.)*

The old railroad station at the north end of town has been converted into the

The Minnesota Zephyr *(left), a 1940s vintage train, takes passengers on a scenic ride along the St. Croix River and through the St. Croix River Valley. It departs from Stillwater. The scenic town of Stillwater (above) is one of the state's most enjoyable places to spend a weekend.*

Stillwater Logging and Railroad Museum. Old photos tell the story of loggers, logging booms, and sawmills of the 1800s. You can still buy tickets at the ticket window at the Stillwater Depot—these for the *Minnesota Zephyr,* a dinner train with the kind of on-board dining I remember as a kid, with white linen table-cloths, heavy silver, and a real five-course meal. The train is made up of five distinctive dining cars, including a domed car built in 1938 and refurbished in 1954 by the Southern Pacific Railroad to accommodate passengers for drinks and lounging. Two 1951 diesel-electric locomotives pull the cars along the route of the Stillwater and St. Paul Railroad, later acquired by the Northern Pacific, up the St. Croix and then west along Browns Creek. After seven miles, the train backs up for the return to Stillwater. *601 Main Street; 651-430-3000 or 800-992-6100.*

You can also take a dinner cruise with music and entertainment on the *Andiamo Showboat,* or take a narrated tour of town aboard a replica of the trolleys that ran in Stillwater a hundred years ago. The trolleys are heated and run year-round.

■ THROUGH THE ST. CROIX VALLEY *map page 205, E&F-1&2*

From Stillwater, Minnesota 95 runs north along the river, past the old boom site, past rolling fields, oak woodlands, and scattered white pine. The pressure to develop riverside homes and suburban tracts is becoming terrific. Residents are concerned about keeping the quaint rural character of their valley and preserving the historic character of towns such as **Marine on St. Croix,** a cluster of white clapboard buildings, where visitors can shop for books, antiques, and ice cream. A short train ride through the valley north of Marine is possible from the historic Osceola Depot, across the river in Osceola, Wisconsin. The trip is more basic and cheaper than the Zephyr and does not include dinner.

From Marine, drive west on County Road 4 then north on Old Marine Trail to Historic Corner. There you'll find the **Hay Lake School** and **Johannes Erickson Log House museums,** operated by the Washington County Historical Society.

Farther up the river lies 1,400-acre **William O'Brien State Park,** named for a logger who bought much of the cutover land once owned by logging companies. Sandstone outcrops along the river are picturesque. Canoeing, picnicking, fishing, and swimming are popular (canoes are available to rent). Hiking trails wind through clearings and wooded uplands. In winter, the ski trails are exceptional. *651-433-0500.*

Just north and west of the park is **Scandia,** founded in 1850 by the first Swedish settlers in Minnesota. The outdoor **Gammelgarden Museum** preserves several

Swedish settler buildings, including the log sanctuary of Elim Lutheran Church, built in 1856, the oldest existing church building in Minnesota. Scandia residents celebrate Midsommar Dag. *651-433-5053.*

A few miles farther to the northwest, strung along US 8, is a cluster of large lakes, including **Forest, Big Marine, South Center, North Center, South Lindstrom, North Lindstrom, Chisago,** and **Green lakes.** They provide good fishing for bass, walleyes, northern pike, and panfish, and attract plenty of tourists and vacationers. The towns intertwined with these lakes—**Forest Lake, Chisago City, Lindstrom,** and **Center City**—were founded primarily by Swedish immigrants, whose heritage is reflected in many small shops throughout the area. The immigrants arrived by riverboat at Taylors Falls in the early 1850s and migrated a short way south and west to this rolling land of lakes, soon to become farmland. Letters and diaries of Andrew Peterson attracted the attention of Swedish writer Vilhelm Moberg during a trip to the area in 1948. Moberg's research lead to four historical novels that became popular in Sweden. The novels formed the basis of the 1971 movie *The Emigrants,* with Max von Sydow and Liv Ullmann, and the 1972 sequel, *The New Land.* Rising above Lindstrom is a water tower resembling a white enameled Swedish coffee pot with the words: Välkommen till Lindström. Townspeople celebrate Karl Oskar Day in August, to commemorate one of Moberg's pioneer heroes. The Swedish festival Sankta Lucia Day falls in December.

■ TAYLORS FALLS AND THE ST. CROIX DALLES *map page 205, E-2*

Approaching Taylors Falls, Minnesota 95 joins US 8 and makes a magnificent descent into town, with a sweeping view of the river valley. At the main intersection, turn left and climb to the **Angel Hill Historic District.** The Methodist church built in 1861 forms the hub of the neighborhood. During the 1850s, circuit riders (itinerant preachers) served the town. The row of houses on Basil Street, virtually all white clapboard, date from this lumber town's earliest days in the mid-1800s. The buildings include the oldest schoolhouse in Minnesota, built in 1852. The Minnesota Historical Society maintains the **Folsom House,** built by Maine lumberman and land speculator William Henry Carman Folsom shortly after he arrived in Taylors Falls in 1850. An early investor in the St. Croix Boom, Folsom set up a store in Taylors Falls. He also helped run a grist mill and other enterprises and served as state representative and senator. His book, *Fifty Years in the Northwest,* remains a respected source of information about the settlement of the region. His five-bedroom house reflects Federal and Greek Revival styles. The outbuildings are

gone, though the well house has been rebuilt. *272 West Government Street; 651-465-3125.*

Taylors Falls is perched on the rim of a rocky canyon where once flowed a long, steep pitch of rapids. All but a short pitch of white water has vanished under a power dam just upstream from town, but the gorge is still known as the **St. Croix Dalles.** "The stream enters a wild, narrow gorge, so deep and dark, that the declining sun is quite shut out," Elizabeth F. Ellet wrote of ascending the Dalles of the St. Croix River by boat in 1852.

> *P*erpendicular walls of traprock, scarlet and chocolate colored, and gray with the moss of centuries, rising from the water, are piled in savage grandeur on either side . . . their craggy summits thinly covered with tall cedars and pines, which stand upright, at intervals on their sides, adding to the wild and picturesque effect.

Ellet can be forgiven her florid prose and sentences that run on like the river itself. Despite the dam and reservoir upstream, the Dalles still inspire the kind of awe that colors her words.

During the logging era, huge log jams formed between the craggy walls of the Dalles, at the sharp bend called Angle Rock. In 1886 logs stacked up through the entire canyon, forming the most spectacular jam ever known. Comprising an estimated 150 million board feet of timber, the jam required 200 men six weeks to clear.

Despite the clear-cutting in the valley above, the Dalles became a popular tourist destination. In 1895 Minnesota created a small park to protect the Dalles from encroaching homes. Wisconsin bought land for a complementary park in 1900, creating the nation's first interstate park.

Prominent in the rocky crags in Minnesota's portion of Interstate State Park are more than 200 potholes, strange geologic formations that look like huge drill holes in solid rock. The potholes formed thousands of years ago when glacial meltwater inundated the valley, drowning cliffs that today tower far above the river. Rocks and pebbles, caught in the current, swirled and rotated in pockets of basalt, drilling holes in the bedrock until retreating waters filled many of the excavations with silt and eventually stranded them far above the river. The widest is more than 20 feet across. The deepest is Bottomless Pit, named in the early 1900s, before workers dug silt from the hole to reveal the bottom at 67 feet below the rim.

Today a trail winds among the potholes. From the safety of a railing, you can

Paul Bergmann hauls large pumpkins from his St. Croix Valley farm.

ST. CROIX RIVER

stare into Bottomless Pit and walk through Devil's Parlor, a chamber of connected potholes. According to a park paper, a 1919 tourist guide also described a Devil's Punch Bowl, Devil's Footprint, Devil's Alcove, and Devil's Kitchen. Tour boat guides will point to a formation in the cliffs called the Devil's Chair.

Naming things for the devil seems big sport, especially a century ago. I often wonder why. Is pristine nature too wild to be associated with goodness? Do we lack the imagination to associate awe and spirits with anything other than evil? Do we simply enjoy the cachet of evil, even as we claim to love goodness? I have been told that many of these features were named by Indians for spirits, and whites could imagine spirits only as devils. But I doubt this is true. While "spirit" might connote quite different things to an Ojibwa and a Swede, I don't think Europeans were so limited that they could not imagine a sublime spirit world, as we profess to do in church. I do know that there seems nothing at all evil about such a majestic and peaceful setting.

The Dalles attracts adventurers. Rock climbers scale the high cliffs. Kayakers play in the short pitch of rapids. Every September, folks gather on the cliffs like mountain goats to watch a white-water slalom in the gorge. Less daring river-rats canoe the calm river below the Dalles (the park rents canoes) or board a tour boat for a view of the gorge from river level. *Taylors Falls Scenic Boat Tours; 651-257-3550, 800-447-4958.*

■ OFF THE BEATEN PATH *map page 205, D&E-1&2*

Follow Minnesota 95 out of Taylors Falls. At Almelund, swing northeast on Chisago 12 to **Wild River State Park,** whose 6,800 acres protect nearly 20 miles of the St. Croix River. The park is a mix of woodlands, savanna, and tallgrass prairie. The park provides 35 miles of trail for hiking and skiing, and 20 miles for horseback riding. Campers enjoy both car and backpack sites, and canoes are available for use on the St. Croix. The land was once the site of Nevers Dam, built of pile-driven logs a century ago to provide a head of water to drive logs through downstream shallows. Floodwaters destroyed the dam in 1954. *651-583-2125.*

The town of **Sunrise** sits on the river of the same name, near its confluence with the St. Croix. The center of town is elusive. No euphemistic suburban names here; names like Poor Farm Road and Ferry Road have significance. The Wild River Inn rents tubes and canoes. When the water level is adequate, the **Sunrise River** is an intimate and enjoyable canoe stream.

During the summer, when I have time or am simply tired of the traffic and droning boredom of Interstate 35, I swing east to the country roads that parallel the freeway through this section of the St. Croix Valley. I drive past tumble-down barns and towns shriveled from lack of attention once the freeway was built. But others are doing okay, able to attract business from the nearby freeway. North Branch, with spiffy houses and bright porches, has lined the street with flags in preparation for its centennial. Kids ride their bikes, and play ball at the playground. Beyond the street grid, you're back in the woods. Forest and fields are verdant, as green as can be. Kestrels and mourning doves perch on the wires. Hay lies in the fields, its aroma heavy and enveloping. Breathe it in. This is country.

At the main intersection of **Rush City** sits the **Grant House**, a simple, unpretentious hotel, built in 1896 (by Russell H. Grant, who claimed to be second cousin to President Grant) and now on the National Register of Historic Places. Once it was a popular stop with traveling salesmen who worked the area. Today its ambiance transports visitors back to the 1940s, with an aging but pleasant decor and simple dinners, good in the "home cooking" sort of way, for under $4 on some days. The air conditioner works overtime on a sweltering day as I stop for iced tea and talk to a young waitress with curly blonde hair and a disposition as sweet as fresh corn. *(See page 327.)*

■ SNAKE RIVER *map page 205, C-1*

During the late 1700s and early 1800s, fur traders built many posts throughout the St. Croix Valley. One such site was the **North West Company Fur Post** on the southern bank of the Snake River, just west of what is now **Pine City**. This wintering post was occupied in 1804–5 by trader John Sayer, his Indian wife (Obemau-Onoqua) and a crew of voyageurs. Sayer, the dominant trader in the area from about 1784 to about 1805, left a journal of his time in this country, an important record of the fur trade in the region. Building his post in only six weeks during the fall, he traded with the Ojibwa through the winter for wild rice and furs. In April he packed the furs to company headquarters at Fort William (Ontario) on Lake Superior. We don't know if the post was ever used again. By the 1960s, when the Minnesota Historical Society began work on the site, the buildings and stockade were long gone, though their location was clearly marked by compacted soil, charred outlines, wood and food residue, and hundreds of artifacts. The post has been re-created in its original location on the banks of the Snake River and stocked with furs, trade goods, and reproductions of furnishings. Guides play the roles of traders, voyageurs, and Indians. *320-629-6356.*

text continues on page 221

HINCKLEY FIRE

About a mile east of Hinckley, in the midst of a country cemetery, rises a dark rock obelisk about 40 feet high. Erected by the state, it is dated September 1, 1894, and dedicated to the 418 victims of the Hinckley fire. Buried in four trenches next to the monument are the remains of 248 town residents who died in the blaze. In an old train station on the west side of town, the **Hinckley Fire Museum** tells the story of one of the state's most notorious disasters. *Open May through October; 320-384-7338.*

In 1894, Hinckley was a prosperous logging town, poised at the intersection of two railroads and the Grindstone River. Eight major logging camps worked the forests surrounding town, but the best timber—the tallest, fattest, old-growth white pines—had already been cut. Their bark and branches lay deep on clear-cut land and scrub forest, drying to tinder in the long drought that plagued the region—for the summer of 1894 had been desperately dry. From May 1 to September 1, less than two inches of rain fell. Lightning, sparks from trains, and careless fires ignited the "slash" left by loggers. All summer small fires burned through the region. Residents of Hinckley and other small towns became inured to the smoke that hung over them like a shroud.

September 1 was no different. Day broke immediately, preternaturally hot and dry. Undoubtedly, Thomas G. Dunn, 25-year-old telegrapher for the St. Paul & Duluth Railroad, felt the bite of smoke in his nostrils and throat as he walked to work that morning. Dunn was in charge of the depot. His boss was out of town for the day. Other workers reported lighting their lamps because of the darkness cast by the thick smoke in the air, and it's natural to think Dunn might have done so as well. By the time Dunn went home for lunch, smoke and cinders were blowing into town from the southwest. As he returned to work, he told his mother he was worried about the fires in the woods. Pack a few things, he advised her, and be ready to leave with the family on the Limited.

Just after lunch, a sudden wind rose, and a wall of flame appeared to the southwest. By 2:30 the Hinckley fire chief, John Craig, assembled a crew of volunteer firefighters to deflect the flames around town.

About 3:00 P.M. Dunn received the message by telegraph that Pokegama, a small town to the southwest, had burned. At the same time, Craig's fire line collapsed. Houses in Hinckley burst into flame. Wood siding seemed to explode from the wood frames. The alarm sounded in the Brennan Lumber Company: the building and piles of timber and lumber began to burn.

Panic spread like the flames. The depot filled with townspeople hoping to leave on the 4 P.M. Limited. Among them were Dunn's own family. By 4:05, with the train still not in sight, the depot caught fire. Passengers fled to the street, but Dunn stayed at his telegraph, appealing for information about the train. As the depot burned around him, Dunn sent his last message: "I think I have stayed too long." Then he too ran into the street, but he was overcome by smoke and died.

Little did James Root, the engineer of the Limited, know of the disaster developing in Hinckley, his next stop. Root, a 14-year veteran of the railroad, drove engine 69, with a tall stack and prominent pilot, or cowcatcher. His Number 4 Limited was the fastest train on the St. Paul & Duluth line. Root left Duluth early that afternoon, bound for St. Paul, with about 125 passengers on board. Twenty-five more boarded in Carlton. As they pulled from the station, Root ordered the headlight turned on because of smoke and darkness. Nothing unusual in that: the crew had run through fires all that summer.

Yet today was worse than usual. A passenger on board Root's trail recalled, "By 3:30 the sky was as dark as midnight and the heat was getting more intense." The poor visibility slowed the train. It was about 10 minutes behind schedule. Shortly after 4 P.M., about a mile from Hinckley, Root realized immediately something was terribly wrong. A crowd of people was running up the track toward the train. As Root stopped, people emerged, as if from the smoke. An older woman, with her daughters,

A mural in the Hinckley Fire Museum depicts the heroic efforts of train crews to outrace the flames. (Hinckley Fire Museum)

cried out, "For God's sake, will you save us?"

Thomas Sullivan, the conductor on Root's train, recalled, "Looking ahead I discovered the fire coming in the shape of a cyclone. . . . Looking around we could see people coming from all directions, making for the train, and to the best of my knowledge I had received in the neighborhood of 150 or 160 men, women, and children. Thinking all were safely on board the train I was about to signal to start to back when screams to my right attracted my attention. It proved to be a mother and her three little children running for their lives, the flames grasping like a demon behind them. Those were the last people that I loaded on my train and then I sprang into the first-class coach and gave the engineer the bell twice. The third pull felt to me as though the bell cord were burned off. I ran into the smoking car and gave the bell cord one more pull and we started back. The train at that time was all on fire with between 300 and 400 lives beneath its roofs. We had only gone a quarter mile when a terrific wall of flame struck us at a terrific rate of speed. . . . It took every window out of the west side of the train. . . . Men, women and children screaming at the top of their voices. This is the hardest sight I have ever seen." Porter John Blair comforted the passengers, wetting towels to cool them and bending to tell a mother with a baby that all would be all right. He was, said Sullivan "as brave a man as I ever saw."

The explosion sprayed Root's neck and head with glass. Bleeding profusely, Root continued to back the train, hoping to make Skunk Lake, a shallow pond about four miles away. By now the train was burning. "I opened the throttle," Root recalled. "Two . . . men got onto the pilot. The one man caught onto the pilot for just a short distance and then fell off and was burned to death."

As the train crested Hinckley Hill, Root passed out from his injuries. John McGowan, the fireman, noticed the train was slowing to a crawl. He discovered Root slumped at the controls, his hand still on the throttle. He splashed Root with water. As Root came to, he saw the steam pressure had fallen to 95 pounds. The engine barely moved. He opened the throttle wide. "My hands were all burned," Root recalled. "I dared not rub them for fear of rubbing the flesh off."

Finally they reached Skunk Lake, no more than a mud hole. McGowan and Blair guided passengers to the water. McGowan came back to the train to carry Root to safety. People tried to find shelter in mud and water barely deeper than a bath.

Passenger James E. Lobdell: "We had all been in the water scarcely half a minute when through a wall of smoke there burst a sea of livid flame crackling and roaring like a thousand demons in search of their prey. The heat was awful. Somebody shouted, 'Get under the water for your lives.' I obeyed the command and I guess everybody else did likewise. I felt as though I was burning up. My mouth got dry and I could feel my tongue swelling. My eyeballs seemed starting out of my head and for a moment I felt the flame above and seemingly all around me. I think I lost consciousness. I don't know how long I had myself completely submerged under the water. I suppose it was only a few minutes, but it seemed like an age. When I raised my head the flames were roaring on at the south shore of the lake. . . . All around the lake the woods were on fire and a wall of flame seemingly 20 feet high hemmed us in. It was an awful awe-inspiring sight which I hope never to witness again. While I was watching the work of the flames all around, a red, lurid glare shot higher and brighter than the surrounding flame and dimly through the smoke and flying sparks I could see that the train was all ablaze. The heat from the burning cars became so intense that once more we were compelled to seek relief under the water, raising our heads at brief intervals to get a breath of air, so impregnated with smoke and fire that it was like poison to breathe it."

Many of the residents of the small towns and countryside were in no position to catch the train. Their fortunes, at that moment, were determined as if by a kind of roulette. Many died; others survived for no apparent reason.

Askov, a dozen miles northeast of Hinckley, was the last town to burn. By 6 P.M., the wall of flame had broken into smaller fires, which crawled toward Duluth and died in the cool evening. By then more than 400 square miles had burned. A page from a Hinckley Bible, carried aloft by the fierce updraft created by the flames, was recovered in Duluth. The glow from the fire was visible in Iowa and central Wisconsin. At the fire's peak, by later calculations, the smoke had reached more than four miles high—nearly the altitude of a passenger jet.

D. W. Cowan, the Pine County Coroner, wrote the report of the victims' deaths. It is stunning in its sparse objectivity, listing page after page of victims, sorted by family if last names were known: Edstrom, Sophie; Edstrom, Mrs.; Edstrom, age eight; Edstrom, age six; Edstrom, age four; Edstrom, age two. Entire families appeared in the pages of Cowan's report: the Fitzgeralds, the Ginders, the Jensens, the Johnsons.

Finally, he listed 102 victims for whom no names were known at all:

Unknown, male, height 5-10, weight 165. Wore heavy, laced shoes, woolen ribbed socks, nothing on body. Found in swamp one-half mile north of Hinckley.

Unknown, boy, age about 12, knee pants, long, black-ribbed stockings, shingle nails found in pocket. Found one-half mile north of Hinckley.

Unknown, girl, age about 13, weight 90 pounds. Found on railroad track near roundhouse in the village of Hinckley, burned beyond recognition.

Unknown, man, age about 24, weighed 160 pounds. Wore a Blousher, laced shoes, and Bedford cord pants, small silver watch case number 25107. $3 in silver. One Yale padlock key. Hair burned off, probably sandy.

[Number] 393, unknown, child, age about 4, only bones left.

[Number] 398, unknown, man, only bones and buckles of heavy shoes left.

In all, 418 were reported dead. Thirty-seven were reported to be still missing at the time of his report.

Aside from Cowan's understated report, the artifact I found most moving was a blackened melted mass of metal, remnant of a railroad car that, under other circumstances, might have carried more victims out of the wake of the worst single-day disaster ever to befall Minnesota.

Digging for bodies in the grisly aftermath of the fire near Hinckley.
(Hinckley Fire Museum)

The **Snake River,** a major tributary of the St. Croix, rises in the boggy country just east of Mille Lacs Lake and runs through wooded country, much of it quite remote. Difficult rapids (class 2 to 4) south of McGrath provide exciting canoeing, but only in exceptionally high water. Otherwise, canoeing is difficult because of the rocks. From Pine City east to the St. Croix, the Snake again runs through frequent rapids, though none here are difficult. Much of the river, especially the stretch below Pine City, provides excellent fishing for smallmouth bass, northern pike, walleyes, and channel catfish.

■ ST. CROIX STATE PARK *map page 205, C-1&2*

Flanking one of the most picturesque stretches of the upper St. Croix is St. Croix State Park, at 34,000 acres Minnesota's largest state park. Owing to its size and the boggy, sparsely settled country that surrounds it, St. Croix is one of the state's wildest parks. Few roads cross it. Gray wolves have taken up residence, preying on the abundant whitetails.

The park has 127 miles of hiking trails, more than twice the mileage of any other park. It also accommodates horses and mountain bikes. In addition to 25 miles of the St. Croix, the park embraces the final seven miles of the Kettle River. Where it runs through the park, the Kettle provides good fishing for smallmouth bass and, in high water, a swift and thrilling canoe ride.

The park was once the site of logging camps, logging railroads, and log drives. The old Fleming Railroad hauled logs to the Yellow Banks on the St. Croix and dumped them into the river. Many of these old logging railroads were temporary—what one worker called "two streaks of rust" through the woods. In the 1930s, the park served as a camp for the Civilian Conservation Corps. Of the more than 150 park structures that date to CCC days, none is more impressive than St. Croix Lodge, built snug as a Roman arch from sandstone blocks and pine timbers.

In the western end of the park stands an old fire tower. Equipped with railings and fencing for safety, it offers a stunning view of the surrounding forest, as well as an intimate view of each layer of forest, from understory to treetops. The park offers canoes and bikes for rent. Both provide a far better view of this country than any car window can. *320-384-6591.*

■ KETTLE RIVER *map page 205, A, B&C-1*

The St. Croix was one of the nation's first federal Wild and Scenic Rivers. One of its major tributaries, the Kettle River, was the first addition to the State Wild and Scenic River system.

The Kettle is a wonderful canoeing stream. The final seven miles through St. Croix State Park are marked by swift, bouldery rapids—great fun for paddlers with even modest experience in a canoe. Beware in low water, however; you may have to drag through long stretches of rocky shallows.

More exciting—and potentially more dangerous—is the stretch of the Kettle known as Banning Rapids or, in reference to one particular drop, Hell's Gate. To paddle this section or simply to take a look at the roaring river and beautiful cliffs and bluffs that surround it, exit Interstate 35 at Minnesota 23 and drive a mile east to **Banning State Park.** *320-245-2668.*

A trail in the park follows the river through the steepest rapids, named over the years by kayakers who have ridden the chain of waves, ledges, and souse holes: Blueberry Slide, Mother's Delight, Dragon's Tooth, Hell's Gate.

I first saw this stretch of river on a canoe trip with my younger brother. We portaged Blueberry Slide, ran Mother's Delight (one of the easier pitches), and made a play at running Dragon's Tooth before pulling out midway through. Luckily, the water was low and the river forgiving, for I was still in that stage of development as a paddler when I confused bravery with expertise. Had the river been high, we might have joined the several other canoeists who had the same misunderstanding and paid with their lives. (In low water, these rapids rate only class 2 in the parlance of river runners, but in high water, they rate class 3 and 4.)

The trail following the river winds through the location of the old quarry town of Banning. Little is left of the town itself, which vacated quickly after the quarry closed in 1905. Today the concrete walls of two old quarry buildings stand vacant and melancholy on the banks of the river.

Just downstream from this traditional whitewater run, a new rapids has appeared. In 1995 construction crews removed the old power dam at Sandstone, exposing a picturesque waterfall about eight feet high that hadn't been seen for a century. To reach the newly revealed falls, drive south (downstream) about a mile from Sandstone.

Just west of Banning State Park is **Willard Munger State Trail,** a complex system of interconnecting trails that eventually will run between St. Paul and Duluth. The partly paved trail, built along the railroad grade that provided escape from the Hinckley fire, accommodates hiking, biking, and horseback riding. Near Duluth, the trail runs through the spectacular scenery of Jay Cooke State Park *(see "NORTH SHORE AND THE ARROWHEAD," page 235).*

N O R T H   S H O R E
A N D   T H E   A R R O W H E A D

■ HIGHLIGHTS

	page
Duluth	227
Ariel Lift Bridge	229
Robber baron estates	233
Gunflint Trail	247
Naniboujou Lodge	249
Grand Portage	250
Boundary Waters Canoe Area	255
Voyageurs National Park	260

Voyageurs National Park • Grand Portage
Boundary Waters Canoe Area
Gun Flint Trail
Duluth

NORTH SHORE &
THE ARROWHEAD
Map page 226

ATOP LAKE SUPERIOR LIES A WEDGE of Minnesota known for its shape as the Arrowhead. Despite the work of fur traders, loggers, and miners, the region retains the character of the great north woods, where thousands of lakes sit in basins scoured from bedrock, and rivers sparkle and tumble through rocky rapids. It is to the Arrowhead that people travel to canoe, hike, snowmobile, and ski in the closest approximation to true wilderness that still exists in Minnesota. For many Minnesotans, the north woods is the quintessential picture of Minnesota—not only how we imagine our state to be, but also how we wish it to be, still forested, still wild, a place where loons call and wolves howl.

■ LAKE SUPERIOR

More than a billion years ago the land mass that eventually became North America began to split apart in a crescent of volcanic paroxysm that stretched from what is now eastern Lake Superior all the way to present-day Kansas. The rifting stopped after a few tens of millions of years, or the valley might eventually have opened to the ocean. Instead, with the close of the last ice age 10,000 years ago, the basin cradles Lake Superior. The ancient outpouring of lava formed the cliffs that now run the length of the North Shore in the United States and Canada. Draped in summer foliage, they flank the lake like a deep green curtain.

At 31,500 square miles, Superior is the largest freshwater lake in the world by area, and second only to Russia's Lake Baikal (which is much deeper) in volume.

NORTH SHORE

Three hundred fifty miles long, and 160 across, it indeed seems an inland sea, connected to far-off ports, a thoroughfare to the rest of the world.

On a calm day, the ebb and flow of gentle swells rolling across the broad fetch of Superior through the wave-rounded rocks on shore resembles breathing, the respiration of a sleeping giant. Awakened by a strong nor'easter, the giant hurls 20-foot waves onto the shore. Superior's storms have sunk hundreds of vessels, from small fishing boats to the 729-foot ore boat *Edmund Fitzgerald.*

In limnological terms, Superior is oligotrophic—the coldest, clearest, and least fertile of all the Great Lakes. From directly overhead, rocks of various colors are clearly visible in up to 30 feet of water. "Every river swarms, every bay is a reservoir of magnificent fish," wrote Robert Barnwell Roosevelt (uncle of President Theodore Roosevelt), who caught lake trout, brook trout, and smallmouth bass at the time of the Civil War.

But the abundance of fish was a bit of an illusion. While brook trout flooded the inshore areas and stream estuaries, the lake, considered as a whole, was largely fishless, so flinty and lacking in nutrients was the basin. The aquatic ecosystem was in its infancy, having formed at the end of the ice age. As a result, the number of species was low and not highly adapted to the lake. By the end of the century, log drives and sawmills had choked tributaries and estuaries with wood bark and sawdust, destroying habitat for several species, including the rapidly disappearing lake sturgeon, which sometimes weighed 300 pounds. During the 20th century, smelt and vampirish sea lampreys entered the Great Lakes through the newly built Welland Canal and preyed upon the primitive community of lake trout, brook trout, and lake herring. Commercial fishing, which had sustained small communities along the shore, collapsed in mid-century. One commercial fisherman told me that in 1950 "one trout in the whole season fishing off Isle Royale had a lamprey scar." Seven years later, he said, "I fished for two weeks [catching about 300 trout] before I had a trout that wasn't lamprey-scarred."

With intensive efforts to eradicate sea lamprey and stock additional lake trout, the lake trout population has partly rebounded. Unfortunately, fisheries managers, at the insistence of anglers, have also introduced West Coast steelhead (migratory rainbow trout) and chinook, coho, and pink salmon. In addition, other exotics—such as river ruff and zebra mussels—have sneaked into the lake aboard the ballast tanks of foreign vessels. What effect this goulash of exotic species will have on the huge lake, which once must have seemed indomitable, will be known only in the future.

Gold Point overlooking Lake Superior on Minnesota's North Shore.

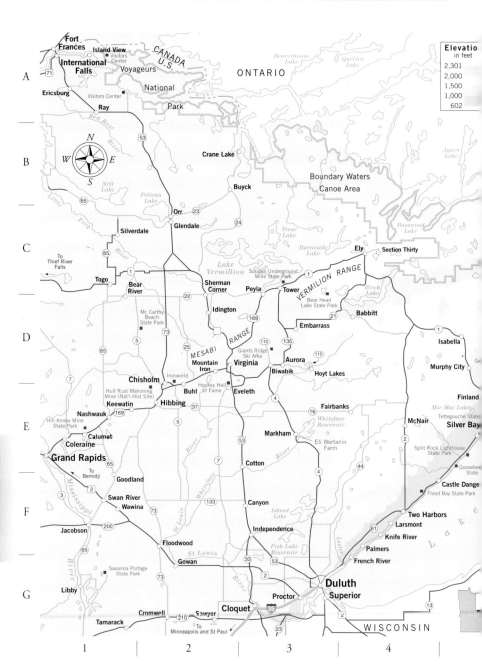

Elevatio
in feet
2,301
2,000
1,500
1,000
602

Fort
Frances   Island View
               Visitors
International Center
   Falls   Voyageurs

Ericsburg   Visitors Center
      Ray

CANADA
U.S.

Beaverhouse
Lake

Quetico
Lake

ONTARIO

National

Park

Red Root

N
W   E
S

Nett
Lake

53

Crane Lake

Boundary Waters
Canoe Area

Aqnes
Lake

Little Fork

65

Pelican
Lake

Buyck

Orr   23

Silverdale   Glendale

24

Trout
Lake

Basswood
Lake

To
Thief River
Falls

65

River

Togo
Bear
River

Lake
Vermillion
22

Soudan Underground
Mine State Park

Sherman
Corner   Peyla

Burntside
Lake

Tower

Ely   Section Thirty

VERMILION RANGE

Birch
Lake

Mc Carthy
Beach
State Park

73

Idington

169

Bear Head
Lake State Park

Embarrass

21

Babbitt

1

5

25

RANGE

MESABI

110 135

Mountain
Iron

Giants Ridge
Ski Area

Virginia

Aurora

110

Isabella

Murphy City

65

7

Chisholm
Ironworld
Hull Rust Mahoning
Mine (Nat'l Hist Site)

Biwabik

Hoyt Lakes

Keewatin
Nashwauk   169

Hill Annex Mine
State Park

Buhl
Hibbing   37

Hockey Hall
of Fame   Eveleth

4

16

Fairbanks

Whiteface
Reservoir

Mic Mac Lake
Tettegouche State Park

Finland

McNair   Silver Bay

5

Calumet
Coleraine

53

Markham

Eli Wertanin
Farm

2

Split Rock Lighthouse
State Park

Grand Rapids   65

To
Bemidji   Goodland

7

Cotton

44

Goosebe
State

Castle Dange
Flood Bay State Park

3
2

Swan River
Wawina   73

133

Island
Lake

Canyon

4

Jacobson   200

Mississippi

Floodwood

Independence

Fish Lake
Reservoir

Two Harbors
Larsmont

61   Knife River

65

St Louis

Savanna Portage
State Park

73

Gowan   33   53

Palmers

French River

Lake

Libby

Proctor

Superior   Duluth

Cromwell   Sawyer   Cloquet

210

Tamarack

To
Minneapolis and St Paul

23

35

2

WISCONSIN

13

NORTH SHORE

1   2   3   4

NORTH SHORE AND THE ARROWHEAD

■ DULUTH: CITY BY THE BAY *map G-3*

Were San Francisco not seven times bigger and already in possession of the name, Duluth (pop. 85,500) might snatch away the sobriquet of City by the Bay. Certainly, very few cities have claimed so lovely a settling, nestled as it is in the cold, rocky embrace of the North Shore cliffs and western tip of Superior. *The WPA Guide to Minnesota* called it "a Lilliputian village in a mammoth rock garden." The city runs along the lake for 24 miles. "Because of the city's narrowness," says the guidebook, "the countryside seems always, in Duluth, to be crowding down to its very back doors." In 1933 a black bear broke into the restaurant of Duluth's largest hotel (since named Black Bear Lounge). People on the outskirts of town routinely shoo bears from trash each fall, and moose occasionally run through town.

Sinclair Lewis, in his novel *Babbitt,* called Duluth "Zenith City," the model of smug, small-minded conventionalism. Truthfully, though I lived in Duluth for two years, I have never been able to picture the city that way. Instead, it seemed hard, a bit gritty, very real, and blessed with a freshwater ocean at its doorstep. Railroads thundered along the hillside, and the deep foghorns of freighters and ore boats sounded outside the harbor. Because of the microclimate created by the lake, Duluth's unofficial motto might be, "Colder by the lake."

The city was named for French explorer Daniel Greysolon, Sieur Duluth, who landed at the spot in about 1679. From the beginning, as the Indian village the voyageurs named Fond du Lac, the community has served water transportation. Located several miles upstream from the mouth of the St. Louis River, Fond du Lac served as a gateway to what is now northern Minnesota and Canada. There, voyageurs in birch-bark canoes would portage the long stretch of rapids at the

6 | 7 | 8

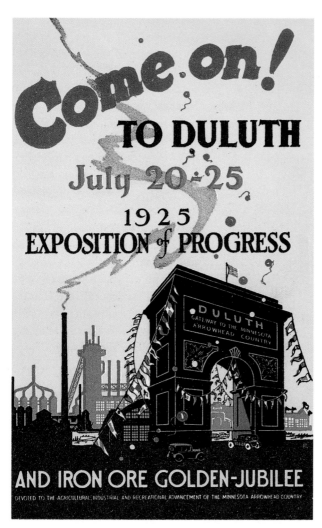

present site of Jay Cooke State Park. Then, they would follow one of two routes: either up the St. Louis and through the Embarrass, Pike, and Vermilion rivers to the Canadian border, or west off the St. Louis, ascending the East Savanna River and crossing to the West Savanna and the Mississippi Rivers by a six-mile portage through small creeks, bogs, and other terrain most eminently suited for mosquitoes. Today, it is possible to hike this historic portage and battle the ancestors of mosquitoes that sucked blood from the voyageurs in Savanna Portage State Park, 50 miles west of Duluth.

A not terribly exciting invitation to visit Duluth's varied industrial sites in the 1920s. (Minnesota Historical Society)

The construction of locks at Sault Ste. Marie at the east end of Lake Superior in 1855 extended shipping to the large eastern cities on the lower Great Lakes. Duluth, as a result, grew dramatically. In 1870 Jay Cooke chose Duluth as the northern end of his Lake Superior and Mississippi Railroad from St. Paul. City fortunes stalled with the panic of 1873, when Cooke went bankrupt. After economic recovery, Duluth rivaled Chicago as a grain-shipping port. In the late 1890s the largest iron mining districts in the world began shipping ore through Duluth. The city swelled with thousands of immigrants coming to work the mines.

◆ DULUTH WATERFRONT

Today Duluth is an international port, shipping pellets of iron ore to steel plants on the lower lakes, and grain and wood products to eastern and European markets. A good place to begin a tour of the town is where the city began, on the lake.

Canal Park and the waterfront have undergone an inspiring facelift in recent years. The park, with fountains and sculptures, produced locally and in Europe, is a great place to walk and hang out for lunch or dinner. Shop at the DeWitt-Seitz Marketplace for eclectic arts and crafts, clothing, and books. Also in the Marketplace are a couple of restaurants and a bakery.

The Aerial Lift Bridge joins the mainland and Minnesota Point, a long sand spit that runs six miles across the mouth of the harbor. A section of the bridge lifts 135 feet to allow boats to pass underneath through the Duluth Ship Canal. The canal is not a natural channel. The natural channel lies on the Wisconsin side of

Giant ore boats berth in Duluth's Harbor Basin. The city is clearly visible in the background.

the sand spit that shelters the harbor, and therein lies an interesting tale. Residents of Superior, Wisconsin, eager to protect the natural advantage of having the ship canal on their side of the harbor, sought to go to court to prevent Duluth from digging its own entrance. But Duluthians got wind of the plan and dug the channel in the night—even regular citizens attacked the sand spit with shovels—to open the passage before Superior could stop them in court.

Minnesota Point, known locally as **Park Point**, is a casual beachside neighborhood, a pleasant place to hike, bike, or watch for birds. (The point is a migration stopover for a great variety of shorebirds and songbirds.) Strong northeast winds kick up a tremendous surf. **Park Point Recreation Center** sits at the tip of the point. Canoe and sea kayak tours are available.

Next to the Lift Bridge is the **Lake Superior Maritime Visitors Center**, dedicated to Great Lakes shipping. You can tour a ship's pilothouse, engine room, and crew quarters, and inspect models of Great Lakes boats, and exhibits of shipwrecks caused by storms in 1905 and 1975. The museum provides a clear view of vessels entering and leaving the harbor. *600 Canal Park Drive; 218-727-2497.*

Docked just inside the harbor, a couple of blocks from the Lift Bridge is the *William A. Irvin,* once the flagship of the U.S. Steel Great Lakes ore boat fleet. Launched in 1938, the 610-foot boat hauled ore to U.S. Steel steel mills until 1978. (Custom dictates that vessels on this inland sea are called "boats" regardless of size.) Walk aboard to tour the engine room, guest staterooms, galley, dining room, and pilothouse.

New along the Duluth waterfront is the **Great Lakes Aquarium at Lake Superior Center** , a 120,000-gallon aquarium representing the deep-water habitat of lake trout, steelhead, and whitefish. Other displays portray the basin's geology, wetlands, beaches, rivers, and forests. *353 Harbor Drive; 218-525-2265.*

For a two-hour sightseeing cruise on Lake Superior call Vista Fleet Harbor Cruises from June to September, *218-529-7745.* Or charter a fishing boat to troll for steelhead, chinook, coho, Atlantic salmon, and lake trout on Lake Superior. Call Boat Watcher's Hotline to learn what just pulled into port: *218-722-6489.*

◆ DOWNTOWN DULUTH

Moving up the hill, you'll find a downtown that has benefited tremendously from efforts to remake itself and stem the decline that has threatened so many Great Lakes industrial towns.

Ore boats trapped in the winter ice of Lake Superior. The lake can be deadliest when winter gales create waves up to 20 feet high. (Underwood Photo Archives, San Francisco)

The old Union Depot, closed in 1969, has been rechristened simply **The Depot** The châteauesque brownstone building, built in 1892, houses several exhibits and attractions. The **Lake Superior Railroad Museum** holds railroad equipment and memorabilia, including one of the largest locomotives built. The **St. Louis County Historical Society** exhibits describe pioneer life, logging, mining, and railroading in the early days of the area. A highlight of the historical society's collections are Indian portraits by American artist Eastman Johnson and examples of Ojibwa beadwork, clothing, and tools. **Depot Square** is a re-creation of a 1910 Duluth street scene at three-quarters scale, with a vintage trolley that runs by commercial storefronts. Other attractions are the **Duluth Children's Museum** and **Duluth Art Institute**. **The North Shore Scenic Railroad** departs from The Depot for a 56-mile round-trip tour up the shore to Two Harbors. Shorter excursions are also available. The locomotive pulls fancy dining cars as well as casual "pizza trains." *506 West Michigan Street; 218-722-1273.*

The 1928 **City Hall** and 1930 **Federal Building** stand farther up the hill on First Street and Fifth Avenue West, sharing the square with the 1909 Beaux Arts **St. Louis County Courthouse** designed by Chicago architect Daniel Burnham.

Old Duluth Central High School.

Cass Gilbert, designer of the State Capitol, designed the Soldiers' and Sailors' Monument in 1921. **The Karpeles Manuscript Museum** boasts original drafts of important documents from many countries, including the U.S. Bill of Rights, Emancipation Proclamation, and Handel's *Messiah.* Many documents are on loan from other museums around the country that, like the Karpeles Museum, were established by Cali-fornia businessman David Karpeles, who grew up in Duluth. *902 East First Street.*

Fitger's on the Lake is a renovated brewery that now houses over two dozen shops and restaurants. *600 East Superior Street; 800-726-2982.*

♦ ROBBER-BARON ESTATES

Northeast from downtown along Superior Street are the one-time mansions of the turn-of-the-century millionaires who built Duluth and the lumber and iron-mining industries: the 1912 Jacobean Revival **Kitchi Gammi Club** at 831 East Superior Street, the 1892 Richardsonian Roman-esque **Traphagen House**, at 1511 East Superior Street, and the 1902 brownstone **Crosby House** at 2029 East Superior Street, built by George H. Crosby, who helped develop the Mesabi Iron Range. All are private. Many other restored Victorian homes make East Duluth the most picturesque residential neighborhood in town.

One of the most luxurious of the robber-baron estates is the **Glensheen mansion.** Built in 1905–8, the historic estate and its

Glensheen mansion, a 39-room Jacobean Revival home.

22-acre landscaped grounds are open for tours. The Jacobean mansion has Georgian, Mission, and Art Nouveau furnishings. The tour focuses on the architecture and history of the estate and family. "Acquaint yourself with a lifestyle that is gone forever," suggests a tourism brochure. The remark is true in more ways than one: Glensheen was the setting for two of Duluth's most notorious murders. In 1977 heiress Elisabeth Congdon was smothered and her nurse bludgeoned. Congdon's daughter and son-in-law were tried. She was acquitted; he was not. The murder, unfortunately, is not covered in the tour. *3300 London Road; 888-454-4536.*

◆ UP AND AROUND DULUTH

Farther up the hill from downtown is the **Duluth campus of the University of Minnesota**, with about 7,800 students. Worth visiting are the **Tweed Museum of Art** (contemporary and historical American and European art), **Sax Sculpture Conservatory**, and **Marshall W. Alworth Planetarium**.

For 27 miles **Skyline Parkway Drive** girdles the towering ridge along the lake, alternately running through woods and then opening to a panoramic view of Superior. Stop where the parkway intersects 18th Avenue West and climb **Enger Tower** for one of the most dramatic overlooks of Lake Superior. The grounds around the tower contain dwarf conifers, Japanese gardens, and picnic areas.

Farther along Skyline Parkway and 600 feet above the lake is the **Hawk Ridge Nature Reserve**. Here, each fall, thousands of hawks, eagles, falcons, and other birds funnel along the shore of Lake Superior in their southward migration. Volunteers spot and count birds and also capture and band birds for research. More than 200 species have been spotted. On some days, tens of thousands of hawks pass by the ridge. Numbers peak in mid-September with big flights of sharp-shinned and broad-winged hawks. Later migrants include golden and bald eagles, goshawks, and rough-legged hawks. Duluth Audubon Society spotters answer questions. *One mile east of Glenwood Avenue.*

Turn your attention westward for a moment to the other end of Duluth—the **West End**, the blue-collar end, built around the cement and steel plants on the waterfront. Watch ore-loading operations from the observation platform overlooking the Duluth, Missabe, and Iron Range Railway Co. docks, which stick nearly a half mile into the harbor, at 35th Avenue West and Superior Street.

The **Lake Superior Zoological Gardens** contains more than 80 exhibits with 500 species on 12 acres. *72nd and Grand Avenues near MN 23; 218-733-3777.* Across from the zoo, catch the **Lake Superior & Mississippi Railroad**, a vintage train that takes a 90-minute, 12-mile round trip though the soaring hills along the

A historic coal-fed steam train departs from Duluth for a scenic ride along the North Shore.

St. Louis River in summer months. *218-624-7549*. **Spirit Mountain Recreation Area** offers downhill and cross-country skiing on the high ridge behind Duluth. The longest run stretches more than a mile, with a 700-foot vertical drop.

Duluth has an impressive **park system** of more than 11,000 acres. Many parks are laid out along the numerous small streams that tumble out of the hills to the lake. Two in particular—**Lester-Amity** on the east end of town and **Magney-Snively** on the west—provide great hiking and cross-country skiing.

At the far western end of Duluth, near the site of old Fond du Lac, gray wolves and deer are often spotted in **Jay Cooke State Park**, an 8,800-acre preserve on the lower **St. Louis River**. The river plunges over beds of metamorphic and sedimentary rocks so tilted and convoluted that the area has an other worldly look. The river is popular with rafters and kayakers. The stretch upstream from the Thomson Reservoir (outside the park) is a pleasant class 2–3 run. Raft rentals are available. The class 4 rapids immediately below the dam at Carlton are the site of one of the Midwest's premier whitewater slalom courses, which attracts international competitors. The class 4–6 (and harder!) stretch of whitewater farther downstream through the park is for suicide squads only. The state park provides good hiking, mountain biking, and some of the best cross-country skiing in the state. *218-384-4610*.

■ NORTH SHORE DRIVE *map page 227*

Through the early 1900s, the North Shore was an isolated shoreline, unreachable by road. It was dotted by Norwegian and Ojibwa fishing communities. Boats brought mail and supplies three seasons of the year; dog sleds handled the task in winter. The North Shore highway, following the route of the present highway for the most part, opened in 1924, inaugurating one of the state's great tourism routes.

Today, US 61 runs along Superior's crooked shore like a thread, generally staying within a quarter mile of the water as it travels about 160 miles from Duluth to the Canadian border. The drive along the lake ranks as a state favorite for its wooded hills, river canyons and waterfalls, and frequent vistas of Lake Superior. Resorts and small rental cabins sit along the lake. Each autumn the hardwoods along the ridges ignite in yellow, orange, and red. In Minnesota the drive and the region are known simply as the North Shore. There's never any need to specify the north shore of what.

(While the shore is great place for anglers, bikers, and sea kayakers, it is decidedly not popular with swimmers. The water along the rocky shore is deep and cold, almost never warm enough for an enjoyable plunge.)

Driving northeast out of Duluth, you cross the **Lester River,** one of dozens of North Shore streams that head up in the North Shore Highlands, wander rather aimlessly near the divide, then gain speed and purpose as they find the swift descent toward the lake, whistling down the mountain of rock through frequent rapids and waterfalls. Historically, it appears, these streams were too small and sterile, too variable in their flow and subject to winterkill, to permanently hold trout. All native brook and lake trout lived in the lake and the very lower ends of the rivers, downstream from the first impassable falls. Today, however, through stocking, the North Shore streams hold brook trout, rainbow trout (a migratory West Coast fish known also as steelhead), and a few brown trout. The lower reaches of the streams attract migratory runs of lake-dwelling steelhead, pink and chinook salmon, and the occasional lake trout and coho salmon.

Just past the Lester River, the highway forks. Skip the expressway, veer right on **North Shore Drive,** and hug the shore where you'll be able to look out over the lake. This is the route of Grandma's Marathon in June, one of the country's largest marathons. The race begins near Two Harbors and ends at Canal Park in Duluth.

About 15 miles out of Duluth, **Tom's Logging Camp Museum** recalls the hardship and hard work associated with the early days of logging on the North Shore, when men clad in wool and armed with hand saws felled huge old-growth white pine. Buildings furnished in period style with old logging equipment form a typical logging camp. There's also a museum on commercial fishing.

Knife River, located on the mouth of its namesake creek, is a good place to stop in one of the little roadside shops for a North Shore delicacy—smoked lake trout and whitefish. Sailboats, cruisers, and runabouts fill the slips, the largest marina along the shore. In the spring, when the Knife River runs full and swift, fishermen will perch along the stream banks to catch silvery steelhead as they swim upstream to spawn.

◆ TWO HARBORS *map page 227, F-4*

Two Harbors, besides Duluth the largest community along the Shore, is named for Agate Bay on the west and Burlington Bay on the east. The first load of iron ore from northern Minnesota's iron mines was loaded and shipped from this port in 1884.

Exhibits in the **Depot Museum,** located in the 1907 headquarters of the Duluth, Missabe and Iron Range Railway, tell of the ore shipments and iron-rich geology of the area. The museum also describes early North Shore logging operations. On display are the Three Spot, a locomotive that started service in the 1880s, and the Mallet 221, one of the largest locomotives in existence, nearly 128 feet long and weighing about 550 tons.

The **Harbor Museum,** located in the light station on Lighthouse Point, tells the story of Agate Bay, where the first shipment of ore departed. The Lake County Historical Society takes care of the *Edna G.* Built in 1896, it was the last coal-burning steam-powered tug on the Great Lakes when it was retired in 1981. Tours of the boat swing through the highly decorated captain's quarters, engine room, and pilot house. The historical society also conducts county tours of five historic and prehistoric sites in a daylong tour; call to make reservations *218-834-4898.*

Burlington Bay, on the east end of town, is a good place to gather **Lake Superior agates.** During the volcanism that threatened to split the continent, the agates formed as minerals filled gas pockets, called vesicles, in the molten lava. Agate picking is best at the western end of the lake.

Two Harbors is also the present terminus of the **Lake Superior Hiking Trail,** the state's premier long-distance hiking trail, which runs about 200 miles to Judge C. R. Magney State Park east of Grand Marais. It's possible to take daytrips, lodge-to-lodge hikes, overnights, and trips of several weeks. The trail passes through several state parks and dozens of campsites as it girdles the steep slopes and crests the high hills along the shore. It has plenty of ups and downs—from the shore of Lake

Superior at 602 feet above sea level to Rosebush Ridge at 1,829 feet—as it wends through old-growth forests of birch and cedar and crosses bald rocky knobs with overlooks of the lake. Simple bridges cross the streams. The trail was designed, built, and is maintained by Superior Hiking Trail Association volunteers. Snowmobilers love the North Shore Corridor Trail, which generally follows the ridge and lies several miles inland from the hiking trail.

◆ POINTS ALONG THE WAY *map page 227, E&F-5*

Castle Danger is one of the most ominously named points along the shore. The name derives, according to *The WPA Guide to Minnesota,* from the shipwreck of the boat *Castle* on the reefs offshore.

A prominent landmark on many early maps of the North Shore, the **Gooseberry River** probably took its name from French explorer Médart Chouart, Sieur des Groseilliers, whose name translates literally as "gooseberry." Today, 1,700-acre

Summer swimming at Gooseberry Falls (above). Some streams tumble 500 feet down bluffs to the lake, forming perfect pools for swimming along the way. Split Rock Lighthouse (left) rests on the rocky shoreline about 50 miles northeast of Duluth.

Gooseberry Falls State Park is one of the state's most popular state parks, with a campground framed by the mouth of the Gooseberry River and the shore of Lake Superior. The readily accessible falls above and below the highway are the focal point of the park, but wooded trails provide good hiking and, in winter, excellent cross-country skiing. The North Shore is the state's snowiest region, and the topography provides plenty of hills and turns. The stone and log work in the old buildings and parking areas in the park provide excellent examples of public-works construction during the Depression. A new visitors center, a rustic yet expansive building constructed of timbers salvaged from a turn-of-the-century warehouse and native stone from a nearby tunnel excavation, overlooks the lower falls and estuary of the Gooseberry River. *218 834-3855.*

The many logging companies that worked the shore during the early years of the century hauled logs to Lake Superior by rail or sent them cascading down the rivers. The Nestor Logging Company gathered logs in the estuary of the Gooseberry and towed the log rafts across the lake to mills in Ashland, Wisconsin, and Baraga, Michigan. The tug *Schoolcraft* made the crossing in eight days with a raft of six million board feet.

Even during the summer months Lake Superior's water temperatures hover around 50° F, making it too cold for most swimmers.

Split Rock Point was the site of the corundum mine opened by Minnesota Abrasive Company in 1901 and soon sold to Minnesota Mining and Manufacturing, later to become 3M. Across the bay is **Split Rock State Park** and **Split Rock Lighthouse Historic Site.** The classic lighthouse, perched on a cliff of anorthosite far above Lake Superior, must be the most photographed landmark on the North Shore, and perhaps in all of Minnesota. The lighthouse was built after autumn storms in 1905 wrecked six boats and killed more than 200 sailors. Metallic deposits in the area deflected compass needles, making navigation along the shore treacherous. Tours of the historic site today take visitors to the light tower (decommissioned in 1969), where the Fresnel lens that focused the beam of light over the lake floats on a bearing of 250 pounds of liquid mercury. Visitors also can see the fog-signal building, residences for three lighthouse keepers and their families, a history center with exhibits on shipping, shipwrecks, and commercial fishing, and an excellent film on the lighthouse. The surrounding park comprises 1,900 acres, with hiking and cross-country ski trails. The Lake Superior Hiking Trail cuts through the park. *State Park; 218-226-6377, Visitors Center; 218 226-6372.*

Beaver Bay is the oldest permanent white settlement on shore. The same day

NORTH SHORE

the town site was platted in 1856, German settlers stepped off a boat to build homes and clear farms. Beaver Bay diminished in importance when the first railroad from the Vermilion Iron Range ran instead to Two Harbors. Buried in the cemetery just outside Beaver Bay is John Beargrease, an Ojibwa who carried mail along the shore from 1879 to 1900, traveling by dog sled in winter and in summer by a small boat he could row or sail. Today, the 500-mile **Beargrease Sled Dog Marathon** runs in early January from Duluth to Grand Portage and back along the North Shore Corridor Trail *(see page 333)*.

Silver Bay is unmistakable for the looming taconite plant lodged between the highway and lake shore. For many years the plant, then owned by Reserve Mining, discharged up to 67,000 tons of tailings, the discards from the taconite concentrating process, into the lake each day. During the 1970s, the company was forced to find an on-land disposal site for the tailings. Today the plant is operated by Cyprus Minerals Company.

Palisade Head, a highway rest area, is a sheer cliff of rhyolite that drops more than 300 feet into Superior's crashing waves. The view of the lake is undeniably dramatic, but keep an eye on your kids. When vertigo subsides, look around for the peregrine falcons that usually nest on ledges in the cliff face. The cliff is popular with rock climbers.

Up the shore a mile is **Tettegouche State Park.** At 9,346 acres, it is the largest park along the shore. It is also one of the most varied and spectacular, with pockets of old-growth forest, picturesque falls and rapids along the **Baptism River,** many spectacular outlooks from bald hilltops, and several small inland lakes. Park names such as Tettegouche, Mic Mac Lake, and Nipisiquit Lake ring with strangeness. They seem out of character in Minnesota's woods. In fact, they are Mic Mac Indian names, bestowed by the Alger-Smith Lumber Company of New Brunswick, which owned much of the present park acreage at the turn of the century. When it had cut the red and white pine from the land, the company sold the lake to the Tettegouche Club, a group of Duluth businessmen who used the land as a hunting and fishing retreat. In 1979, the land and a few buildings on the interior lakes were donated for use as a state park. The Baptism provides fishing for brook trout (primarily in the upper reaches), lake-run steelhead, and chinook and pink salmon. Lake trout swim off the river mouth. The park contains campsites and more than a dozen miles of hiking and cross-country skiing trails. *218-226-6365.*

The North Shore is a spectacular site for sea kayaking because of its soaring rock cliffs. But because of those cliffs and scarcity of protected beaches where you might launch or take shelter in a wind, it is also one of the most inhospitable and hazardous parts of the lake. The Minnesota Department of Natural Resources is working with recreation groups, resorters, and other government agencies to open the Lake Superior Water Trail, a network of kayak landings and campsites along the lake. So far, only a few sites have been established. Eventually the network will circle the lake. You can rent sea kayaks at several locations along the North Shore.

◆ **MN 1 TO ELY** *map page 227, C,D&E-4&5*

A great side trip from the North Shore to Ely, narrow, winding **MN 1** cuts through remote land, passing by deep forest and rocky lakes, the epitome of Minnesota's north woods. Watch for moose, because they can make a mess of an automobile if you hit one, and vice versa. Not far inland, you'll pass through **Finland**, which true to its name was settled by Finns, most of whom lived on small farmsteads in the surrounding countryside, growing vegetables and hay for livestock.

If at Finland you turn southeast on Lake County 6, you'll soon come to **Wolf Ridge Environmental Center**, one of several such centers in the state. Wolf Ridge puts on programs about nature and outdoor skills with a decided aversion to classroom time. Time is spent mostly outdoors. You may climb ropes, paddle a replica of a voyageur canoe, learn to fly-fish, study geology, or identify birds. School kids, adults, and families all participate. *6282 Cranberry Road; 218-353-7414.*

If at Finland you head northeast on Lake County 7, you soon arrive at **Crosby Manitou State Park**, with 5,300 acres flanking the lower reaches of the Manitou River and established on a unique premise: All travel is by foot. No cars are allowed beyond the parking lot. About two dozen campsites are scattered along tiny Bensen Lake and the rocky shore of the **Manitou River**. Manitou, by the way, is Ojibwa for "spirit." Indeed, the dark canyon and lively rapids are so enchanting as to seem supernatural. The Lake Superior Hiking Trail *(see page 237)* bisects the park. Trails are hilly. *Information from Tettegouche State Park; 218-226-6365.*

◆ **ALONG THE SHORE TO GRAND MARAIS** *map page 227, C,D&E-5,6&7*

If you stick to the shore rather than head inland, you soon come to the Caribou River, a nondescript stream where it passes beneath the highway bridge. But if you park the car and hike upstream about a half-mile, you will discover one of the most spectacular and (had you not read this) unexpected falls on the North Shore. Sorry to give away the secret.

Taconite Harbor is exactly what it says—a facility to load ore from LTV Mining's taconite operations in Hoyt Lakes on giant ore carriers, up to 1,000 feet long, which carry the ore to blast furnaces down the lakes. Despite the size of the boats,

each can be loaded in a mere four hours. An observation dock sits on the west side of the facility.

At **Cross River,** a stunning waterfall appears on your left as you drive up the shore. A small sign on the road directs you to Father Baraga's Cross—in its present incarnation, a concrete cross at the mouth of the river. The original, made of wood, was erected by Austrian priest Frederic Baraga out of gratitude after he survived a stormy crossing of Superior from the Apostle Islands (in Wisconsin) in 1843.

The **Temperance River** is so named because it doesn't have a bar at its mouth. Never mind that some other rivers, too, lack a gravel bar. Trails wind along the river, which runs through a narrow canyon in its final plunge to the lake. The Ojibwa name, *Kawimbash,* translates as deep, hollow river.

Three fairly easy hikes make it possible to view the shore and lake from the perspective of some of the highest peaks in the region. At Tofte, turn up the Sawbill Trail a couple of miles to the short hiking trail up **Carlton Peak.** Beyond Tofte, about halfway to Lutsen, is the turnoff for Forest Road 336, and the trailheads for

(Above) Schoolchildren help Cree (part wolf) howl at the Wolf Ridge Environmental Learning Center near Finland. Bill Cronberg (left), proprietor of the fish and sporting goods store The Beaver House in Grand Marais will tell you all you need to know about fishing the local waters.

hikes to the summits of **Oberg Mountain** and **Leveaux Mountain.** These are mountains only in a flatlander's vernacular. No oxygen is necessary—unless you try to run to the top. The Oberg hike is 2.2 miles one way; the Leveaux trail, 3.4 miles. Farther up the shore, at the junction of forest roads 153 and 158, is the trailhead for the 3.5-mile hike up **Eagle Mountain,** Minnesota's highest point at 2,301 feet.

At the mouth of the **Poplar River** is **Lutsen Resort,** *(see page 318),* perhaps the oldest resort on the shore, begun as C. A. Nelson's private "Lutzen House," a hunting retreat for Nelson's friends at the turn of the century. The present lodge was built in 1952. Up the hill is **Lutsen Mountains Ski Area.** The longest run stretches more than a mile and has a vertical drop of nearly 1,000 feet. In summer, an Alpine slide carries riders down the hillside. A gondola ride to the top of the run provides a stunning view of the countryside. Lutsen provides about 20 miles of mountain bike trails.

The **Cascade River** slips from its dark canyon of rock like a beam of light from darkness. The river is named for the series of thunderous waterfalls in its final descent to the lake. Many years ago, some friends and I tried to run the final three miles of whitewater in kayaks. After several excruciating portages along cliffs and steep bluffs, and several unscouted and frightening descents down tumultuous rapids, I simply carried my boat back to the car. I think the final tally was something like this: Of three miles of river, I had portaged two. As difficult as these falls are to paddle, they are extremely easy to look at. Park at the river's mouth and follow any of several trails up the river and into the rugged hills, which make up **Cascade River State Park.** The 2,800-acre park includes the Jonvik deer yard, largest in the state, where deer gather to take advantage of the south-facing slope of the shore in the winter, tilted to the sun as if it were a solar oven. Some oven—temperatures still plunge below zero, but this lake-influenced "microclimate" is far more temperate than the climate that prevails only a few miles inland, over the crest of the hills. In winter, in addition to deer, you're also likely to see coyotes and gray wolves looking to make a meal of a dead or vulnerable deer. One trail leads to Lookout Mountain, 600 feet above Lake Superior. The Superior Hiking Trail follows the river, cutting through the park. The park has five backpacking campsites and plenty of hiking and skiing trails. The trails are knit into the **North Shore Mountains Ski Trail System,** a network of about 120 miles of trails winding through the North Shore highlands between Schroeder and Cascade River. **Cascade Lodge,** *(see page 318)* nestled next to the park, caters to tourists year-round.

At the east end of the park is **Butterwort Cliffs Scientific and Natural Area.** You'll need a permit from the park office to enter. Here grows the butterwort, a delicate purple flower, holdover from the ice age. Several other tundra plants grow in tiny areas along the shore, remnants of larger populations that existed as the ice was retreating from the area thousands of years ago. *218-387-3053.*

Thomsonite Beach is a repository of its semiprecious namesake mineral, which formed in vesicles in molten lava 1.1 billion years ago, much as agates did. Embedded in dark basalt, thomsonite is banded green, white, and pink.

◆ GRAND MARAIS *map page 227, C-7*

Grand Marais started as trading post of fur magnate John Jacob Astor. White settlers arrived in the wake of treaties with the Ojibwa in 1854. Today, the gentle ambiance of a harbor-centered village struggles against the corrosive crush of growing tourism. As you'd expect in a picturesque tourist town, Grand Marais has good restaurants, stores, wilderness outfitters, craft shops, and galleries.

The **Cook County Museum** is located inside the 1896 lighthouse keeper's quarters, for exhibits about the commercial fishing and logging that were so important to the area early in the century. Take a walk down **Artist's Point,** a sheltering finger of land separating the harbor from East Bay.

Grand Marais is also the starting point of the **Gunflint Trail**, which runs 58 miles to Saganaga Lake on the Canadian border. The trail, now paved, traverses some of the prettiest country in northern Minnesota. Just a couple miles from Grand Marais, by way of Cook County 53, is the **Pincushion Trails System,** excellent for cross-country skiing. Several good resorts and restaurants lie along the trail. In winter, it's possible to set up lodge-to-lodge cross-country skiing trips; your luggage will be shuttled ahead to your next stopover. *Gunflint Trail Association; 800-338-6932; www.gunflint-trail.com.* In the summer, travel the trails by mountain bike. Many of the lakes provide excellent fishing, variously for northern pike, walleyes, smallmouth bass, and trout. There are plenty of camping sites in Superior National Forest. *218-626-4300.* The Gunflint Trail is a take-off point for the Boundary Waters Canoe Area Wilderness *(see page 255).*

◆ ON TO GRAND PORTAGE *map page 227, C-7&8*

A mile farther up the shore from the Gunflint Trail is **Chippewa City**, now abandoned. All that remains of this turn-of-the-century Ojibwa community is a small cemetery and St. Francis Xavier Church, built in 1895.

NORTH SHORE

If you're willing to hike through water and scramble over rocks, try walking the Kadunce and Devil Track river canyons to hidden waterfalls in the deep folds of the rocky cliffs. Don't try this if the water is high or conditions are wintery; it's a good way to drown, break bones, or die of hypothermia. But in the summer, if the water is low, the scenery in the secluded river gorges is stunning. The Devil Track provides an instructive example of how early settlers corrupted poetic and perfectly apt Indian place names, preferring instead, a kind of devil fetish. The Ojibwa name for this stream is *Manido Bimadagakowini Zibi,* translated as "Spirits' Walking Place on the Ice River."

Judge C. R. Magney State Park, with 4,500 acres, is a particularly dramatic North Shore park. It is named for the lawyer, Duluth mayor, and justice of the state Supreme Court who advocated the creation of a large system of just such parks along the North Shore. The spine of the park is the **Brule River,** sometimes called the Arrowhead. One of the largest rivers along the shore, it provides a thrilling and potentially hazardous route for whitewater paddlers, with several miles of class 3–5 rapids and several portages. About a mile upstream from the highway, the river tumbles over a spectacular and puzzling waterfall. The current

Dining room and lounge of Naniboujou Motor Lodge and Resort, a onetime hangout for sports stars and Hollywood types. (Minnesota Historical Society)

A reconstruction of the North West Company Fur Trade headquarters in Grand Portage.

splits around a boulder and half falls freely over a tall drop. The other half of the river's volume disappears into a huge hole. Efforts to find where this plume rejoins the river or Lake Superior have been unsuccessful. The falls is named, not surprisingly, Devil's Kettle.

Just east of the river's mouth sits the Jazz Era curiosity, **Naniboujou Lodge** *(see page 318)*. The resort opened in 1929 as a retreat for the wealthy. Jack Dempsey, Babe Ruth, and Ring Lardner were reported to be investors. The stock market crash put an end to the most ambitious of plans, including the riding stables, tennis courts and cottages, but the lodge had been built—and what a structure it is. Eastern Cree designs decorate the walls and ceiling. Two hundred tons of wave-rounded stone gathered from the beach form the fireplace in the main room. The rooms are small and it's a bit primitive by modern standards, but the Naniboujou is worth a visit for the architecture and location on the shore of the lake.

The hills inland from **Hovland,** along the **Arrowhead Trail,** are some of the most beautiful along the North Shore in autumn, when maples turn to red and birches to yellow amid still-green conifers. On crisp days in late September, the lake seems impossibly blue.

NORTH SHORE

VOYAGEURS COME TO TOWN, 1790S

*T*hese *voyageurs,* mostly French, were an extraordinary group of men; the majority came from Canada in the region of the St. Lawrence River. Short of stature, they were nevertheless exceedingly strong; unmoral and boastful, it was their faithfulness and loyalty to their contracts that made the vast fur trade possible; taking great pride in their manners, their dancing and singing, they were yet voluntary exiles, their ambition being to become "les gens libres" or free traders. . . .

Trading negotiations were usually completed in July, after which there always followed a celebration to which factors, *voyageurs,* and Indians—all who could possibly get there—came from miles around. The opening banquet was followed by a dance in the mess hall whose puncheon floor was 60 feet long. Gallons of rum were drunk, and to the music of bagpipe, violin, and flute, they danced the night through with their Indian girl partners. The fiesta over, the *voyageurs* set off once again in their canoes, loaded now with trade goods and camp supplies, and cheered by their own songs, paddled and portaged back through the wilderness to face long months of hardship and loneliness. In the shipping of furs on Lake Superior the average canoe carried more than 5 tons of furs and supplies, and was manned by 8 *voyageurs.*

—WPA Guide to Minnesota, 1938

◆ GRAND PORTAGE *map page 227, B-8*

The Ojibwa name for **Grand Portage** was *Gitche Onigaming*—Great Carrying Place. The portage was known to American Indians for centuries as the gateway to the waterways that lead west and north to the heart of the continent. The trail runs nine miles and rises 760 feet to bypass the most violent of the falls and rapids of the lower Pigeon in its descent to Lake Superior. The North West Company, a partnership of Scottish traders, established a post at Grand Portage in the 1770s to act as a depot and exchange for voyageurs traveling the Great Lakes and those headed inland to trade with remote Indian tribes. As furs, trade goods, and supplies flowed along this conduit, Grand Portage was one of the most important and busiest centers of commerce in the wilderness. Grand Portage's importance was short-lived, however; in 1803, the North West Company, fearful that the United States would tax its operations, moved those operations north to the present site of Thunder Bay, Ontario.

Pierre "Gray Fox" and his friend "White Fox" attend a rendezvous at the Grand Portage National Monument.

Today at **Grand Portage National Monument** you can tour the restored head-quarters of the North West Company, where voyageurs, Indians, and company partners and clerks rendezvoused each July during the heyday of the fur trade. As traders all trickled in from remote outposts, the fort's population swelled to more than 1,000.

The post stands much as it did two centuries ago, surrounded by a stockade of vertical pickets. Exhibits on the fur trade are found in the Great Hall, where business was conducted during the day and entertainment staged in the evenings. Outside the stockade is the canoe warehouse with replicas of the 36-foot canoes that carried goods from Montreal across the Great Lakes to Grand Portage, and the smaller 24-foot canoes that carried goods inland. Guides in period costumes answer questions. *218-387-2788.*

You can hike the historic Grand Portage, a round trip of 18 miles on a main-tained trail that isn't particularly rugged. To shorten the trip, drive in on the old highway (north from Mineral Center), which bisects the trail and reduces the round trip to about 10 miles. By the way, in these parts, "portage"—whether you refer to Grand Portage or the act of carrying a canoe—is pronounced with the ac-cent on the first syllable. I have never heard a native say *por-tazh'*. The French pro-nunciation apparently died with the *vwa-a-zher*.

The national monument is the departure point for the ferry that runs to **Isle Royale**, Lake Superior's largest island. Isle Royale, despite its proximity to the North Shore, is actually part of Michigan. The island was known by Indians for copper nuggets. Perhaps it was a source of nearly pure copper used by Archaic In-dians for tools and other goods. Today, the island is preserved as a national park and is a popular destination with backpackers. *906-482-0984, Isle Royale Trans-portation Line; 888-746-2305, 715-392-2100.*

Around Grand Portage lies the **Grand Portage Indian Reservation**. This Ojib-wa reservation comprises some of the least settled land along the Minnesota shore. It is also some of the most rugged, providing far vistas as the highway crosses the long ridges running down to the lake. The land is so rugged, the highway along the lake was not completed until the early 1960s. Hunters and anglers will need a permit (available in Grand Portage) to fish or hunt on the rez. It is no longer pos-sible to visit the **Spirit Little Cedar,** an ancient white cedar long known by whites as the Witch Tree for its gnarled appearance. Believed by some Ojibwa to harbor a spirit, it has grown from a rocky crevice next to Lake Superior for at least 400 years. The cedar was being destroyed so it has been made off limits to the public. It can be seen, however, from the ferry boats going to Isle Royale *(see above).* At the eastern end of the reservation are the **Susie Islands,** a picturesque archipelago, where several subarctic plants, refugees from the ice age, cling to the rock and life. **Pigeon Point** reaches out to within a mile of Michigan.

The **Pigeon River** forms the border between the United States and Canada. The long series of rapids and falls bypassed by the Grand Portage is now protected by, on the Minnesota side, **Grand Portage State Park,** and on the Ontario side, Middle Falls Provincial Park. Swing into the park entrance right before you reach the border, and hike about a half mile to **High Falls,** at nearly 120 feet, the highest waterfall in Minnesota. A log flume, still visible on the Canadian side of the falls, once carried logs around the falls. A three-and-one-half-mile trail leads to Middle Falls, another cascade to curse the voyageurs. Grand Portage is the only Minnesota state park managed in cooperation with an Indian tribe. State park naturalists are tribe members knowledgeable about Ojibwa history in the area. *218-475-2360.*

■ VOYAGEURS' HIGHWAY *map page 227*

From Grand Portage, the French Canadian voyageurs working for the North West Company carried their 25-foot birch-bark canoes up the Grand Portage nine miles to the Pigeon River. For the most part, the men were small—a six-footer simply took up too much room in a canoe—but they were strong. At a minimum, those who did not carry a canoe lugged two 90-pound bales across the portages. The strongest men carried extra bales for extra wages. The voyageurs, by all accounts, drank hard, swore hard, and played hard, while showing utmost loyalty to their contracts to haul trade goods to the interior of the continent and return to Lake Superior with furs.

After their long portage, the voyageurs followed the Pigeon River and then a chain of lakes to the "height of land," the major divide separating the Great Lakes drainage from the Hudson Bay drainage. From Grand Portage to Rainy Lake the voyageurs crossed 36 portages. From Rainy to Lake Winnipeg (now in Manitoba), they crossed 26 more. Not surprisingly, men occasionally died from strangulated hernias.

It's no coincidence that the first leg of the voyageurs' route followed the international border. A series of treaties following the Revolutionary War, well into the 1800s, would define the border as the "water communication" between Superior and Lake of the Woods—that is, the very water route followed by the voyageurs, and before them, many generations of Indians.

The land along the voyageurs' highway was spectacular for its rocky lakes and

cliffs, the result of volcanic activity 2.7 billion years ago. Underwater outflows of lava, intrusions of magma, and intense uplifting and folding created the mammoth sheets of greenstone, granite, gneiss, and other volcanic rocks that today characterize the topography from northern Minnesota to Hudson Bay. The landscape was scraped clean by the glaciers. With the retreat of the ice, clear lakes filled the basin and a somber forest of pine, spruce, fir, and birch crept across the hills to the water's edge. Yet, everywhere, cliffs and outcrops of rock jut out like the old bones of the continent.

■ BOUNDARY WATERS CANOE AREA WILDERNESS *map page 227*

While the outboard motor has replaced the paddle through most of Minnesota, much of the voyageurs' route remains the domain of canoes. The Boundary Waters Canoe Area Wilderness (part of Superior National Forest), stretches more than 100 miles along the Canadian border. Up here it's known simply as the Boundary Waters or Border Country or Canoe Country. In bygone days, according to one explorer's map, it was called only "region of rocks and water."

It is those things and more. It is a land of 1.1 million acres of unbroken forest and some 2,500 lakes. It is a place where loons call and wolves howl. With few exceptions, it is a land where motors are not allowed and progress is measured by the firm bite of a paddle in clear water and the weight of a canoe and pack on your shoulders.

◆ BOUNDARY WATERS BY CANOE OR BY FOOT

Canoe travel is possible over an infinite combination of water routes and portages that might require a part of a day to more than a week. The best time for a Boundary Waters canoe trip is late May to mid-September.

It's possible to hike through the Boundary Waters. Two trails are particularly noteworthy. The first is the Border Route Trail, a 38-mile wilderness route along the high cliffs of the Minnesota-Ontario border. It is a rugged trail for experienced hikers but does provide spectacular views. The second trail is the notoriously rugged 40-mile Kekekabic, which angles across the eastern half of the Boundary Waters, linking the Fernberg Road (out of Ely) with the Gunflint. The trail is maintained by volunteers. It crosses some hellish country, with wetlands and deep forest, so expect deadfalls and slow going. It lacks high ground and vistas, but has

(left) Canoeing near the scenic Boundary Waters Canoe Area Wilderness.

plenty of lowlands and mosquitoes (and moose, wolves, and bears). When you finish, you can say that you've done it.

Many campers enter the Boundary Waters from North Shore routes such as the Sawbill Trail (north from Tofte) or Gunflint Trail (northwest from Grand Marais). The most popular entry point is Ely, an old iron-mining town whose life blood these days, as much as some residents hate to admit the fact, are the tourists heading into the Boundary Waters.

If you're passing through Ely on your way to the woods, take time to check out the acclaimed Wolves and Humans exhibit at the **International Wolf Center,** dedicated to North America's largest and most demonized wild dog. Northern Minnesota long harbored the only significant population of gray wolves in the Lower 48. With protection under the federal Endangered Species Act, the state's population has grown to about 2,000 animals. Many of these wolves have migrated east, bolstering remnant populations in Wisconsin and Upper Peninsula of Michigan. Others have drifted west into North Dakota. Several captive wolves live at the center. Exhibits tell about the biology of the gray wolf, its pack structure and behavior, and its struggle to survive as more and more of its habitat has been logged or settled. The center provides various wolf activities. For example, you can ski, snowshoe, dogsled, or fly into wolf country to examine a kill site. During warmer weather, you can track radio-collared wolves. Who knows, you may see a wild wolf. *For information, call 800-ELY-WOLF, or look up www.wolf.org.*

The Echo Trail winds northwest from Ely through the wilds of Superior National Forest. Much of the land just outside the Boundary Waters is still heavily logged for pulpwood, primarily aspen. The Echo Trail, unpaved for much of its length, provides easy access to several lakes and streams in the Boundary Waters. One of the most interesting of these day trips is the half-day canoe trip to the **Hegman Lake pictographs.** Drive up the Echo Trail north of Ely to South Hegman Lake. There, launch a canoe, take the short portage into North Hegman Lake, and paddle into the narrows at the far north end. The pictographs will be on the left, several feet above the waterline, painted in red ochre on a cliff. The figure of a man stands as if in surprise, with arms outstretched and fingers spread apart. Standing with him are a moose and a dog (or wolf). Crescent-shaped canoes float on the rock face. This tightly composed picture is one of the clearest of the many Indian pictographs scattered throughout the Great Lakes region of United States and Canada. But while the images are clear, their meaning, origin, and purpose are

(left) Jeremy Canfield portages his canoe through the Boundary Waters Canoe Area Wilderness. (following pages) An aerial view of Voyageurs National Park, one of the most extensive wilderness areas in the United States.

not. They are probably Ojibwa, but even of that we are not sure. Their age is un-known. Some pictographs (not these) were described by early European explorers more than 250 years ago.

Boundary Waters travel requires some specialized camping equipment, includ-ing a fast, light canoe. If you don't have your own gear, work with an outfitter, who can help plan your trip and supply everything you'll need, including food. At the end of the Sawbill Trail, try Sawbill Outfitters. On the Gunflint Trail, call Tuscaro-ra Outfitters. In Ely, call Piragis Northwoods Co. In the Twin Cities, call Wilder-ness Inquiry. These outfitters also offer guided trips, for wilderness wanna-bes with no canoeing experience. *For general information and outfitters call Superior National Forest; 218-626-4300, www.fs.fed.us/r9/superior, www.bwca.org. For permits for overnight travel call 877-550-6777. Another excellent source of information is the Gunflint Trail Association; 800-338-6932; www.gunflint-trail.com.*

■ VOYAGEURS NATIONAL PARK *map page 227, A&B-1&2*

Farther west along the old voyageurs' highway of lakes and rivers is the aptly named **Voyageurs National Park,** a kaleidoscope of islands, lake, rock, and forest. Of its 218,000 acres, a third is water. The park comprises parts of several large

The first mining camp near Mountain Iron in 1893. (Minnesota Historical Society)

lakes: **Crane, Sand Point, Namakan, Kabetogama,** and the giant **Rainy.** In many ways, this area is like the Boundary Waters: Fishing is good for northern pike, smallmouth bass, and walleyes. Wolves, bears, moose, deer, and lynx are common in Voyageurs' forest, much of which is second-growth from turn-of-the-century logging. The two areas differ in this way: whereas the BWCA is wilderness, motorboats ply the big lakes of Voyageurs in summer. In winter, snowmobiles race around much of the park. *218-283-9821, www.nps.gov/voya.*

Prospectors flooded to the area during a short-lived gold rush in the 1890s. Loggers worked the woods in the early decades of this century. Still visible in Hoist Bay are log pilings that supported a railroad trestle over the water.

The **Kettle Falls Hotel** sprung up in 1913 to serve the lumberjacks and rising tide of bootleggers, prostitutes, prospectors, and sportsmen. Accessible only by boat or plane, the hotel still serves the public with rooms, a restaurant, and bar. *(See page 332.)* Hiking and backpacking are possible on the **Kabetogama Peninsula,** which is nearly surrounded by the large lakes of the national park. More than 20 small lakes dot the peninsula. For an unusual way to enjoy the park, rent a houseboat. Sleep aboard or at any of the island or shoreline campsites.

The gateway to Voyageurs is **International Falls,** long known as Icebox of the Nation. It is a paper-mill town, like Fort Frances, its twin across the international border. The **Koochiching County Historical Museum** provides exhibits of the local history. In the same building is the **Bronko Nagurski Museum,** which celebrates the achievements of this local hero and one-time National Football League player. *214 Sixth Avenue; 218-283-4316.*

◆ GRAND MOUND

On the south bank of the Rainy River, 17 miles west of International Falls on Minnesota 11, is stunning evidence of prehistoric people in northern Minnesota. There sits the prehistoric burial site known as Grand Mound. Measuring 25 feet high and 100 by 140 feet at the base, the hill is the largest prehistoric manmade structure in Minnesota. It contains almost 5,000 tons of earth and the remains of 2,000 to 5,500 people.

Grand Mound and several smaller burial mounds were constructed from 500 B.C. to A.D. 800, during what is loosely known as the Woodland Period, when Indians in this region made pottery and buried their dead in various kinds of mounds. In particular, the Indians who built huge burial hills such as Grand Mound were termed the Laurel Culture. They lived in small villages on the river banks and fished the Rainy and Big Fork rivers for lake sturgeon of up to 250 pounds with toggle-headed harpoons that resembled those of subarctic tribes. In fact, the very abundance of food supported a population large enough to require or construct the mounds. By appearances, corpses were set on platforms to decay or were buried and then unearthed. The large bones were bundled for burial in the Grand Mound and other large mounds. The mounds do not appear to contain all those who would have died during the roughly 1,300 years the Laurel used the mounds, yet the remains are of all ages, male and female.

After A.D. 800, the habits and artifacts of the inhabitants shifted. Pottery changed. The bow and arrow replaced the atlatl and spear. Wild rice assumed greater importance as food. This new culture, known as the Blackduck, interred their dead whole, soon after death, placing them in smaller mounds or simply adding to the Laurel mounds. They often placed pots, tools, copper jewelry, shell necklaces, and clay masks in the graves. What blood ties might have existed between the Laurel and Blackduck? Did the Laurel evolve to become the Blackduck? Or did the Blackduck drive the Laurel from the region? These questions still puzzle archeologists. What might have become of the Blackduck? When French explorers such as Jacques de Noyon passed through the area in the late 1600s, the

The red rock of iron ore deposits at Ironworld near Chisolm.

area was only sparsely settled by Dakota, Cree, and later, Ojibwa. The Blackduck might have become any of these tribes, or for that matter Assiniboin, Cheyenne, or Arapaho.

Since the late 1800s, Grand Mound has attracted archeologists and grave robbers. In 1933 Albert Jenks of the University of Minnesota completely excavated one of the smaller mounds. In 1991, as sensitivity over the sanctity of the graves superseded our curiosity about their contents, all human remains were reinterred, with a private ceremony by Ojibwa and Dakota. Exhibits at **Grand Mound Center,** managed by the Minnesota Historical Society, tell the story of the people who built these mounds. *6749 Highway 11 in International Falls; 218-285-3332.*

■ HOME ON THE IRON RANGE *map page 227, C-3*

When prospectors rushed to northern Minnesota in an abortive gold rush in 1865, most, like state geologist Henry H. Eames, were blind to the real treasure beneath their feet. Eames reportedly dismissed reports of iron ore with the retort, "To hell with iron. It's gold we're after."

U.S. Steel mining operations in Virginia, Minnesota. Here ore is scooped up into railroad cars.

George Stuntz, too, had traveled north in quest of gold. Yet when the rush was over, Stuntz was convinced that iron deposits would build northern Minnesota. With Duluth banker George Stone and Philadelphia investor Charlemagne Tower, Stuntz formed the Minnesota Iron Mining Company in 1882 at the site of Soudan Underground Mine State Park. The first train load of commercial-grade ore was shipped in 1884. Townspeople gathered by the tracks and tossed chunks of iron ore in the cars as the train pulled out for Two Harbors.

There are actually three iron "ranges" in Minnesota. All had their origin about 2 billion years ago, as marine organisms became abundant enough to create an atmosphere rich in oxygen, a by-product of photosynthesis. Iron dissolved in seawater combined with the oxygen and precipitated to the bed of prehistoric seas. These deposits were further concentrated by the flow of warm oxygen-rich water, which dissolved much of the silica, leaving oxidized iron minerals until the richest reached concentrations of about 66 percent iron.

Stuntz's Soudan was the first mine in the **Vermilion Range,** which lay between the present towns of Tower and Ely. The iron occurred as hard, nearly vertical layers of hematite. Mining began with open pits, but soon underground mining was necessary to reach ore. By the time the Vermilion mines closed in 1967, they had shipped 104 million tons of ore.

Farther to the south, according to Ojibwa legend, lived a red giant called *Mesabe* who slept in the earth. In 1890, J. A. Nichols, working for the legendary Merritt brothers, discovered ore that was 65 percent iron. The deposit was immediately called the name it still carries: Mountain Iron. Thus was born the **Mesabi Range.** Eventually, prospectors would uncover a body of ore lying in a rough zigzag, like a lightning bolt, 120 miles from Hoyt Lakes to Grand Rapids. Much of the ore was so rich, so concentrated, so soft, and so shallow and horizontal in its configuration, it could be dug from the earth in large open pits. The Mesabi has proved to be one of the biggest ore bodies in the world, yielding more than three billion tons of ore. During most of the 20th century, the Mesabi Range, the largest domestic iron range known, supplied most of the nation's iron ore, feeding the mills down lake at Chicago, Gary, and Cleveland. Mesabi iron built the guns, tanks, and armament that won World War II. For years, Minnesota produced 25 percent of the world's iron ore. When someone says he's from the Range, he means the Mesabi.

Farther south, near Crosby, lies the **Cuyuna Range** (*see* "GLACIAL LAKES" *pages 282–310*). Unlike the Vermilion and Mesabi, the Cuyuna provided no outcrops, ridges, or other telltale topographic clues to prospectors. Covered by glacial drift and topsoil, the ore body was discovered only by the puzzling deflection of compass needles. Prospectors drilled on these magnetic anomalies. In 1904 Cuyler Adams found ore. At his wife's suggestion, the range was named with a combination of Adams' name and that of his dog, Una. In 1909 the first Cuyuna ore was shipped to the port of Superior, Wisconsin. The Cuyuna, now largely exhausted, has given up about 100 million tons of ore.

Owners of Vermilion Range mines, in need of skilled labor, recruited Cornish miners, nicknamed Cousin Jacks, many from Michigan mines. Later, skilled Scandinavian miners took the place of the Cousin Jacks. At the turn of the century, underground miners worked 10- to 12-hour days, and six-day weeks. On a piecework contract system they could earn about $3 a day, but paid for their own tools and materials.

In the gaping open-pit mines of the Mesabi, skilled labor was not needed so much as human beasts of burden. The mines recruited unskilled labor anywhere they could find it. "Both Hibbing and Virginia were literally chopped out of the forest," reports *The WPA Guide to Minnesota,*

> *I*nto this rip-roaring melting pot, labor agencies dumped Slavs, Finns, Germans, Scandinavians, Greeks, English, and Celts. Praying, swearing, and love-making were carried on in 20 different languages and dialects. . . . The very multiplicity of languages, however, proved to be a flux in the melting pot. With so many mother tongues, English was agreed upon as a common medium of communication.

The mines drew workers from more than 40 countries. By far the largest number of foreign-born Range residents in 1910 were Finns, who fled to the United States to avoid conscription and escape the Russiafication policy of Czar Nicholas II. In descending order by population were Slovenes, Italians, Swedes, Croatians, Norwegians, English-speaking Canadians, British, Poles, Montenegrins, Germans, Serbs, French Canadians. On the Mesabi in 1910, just under 50 percent of the residents in towns were foreign born; in the unincorporated areas, about 60 percent were foreign born. Not surprisingly, perhaps, the vast majority of those who died in mining accidents were immigrants. The English language and optimistic drive to succeed united this polyglot. So too, did the polka, which takes distinctive forms among Slavs, Germans, Finns, Scandinavians, Mexicans, and the native-born to the present day. Polka masses have remained a fixture on the Range.

That the Mesabi and other Minnesota ranges would suffer the natural death of all mining districts was articulated as early as 1918 by Edward W. Davis, of the

University of Minnesota Mines Experiment Station. He compared the iron formation to raisin cake. In the near future, Davis warned, the raisins would be eaten, leaving only the low-grade cake. This low-grade ore is known as taconite. Davis and others studied methods to crush the nearly indestructible taconite and "concentrate" the low-grade ore to produce merchantable pellets to use in blast furnaces. An early experimental taconite plant opened near Babbitt in 1919. It couldn't compete with higher grade ores and closed in 1924.

What had taken a million years to form required only a century to mine. By mid-century, many mines closed as high-grade ores were depleted. In 1955 the state's first commercial taconite plant, at Silver Bay on the North Shore, began shipping pellets. The state's Taconite Amendment of 1964 encouraged investment in additional taconite plants by limiting state taxes on taconite for 25 years. During the next two decades, seven more mammoth taconite plants sprang up along the Range to prolong the economic life of the area. Despite recessions and repeated layoffs, iron mining remains the chief industry of the area, employing nearly 6,000. The Iron Range area provides good fishing, camping, hiking, and tours of mines and historic sites.

Iron ore is processed at this plant in Virginia, Minnesota.

NORTH SHORE

Franklin Mine, *1932, by Dewey Albinson.*

■ DRIVING TOUR *map page 227*

◆ TOWER *map page 227, C-3*

Perhaps the best way to see Minnesota's iron districts is to start where mining began, at **Soudan Underground Mine State Park** near the town of **Tower** (about 210 miles north of the Twin Cities and 85 miles north of Duluth on US 53 and MN 169). Step aboard the "cage," the loud (but perfectly safe), partly open elevator, a bit off vertical, that takes you almost a half mile below the surface. Once you are deep into the earth, ride the mining train three-quarters of a mile. A short walk brings you to the Montana stope, where iron ore was once mined. (Be sure to bring a sweater—the temperature is a constant 50 degrees.) The state park has preserved the mine much as it appeared in 1963, when the last load of ore was hoisted to the surface. Back on the surface, you can tour old mine buildings or follow

NORTH SHORE

hiking trails through natural areas. Nearby, the Tower-Soudan Historical Society has a **railroad coach museum**, open during summer, which portrays days of gold and iron mining in the area. *1379 Stuntz Bay Road; 218-753-2245.*

Next to town is **Vermilion Lake**, a large rock-bound basin studded with islands. The site of many resorts, it provides good fishing for northern pike, smallmouth bass, and walleyes.

◆ FINNISH FARMSTEADS *map page 227, D-3*

Though the name of the town of Embarrass is French (meaning obstruction, as on the Embarrass River), the heritage of the community and surrounding area is pure Finnish. Finns, more than any other ethnic group, were identified with leftist politics and were major organizers and participants in the Mesabi miners' strike of 1907. Many Finns were blacklisted for participation in the strike. Animosity with mining companies often drove the Finns to the countryside where, in imitation of their life in the Old Country, they carved small farms out of the woods, worked as loggers, and honed their skills as consummate woodsmen and craftsmen. Up here, Finnish homesteads are known especially for tightly built square-log cabins with complicated and exquisitely fitted corner joints. The organization Sisu Heritage has restored a number of Finnish settler buildings and hopes to preserve several more. (*Sisu* is Finnish for fortitude or determination.)

At the intersection of Minnesota 135 and St. Louis County 21 is the Embarrass Visitor Center. From here start the Sisu Heritage Homestead Tours. A guide will get into your vehicle and direct you to Finnish farmsteads through the area; *218-984-3672 or 2106.* Also visit the **Sisu Tori Craft Shop** for Finnish crafts. East on County 21 and south on County 362 is the **Finnish Heritage Homestead** *(see page 317),* a bed-and-breakfast on a Finnish homestead built by John Kangas in 1891. The Kangas home served as a boarding house for loggers and railroad workers. Lodging is in the old hand-hewn log farmhouse, with period furnishing and artifacts from the original homestead. Spend a few days in bucolic surroundings and take an authentic Finnish sauna.

◆ AURORA AREA *map page 227, D-3*

Drive south on Minnesota 135, a surprisingly hilly and winding road in such generally flat country. Near Aurora, view the active LTV Steel Mining Company **open pit taconite mine** and tour the plant that concentrates low-grade ore into pellets ready for the down-lake blast furnaces. *218-229-2614.*

Swing east for a slight detour. Three miles north of **Hoyt Lakes** on St. Louis County 110 you'll find the **Longyear Drill Site,** maintained by the Iron Range Historical Society in Gilbert; *218-749-3150.* In 1890, E. J. Longyear first used a diamond drill to take a core sample in an effort to find iron. Taking drill cores, rather than the slow and laborious digging of test pits, quickly became the usual method for locating deposits. The exhibit, located at the end of a pleasant quarter mile walking trail through the woods, includes period drill equipment set up at the site of the first test borings. Longyear eventually drilled more than 7,000 holes on Minnesota's iron ranges. The business he started became a worldwide mineral exploration and equipment corporation.

The **Eli Wirtanen Farm,** just to the south on St. Louis County 4 in Markham, provides an example of the Finnish homesteads that dotted these woodlands early in the twentieth century. This 40-acre homestead of a Finnish bachelor looks much as it did in 1904. Wirtanen, like many Finns, worked at several jobs, mostly logging, and farmed for subsistence. The farm comprises many small buildings, including a smoke sauna, with the traditional rock hearth. Prized for its dark sooty interior and the "softness" of its warmth, the smoke sauna filled with smoke as it heated up and was vented by way of a window and door before it was used. *For information, call the St. Louis County Historical Society; 218- 733-7580.*

◆ VIRGINIA AREA *map page 227, D-2*

In **Virginia** is another of the many open pit mine observation areas on the Range. The so-called Mine View of the Sky is located on the south edge of Virginia, on the lip of the gaping **Rouchleau Mine.** Keep an eye out for peregrine falcons, which nest on the cliffs. For opportunities to view bald eagles, ospreys, loons, and various waterfowl, visit Silver Lake in Virginia. In addition to being surrounded by iron mines, Virginia was home to the huge Virginia & Rainy Lake Company, where 1,200 men ran the world's largest white-pine sawmill. **Finntown- Kaleva Hall,** *Second Avenue and Third Street,* was a Finnish fraternal society. Today the building houses an interpretive museum. The **Virginia Heritage Museum** in a city-owned historic home in the Olcott Park neighborhood exhibits photos and artifacts from logging and mining days.

Rangers can be a tough bunch. Slapping a puck around the ice is their game. A friend of mine, who grew up and still lives on the Range, wears what is one of my favorite T-shirts. It says: "Give Blood. Play Hockey." And so it's natural that if there were such a thing as a **U.S. Hockey Hall of Fame**, it would be on the Range. In fact, it is in **Eveleth**, right next to US 53. The exhibits highlight the achievements of U.S. players in a game where Canadians have dominated. There's even a history of the ice-resurfacing machine known as a Zamboni. Only on the Range! *801 Hat Trick Avenue; 800-443-7825, 218-744-5167.* A mile west of Eveleth on County 101 is the **Leonidas Overlook,** where you see a panorama of Eveleth Taconite and Minntac operations.

Mountain Iron is where the Merritt Brothers would win and lose their fortune, and in the process, open up the Mesabi. After they discovered their mountain of ore in 1890, the family brought the first steam shovel to the Mesabi to strip overlying soil and sand and scoop ore. They built miles of railroad. By 1892 they were shipping ore over their own rails to docks in Superior, Wisconsin. Unfortunately, the panic of 1893 checked their expansion. Short of cash, in the midst of railroad and dock construction, the Merritts entered into lease and loan agreements with two groups: Oliver Iron Mining Company (with close ties to Carnegie Steel Corporation) and the American Steam-Barge Company, controlled by John D. Rockefeller. Merritts' money ran out in 1893. Laborers rioted. Rockefeller advanced

The sharp light of an autumn afternoon in northern Minnesota.

money, but by 1894, the Merritts were forced to sell their assets and lost control of their empire. They opened up the country and then got screwed—folks a miner can identify with. Mountain Iron is also the site of the largest taconite plant on the Range, **Minntac,** owned by U.S.X. (formerly U.S. Steel). *Scheduled tours run during the summer; 218-749-7588.*

Travel west on US 169, through a string of tiny Range towns, and soon you arrive in Chisholm, home of the **Minnesota Museum of Mining**. The exhibits recall the history of the Mesabi. They include locomotives, steam shovels, ore cars, and smaller mining equipment. The wheels of a 127-ton dump truck used in the mines today stand half again as tall as a person.

The best and most comprehensive exhibit to describe the history and people of northern Minnesota's mining districts lies just south of Chisholm on US 169, on the precipice of the old Glen Mine. It is **Ironworld USA**. The setting is impressive enough: the Glen, which gave up more than 13.5 million tons of ore before it closed in 1957, looks vaguely like a gaping natural canyon. Trains carry visitors through the area around the Glen Mine. Inside, exhibits describe the geology of the ore bodies in the Lake Superior region and the discovery of ore in Minnesota's three iron ranges. They tell the story of immigration, work, politics, labor strife,

A stand of pines choked by the encroaching waters of a swamp.

and everyday life in the mines and the communities that surrounded them. Iron-world hosts several festivals during the year. One of the best is Minnesota Ethnic Days in July, which celebrates the diverse roots of the Iron Range residents. Also on the grounds is an outdoor amphitheater, and library, archives, and research center with immigration and genealogical records, collections of personal papers, maps, and business records. *800-372-6437 or 218-254-0011.*

◆ HIBBING *map page 227, E-2*

In 1893 Frank Hibbing, a prospector working along the ridge that defines the Mesabi, poked his head out of his tent on a morning when the mercury read minus 40 degrees and proclaimed, "I believe there is iron under me. My bones feel rusty and chilly." At minus 40, most anyone's bones would feel chilly regardless, but the prospector's intuition served him well. He did find iron—the largest deposit of naturally enriched iron the world has ever known. A century later, huge so-called production trucks would still be hauling iron from the Hull-Rust-Mahoning, a combination of 50 mines that had merged to form a pit more than three miles long, two miles across, and 535 feet deep. Open-pit mining was first made possible by wood-burning steam shovels. By one account, "when one dug into a bank, the tail end reared, the stack shivered and belched forth fire, cinders, smoke and steam." Eventually, in the production of more than 800 million tons of ore, miners excavated more than twice the material moved in the building of the Panama Canal.

The town of **Hibbing** grew on the lip of the Hull-Rust. In a miscalculation, the town founders sited the community squarely on the ore body. In 1919, log haulers towed houses and commercial buildings two miles south to make way for the expansion of the mine. Christ Memorial Church was disassembled stone by stone, moved, and rebuilt by Cass Gilbert's original plan. Graves were simply scooped up with steam shovels. The remains of **North Hibbing,** as it is now called, perch precariously on the edge of the pit. Signs, street lights, and a few old foundations line a grid of old streets. Interpretive signs tell of the buildings that once stood here. At this old site, with its restrained restoration and interpretation, Range residents have preserved a place for their ghosts. To reach the pit, follow Third Avenue East north from downtown Hibbing about two miles. The **Hibbing Historical Society and Museum** in the Memorial Building portrays life in the early mining era. Models depict the relocation of the town.

As Hibbing was being moved, townsfolk needed to travel from the old town to the new. Andrew Anderson and Carl Wickman began shuttling passengers between the two sites in a Hupmobile for 15 cents a ride. Their company grew to become Greyhound Bus Lines. The story of the company is told at the Greyhound Bus Origin Center; *23rd Street and Fifth Avenue East.*

One of the first public buildings completed on the new site, and certainly the most impressive, was Hibbing High School, built in the early 1920s at a cost of $4 million, much of it paid for by taxes on mining companies. Even today it is a palatial example of public architecture. It stretches nearly the length of two football fields. Inside are two gyms and a running track. The auditorium, which seats 1,800, was modeled after New York's Capitol Theater and built with a rare Barton pipe organ. Cut-glass chandeliers hang from the ceilings. Murals of history and industry decorate the walls. Box seats overlook the stage.

The **Paulucci Space Theatre**, *US 169 and East 23rd Street in Hibbing,* with a wrap-around screen and planetarium, puts on multimedia presentations on natural history, from dinosaurs to astronomy. Call the Hibbing Chamber of Commerce for information about a bus tour of the area, including the Hull-Rust Mahoning Mine, the Paulucci Space Theatre, planetarium, and a nearby taconite plant; *218-262-3895.*

About 20 miles north of Hibbing on St. Louis County 5, **McCarthy Beach State Park** sits among a knot of lakes in a region of glacial hills. The park is known for its namesake beach on Sturgeon Lake. The park really shines in the winter; its cross-country ski trails are beautiful, winding among often pure stands of birch and red pine. *218-254-2411.*

If by now you can't imagine what a big hole in the ground must look like, stop in **Nashwauk** at the overlook to the **Hawkins Mine**, the first iron ore mine in Itasca County when it opened in 1902. Production ended in 1962 when the natural ore ran out.

Hill Annex Mine State Park near **Calumet** provides yet another tour of a big pit. This one lasts one and a half hours by bus along the roads trucks once traveled to haul ore from the mine. In the visitor center are early photos of the Hill Annex Mine and surrounding communities, as well as marine fossils, such as ammonites and sharks' teeth of 75 to 85 million years ago, when the bedrock of the mine site lay at the bottom of a shallow sea. *218-247-7215.*

NORTHERN REACHES

■ HIGHLIGHTS   *page*

Lake of the Woods   274
Zippel Bay State Park   278
Peatlands   278
Agassiz National Wildlife Refuge   281
Thief Lake State Wildlife Area   281

NORTHERN
REACHES
Map page 276

ALONG MINNESOTA'S LONG LONELY border with Canada lie vast stretches of peatland and low-lying spruce forests that, at first glance, look stupendous if only for their emptiness. At second and third glance, the view changes hardly at all. Nonetheless, this land, vacant though it may seem, offers up a few good stories.

■ HISTORY, TREATIES, AND ANGLES

TWO QUESTIONS, WITH THE SAME ANSWER:
• What is the northernmost point of the contiguous United States?
• What is the only part of the Lower 48 that you can drive to only by way of a foreign country?

The answer is the **Northwest Angle**, the odd appendage on Minnesota's northern border, created by the Treaty of Paris, which ended the Revolutionary War in 1783. The treaty set the border between the former colonies and British holdings to the north along the "water communication" between Superior and Lake of the Woods "thence through the said lake [Lake of the Woods] to the most northwestern point thereof, and from thence on a due west course to the river Mississippi."

Ooops. Therein lies the problem. Actually, three problems.

Problem one: establishing the "water communication." Before negotiators agreed on the route that follows the present border, they played these two gambits: The British proposed the St. Louis-Pike-Vermilion route, which would have claimed much of what is now northern Minnesota for Britain. Americans had countered with the Kaministikwia River, which would have appropriated part of southern Ontario. The particulars were not settled until the Webster-Ashburton Treaty of 1842. Even then, the final field work required to mark the border precisely was not completed until 1926.

Problem two was conceptually more intriguing: Where was the northwestern point of Lake of the Woods? Original treaty-makers had referred to a map that showed the huge lake as elliptical with a discernible northwestern point. But the real lake was nothing like that. Instead, its western and northern edges are made up of several large bays, any one of which might be the northwestern corner. Finally, astronomer and mathematician Johann Ludwig Tiarks proposed, in effect, that the point be established on a map by drawing a line angled 45 degrees to the northeast and then moving this line toward Lake of the Woods directly from the

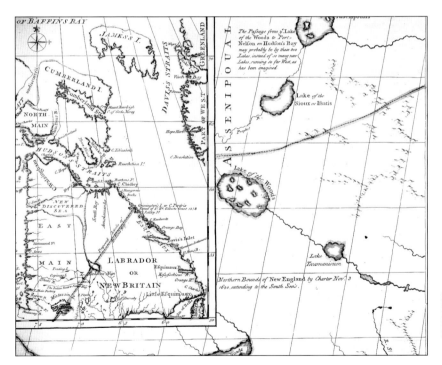

The Mitchell map of 1755 showing Lake of Woods as elliptical with a definite northwest corner, thus confounding border negotiations when it was discovered that Lake of Woods had no easily discerned "northwestern point." This confusion ultimately led to the oddity of the "Northwestern Angle," that little bit of the United States beached in Canada. (James Ford Bell Library, University of Minnesota)

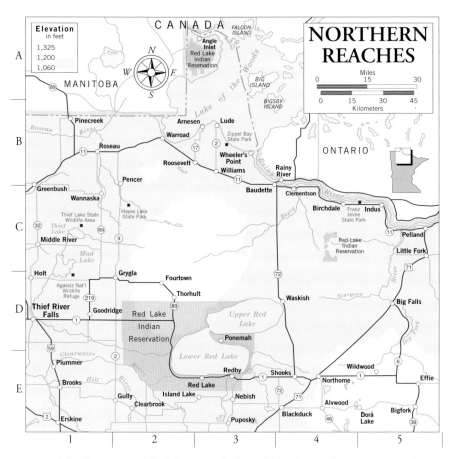

west. The first point of the lake it touched would be the northwest point. And so it was that Northwest Angle Inlet became the northern border of the United States.

Problem three was the location of the Mississippi. Contrary to the understanding of treaty negotiators, it lay far south of Lake of the Woods, rendering the "due west course to the river Mississippi" impossible. That conundrum was resolved in 1818, when negotiators determined that the border would drop due south to the 49th parallel from the northwest corner of Lake of the Woods.

Today, the Northwest Angle seems hardly to have been worth the trouble. (And of course, it wasn't. Everything else was worth the trouble.) Standing on the northernmost point of the contiguous United States, as one friend remarked, "is not exactly a magic moment." Well, no. Mainly I am surrounded by boggy country with a sweep of marsh and low islands in front of me. But it is worthwhile to mail a few postcards from the self-proclaimed "most northerly P.O. in contiguous U.S." I also make a few phone calls from the pay phone stuck in the dirt parking lot next to the boat landing at Young's Bay, undoubtedly the most northerly pay phone in the contiguous United States.

An all-weather road was built to the Angle in the 1960s. Electricity arrived a decade later. The state's only one-room schoolhouse, serving kindergarten through eighth grade, operates here. The boggy interior of the angle is owned by the Red Lake Indian Reservation. Whites own the many resorts along the scenic lakeshore and islands. "It's a typical white Anglo-Saxon screwing we gave them," acknowledged one resort owner. The biggest draw is for sportsmen. Lake of the Woods is an incredible expanse of water: 90 miles long, 55 miles wide, covering nearly 1 million acres. The lake, with 65,000 miles of shoreline, contains 14,000 islands. Fishing is excellent for walleyes, smallmouth bass, and northern pike. The lake offers perhaps the best muskie fishing in Minnesota. The ducks fly heavy in the fall. During the winter, snowmobiles and tracked vans carry ice fishermen to ice houses scattered over the lake.

On Magnusons Island is a replica of **Fort Saint Charles,** established there by La Vérendrye in 1732.

Ice fishing is a community activity in the towns of northern Minnesota.

A ferry service will carry you to the islands or resorts strung along the shore but not served by road. *Lake of the Woods Tourism Bureau: 800-382-3474, 218-634-1174.*

In **Baudette,** near the mouth of Rainy River, the **Lake of the Woods County Museum** provides exhibits on the area's Indians, logging, and commercial fishing on Lake of the Woods. *218 634-1200.*

I first went to **Zippel Bay State Park,** not because of its location on huge Lake of the Woods, or because of its reputation for possessing the best sand beach in Minnesota, but out of simple curiosity about its name. It turns out to have been named after one of the first white settler families of the area, who commercially fished the lake. The beach is lovely—lonely and windy, looking out toward Canada and the far tip of Lake of the Woods, 80 miles away. It is three miles long, with areas of black sand. The park, at 3,000 acres, provides breeding habitat for the rare piping plover. *3684 54th Avenue NW in Williams; 218-783-6252.*

■ PEATLANDS *map page 276*

When Glacial Lake Agassiz retreated from northwestern Minnesota at the close of the ice age, it left a landscape of utter flatness. In north-central Minnesota, from the Red Lakes north to Lake of the Woods, the combination of poor drainage and cool climate created ideal conditions for the formation and accumulation of vast, flat bogs. In the waterlogged soils—without oxygen and the usual mix of bacteria, worms and other agents of decay—mosses, sedges, trees, and other plants accumulated in a mucky and often spongy mass, called peat. As successive peat accumulated and further inhibited drainage, it created its own growing, organic topography.

From ground level, these bogs seem as flat as they can be. But from the air, the subtle vegetational features—water tracks, ovoid islands, and strange ridges and pools called strings and flarks—suggest a fleet of ships on a wavy sea or the ridges of oil in a painting.

Wet and jellylike, devoid of soil fertility, peatlands are inhospitable to most terrestrial plants and animals. The going is tough. Mosquitoes are atrocious. Even wolves, moose, and deer are likely to skirt the edges of the bogs. The exceptions, however, provide insights into adaptive evolution. Black spruce, cedar, and tamarack avoid drowning by sending out new roots from their trunks into the uppermost and best oxygenated layers of a bog. As a result, the base of a trunk may lie buried beneath many yards of peat. A number of colorful orchids flourish in peatlands, including the ram's-head lady's-slipper with its delicate pouch of white and blood-red veins. Several mosses and sedges grow nowhere else. Pitcher plants, bladderworts, and sundews, some of them rare, have adapted in unique ways to this water-rich, nutrient-poor environment. Unable to draw sustenance from the acidic soil, they instead devour insects.

In summer several species of frogs, turtles, and snakes are common. Some small mammals also live in peatlands. Two that are particularly well suited to this habitat are the southern bog lemming and its rare cousin, the northern bog lemming. These chubby, nearly indistinguishable voles dote on grasses and sedges and nest in clumps of sphagnum. Some threatened and rare birds, such as the sharp-tailed sparrow, sora rail, great gray owl, short-eared owl, and greater sandhill crane depend on peatlands to survive. Others, such as palm warblers and Connecticut warblers, are found in greatest numbers in bogs.

But some endangered species have not fared well. Woodland caribou once grazed on lichen and sedges, their large hooves carrying them over the boggy ground. They survive in Canada but disappeared from Minnesota peatlands a half-century ago as settlement in areas surrounding the vast peatlands fragmented herds and restricted their movements.

The state recently added 18 large peatlands, about 150,000 acres of the state's most pristine bogs, to the state's scientific and natural areas system. The peatlands, nearly all of which are state land, will be protected from logging, mining, ditching and road building. In a way, it was protection by default. Minnesota's bog country was really protected by its remoteness, inaccessibility, and simple lack of utility.

To see this country, drive north out of **Blackduck** on State Highway 72 and wander the back roads of Pine Island State Forest, Beltrami Island State Forest, or the Red Lake Wildlife Management Area. Try not to get turned around in a sea of stunted spruce with few outstanding landmarks to set you straight. And don't slip off some unmarked path and mire your car in peat moss up to the fenders.

If it's summer, slip on your hip boots, slap on some bug dope, and head into the forest to contemplate delicate orchids and feathery sphagnum beneath a cloud of hovering insects. Better yet, wait till winter, step into skis or snowshoes and cross the frozen bog along an old forestry trail flanked by gloomy spruce.

This bogtrotting won't catch on anytime soon. There is, after all, nothing to do in a bog—no mountains to climb, no rivers to cross, nothing to distract us from

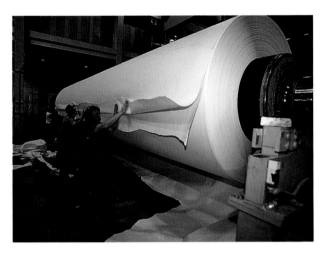

This Boise Cascade paper plant is on the U.S.-Canadian border in International Falls.

the numbing sameness of topography and vegetation. Yet in the reddening light of a winter afternoon, it is possible to appreciate the enveloping solitude and the resistance—the sheer pigheadedness—of a landscape that resists something so elemental and universal as decay.

In the midst of this region is **Red Lake Indian Reservation**, which, unlike other Ojibwa reservations (and most Indian reservations in the nation) refused to cede the land to the U.S. government, to allot tribal land to individual members, and to sell land and timber to non-Indians.

In a region with a paucity of state parks and open water, **Hayes Lake State Park** stands out. Its 2,950 acres lie along an impoundment on the North Fork Roseau River. Moose, black bears, wolves, and other large mammals roam this forested park. Camping, hiking, and swimming are available. *218-425-7504.*

On the western fringe of the peatlands, about 20 miles northeast of Thief River Falls, is **Agassiz National Wildlife Refuge**, a complex of wetlands and forest, a haven for mammals, waterfowl, shorebirds, and upland birds. Just north of Agassiz is **Thief Lake State Wildlife Management Area**, a premier wildlife watching area of 53,000 acres. Among the species you might see are elk (a small and struggling herd reintroduced to Minnesota decades ago), moose, deer, various ducks and geese, western and eared grebes, sandhill cranes, Forster's terns, and sharp-tailed grouse.

In **Roseau,** entrepreneurs Edgar and Allan Heteen and David Johnson started Polaris Industries in 1954 to make farm equipment. Johnson and Allan Heteen scrounged parts to build a snow machine to use in winter. Edgar, who thought the thing frivolous and was angry at the time the other two spent in building it, sold the machine to a local businessman to help pay the company's bills. Johnson and Allan built another "iron dog." Edgar sold that one too. Today, Polaris Industries, the largest manufacturer of snowmobiles, employs more than 1,000, 1995 sales exceeded $1 billion.

In all, Minnesotans are a bit snowmobile crazy. Every Labor Day weekend Eveleth puts on snowmobile drag races—on grass; *218-744-1940.* Minnesota has thousands of miles of snowmobile trails on public land as well as long "corridor trails," such as the Arrowhead, Taconite, and North Shore. *For information call the Minnesota Department of Natural Resources; 651-296-6157.*

The first successful snowmobile was invented by Carl Eliason of Wisconsin in 1932. (Underwood Photo Archives, San Francisco)

G L A C I A L L A K E S

■ HIGHLIGHTS   *page*

Paul Bunyan Territory   287, 295
Chippewa Trails   289
Forest History Center   292
Mille Lacs   297
Sinclair Lewis   302
Kensington Runestone   305

GLACIAL LAKES
Map page 285

A GLACIER IS AN AWESOME MACHINE for the rearranging of a landscape—part bull-dozer, part conveyor belt, part sluice, all on a continental scale. Glacial meltwater, subglacial streams, ice that simultaneously advanced as its margins retreated—during the last ice age all these forces combined to form hills and swales, ridges, cone-shaped kames, worm-shaped eskers, fields of parallel drumlins. The most obvious blessing of the glaciers are the thousands of lakes that formed in this irregular topography. The greatest concentration of these glacial lakes runs in an arc from the headwaters of the Mississippi (around Bemidji), southwestward through Detroit Lakes, and then south and east toward the Twin Cities. Another patch of hundreds of lakes occupies the region north of Mille Lacs Lake and Brainerd. As galaxies fill the sky, glacial lakes fill the firmament of central Minnesota.

Minnesotans are always headed "to the lake." We're headed—most of us, any-way—to Glacial Lakes country, to luxuriate in lake life: fishing, boating, swimming. (The basins may be glacial in origin, but the lakes have had plenty of time in the ensuing 10,000 years to warm up to pleasant swimming temperature.) Up here are resorts, golf courses, and tourist traps aplenty. Thousands of lakes provide good fishing for largemouth bass, northern pike, walleyes, sunfish, and some trout and muskies. Central Minnesota's glacial lake country may not have the gloomy solitude of the far north, the stunning drama of the North Shore, or the awesome space of the western prairies, but the rolling, wooded hills are undeniably pleasant. In many ways I find it the least interesting but most pleasant part of Minnesota.

■ DOWN THE MISSISSIPPI

Rising in the springs, bogs, and tiny creeks surrounding Lake Itasca in northern Minnesota, the nation's mightiest and most famous river glides northward before turning gradually east and finally south as it embraces central Minnesota in a curving arm of water leading to the Twin Cities. Its path might be said to describe a question mark or fish hook. Either symbol would be apt, for the uppermost reaches of the Mississippi long remained unknown and uncharted, and few tasks hooked the imagination of early white explorers like that of finding the headwaters of the Great River.

A steady parade of European explorers moved up the river, beginning in 1541, when Hernando De Soto battled Indians along its lower reaches. In 1673 Jacques Marquette and Louis Joliet, looking for a passage across North America, encountered the Mississippi at its junction with the Wisconsin River, just south of the Minnesota border. In 1680 Father Louis Hennepin was taken captive by Dakota Indians and hauled up the Mississippi through the region now occupied by the Twin Cities. Jonathan Carver explored the upper Mississippi in the late 1760s.

By the late 1700s, the search for the river's headwaters had reached northern Minnesota. In 1798 English surveyor David Thompson claimed Turtle Lake north of Bemidji as the source. Lt. Zebulon Pike led an expedition up the river in 1805, identifying two sources: Leech Lake and Cass Lake (then known as Red Cedar Lake).

Lewis Cass, governor of the Michigan Territory (which included Minnesota east of the Mississippi), ascended the Mississippi in 1820 and, like Pike, concluded that Upper Red Cedar Lake was its source.

Carrying his trademark red umbrella, Italian nobleman Giacomo Constantino Beltrami came to Fort Snelling in 1823 on the *Virginia,* the first steamboat on the Upper Mississippi. He accompanied Maj. Stephen H. Long, but after a quarrel with the commander, quit the expedition and canoed back to Fort Snelling, claiming, in the process, to have discovered not only the source of the Mississippi but also the headwaters of the Red River—all in the same body of water, which he named Lake Julia.

Of course, the various pretenders to the discovery of the Mississippi had no real right to the claim. Various Indian tribes have occupied the headwaters region of the river for millennia. For hundreds, possibly thousands, of years, Indians had traveled these waterways in birch-bark canoes. And many explorers' journals make it clear that the local Indians knew that the lake they called *Omushkos* (that is, Elk Lake) ultimately fed the Mississippi. At most, white explorers could claim to be documenting by written notes and reasonably accurate maps the location of the river's headwaters.

One of these explorers was Henry Rowe Schoolcraft, geologist for the Cass expedition. Schoolcraft, historian William E. Lass notes, "dutifully reported that Cass had found the Mississippi's 'true source'; but he obviously did not believe it, for later on in the same report he noted that two rivers entered the lake."

It would be 12 years before Schoolcraft would return to the headwaters country. In the intervening years, Schoolcraft landed at Sault Ste. Marie as Indian agent. From his British-Ojibwa wife and her relatives he learned Ojibwa. He recorded Indian legends. He served in the Michigan legislature and founded the Michigan Historical Society. In 1832 Schoolcraft was asked by the federal government to visit Indians along the Upper Mississippi.

Lured by the honor of finding the headwaters of America's great river, Schoolcraft mounted an expedition out of proportion to the rather simple task of tagging

HERE 1475 FT ABOVE THE OCEAN THE MIGHTY MISSISSIPPI BEGINS TO FLOW ON IT'S WINDING WAY 2552 MILES TO THE GULF OF MEXICO

GLACIAL LAKES

(above) The headwaters of the Mississippi River at Itasca State Park.

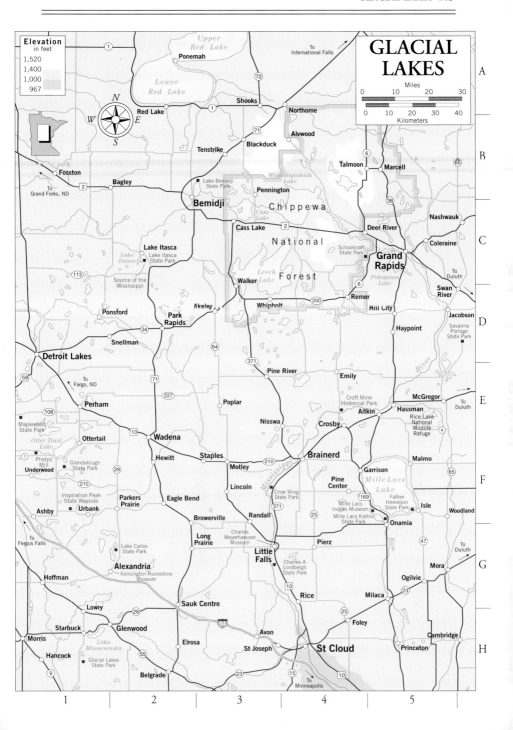

GLACIAL LAKES

Elevation
in feet
1,520
1,400
1,000
967

Miles
0   10   20   30
0   10   20   30   40
Kilometers

N W E S

Upper Red Lake
Ponemah
To International Falls
Lower Red Lake
Shooks
Red Lake
Northome
Alvwood
Tenstrike   Blackduck
Fosston
Bagley
Lake Bemidji State Park
Pennington
Bemidji
Winnibigoshish Lake
Talmoon   Marcell
Chippewa
Cass Lake
Cass Lake
Deer River
Nashwauk
Lake Itasca
Lake Itasca   Lake Itasca State Park
National
Schoolcraft State Park
Grand Rapids
Coleraine
Source of the Mississippi
Leech Lake
Walker
Forest
Pokegama Lake
To Duluth
Swan River
Ponsford
Park Rapids
Akeley
Whipholt
Remer
Hill City
Jacobson
Haypoint
Savanna Portage State Park
Snellman
Detroit Lakes
Pine River
Emily
McGregor
To Duluth
To Fargo, ND
Perham
Poplar
Croft Mine Historical Park
Aitkin
Hassman
Nisswa
Crosby
Rice Lake National Wildlife Refuge
Maplewood State Park
Ottertail
Wadena
Hewitt   Staples
Motley
Brainerd
Malmo
Otter Trail Lake
Phelps Mill
Underwood
Glendalough State Park
Lincoln
Crow Wing State Park
Pine Center
Garrison
Mille Lacs Lake
Inspiration Peak State Wayside
Parkers Prairie
Eagle Bend
Browerville
Randall
Mille Lacs Indian Museum
Father Hennepin State Park
Isle
Woodland
Ashby   Urbank
Mille Lacs Kathio State Park
Onamia
To Fergus Falls
Long Prairie
Charles Weyerhaeuser Museum
Pierz
To Duluth
Lake Carlos State Park
Little Falls
Charles A Lindbergh State Park
Mora
Alexandria
Kensington Runestone Museum
Ogilvie
Hoffman
Rice
Milaca
Lowry
Sauk Centre
Foley
Cambridge
Starbuck   Glenwood
Avon
Princeton
Morris
Lake Minnewaska
Elrosa
St Joseph
St Cloud
Hancock
Glacial Lakes State Park
Belgrade
To Minneapolis

along with local Indians on a long canoe trip. In the words of Mississippi River historian Timothy Severin, "It was a sledgehammer to crack a rather insignificant nut."

Though he knew the Indian name for the headwaters lake, Schoolcraft apparently thought *Elk Lake* too prosaic for the birthplace of the Mississippi. So he coined his own name, asking Rev. William Boutwell for Latin translation for "true source." Boutwell's facility with classic languages was apparently rusty, for he said *veritas caput,* "true head." By joining portions of the two words, Schoolcraft fabricated *Itasca.* As Lass wryly notes, "Once he had the name he had only to reach the lake."

Schoolcraft hired the Ojibwa Ozawindib as his guide. For the record, which had Ozawindib speaking a stilted Hollywood noble savage dialect, the Ojibwa told Schoolcraft: "My brother, the country you are going to see is my hunting ground. I will myself furnish the maps you have requested and will guide you onward. I shall consult my band about the canoes and see who will step forward to furnish them. My own canoe shall be one of the number."

Ozawindib, in fact, knew the country well enough to take a shortcut. From Lake Bemidji, he ascended the Schoolcraft River. Then, leading the way and carrying one of the canoes, Ozawindib portaged west to the fledgling Mississippi. In his diary, dated 13 July 1832, Schoolcraft wrote: "On turning out of a thicket, into the small weedy opening, the cheering sight of a transparent body of water burst upon our view. It was Itasca Lake—the source of the Mississippi."

Perhaps with our present ease of surveying topography—by airplane and even satellite—it is difficult to understand the allure of unmapped and unexplored land and the romance of finally pinning a source on the Mississippi River. Likely, the search for the river's headwaters seemed arbitrary and rather pointless to Ozawindib or the other Indians who led these explorers. After all, what is more arbitrary than naming a river's source? A river heads up in many places. Why not the Schoolcraft River, which is roughly as long as the upper stem of Mississippi. Or the Missouri River, which is longer than the upper Mississippi, or the Ohio, which has greater volume? Still, Schoolcraft's Itasca had the ring of truth to it, for the debate about the source of the river largely died.

The documentation and mapping of the river's headwaters did have the practical effect of resolving some longstanding border questions with the British colony of Canada. And, on a different level, the search affirmed our fascination with exactitude and comparatives—where things begin, where they end, and what is most, farthest, largest. The search for the source of the Great River was a quest in our many quests for superlatives.

■ IN THE BEGINNING

We expect a river as magnificent as the Mississippi to burst forth in immediate splendor. It is, after all, the mightiest river on the continent, and to see it glide gently from the sandy shore of Lake Itasca, trickle through a line of boulders, and set merrily on its way—all of 20 feet wide—is, well, confounding. Hard to imagine why just about every white explorer from the mid-1700s to the mid-1800s, from Jonathan Carver to Willard Glazier, would claim for himself the honor of discovering something so puny as the headwaters of the Mississippi, as if the Ojibwa hadn't known about it all along.

But after you stand at the headwaters, hands in pockets, and contemplate this paradox for five minutes, you can set about discovering the real treasures of **Itasca State Park**. At 32,000 acres, it is Minnesota's second-largest state park and one of its grandest. From the headwaters, continue on **Wilderness Drive**, the 11-mile-long one-way that loops west and swings around to Douglas Lodge. It's a great drive—even better by bicycle. On your way, you'll wind beneath a towering forest of old-growth red pine and white pine. Take a side trip on the Bohall Trail into the park's Wilderness Sanctuary. Loiter awhile at the Bison Kill Site, where spear-wielding Indians ambushed and butchered a herd of bison 8,000 years ago, when prairie still extended to the headwaters of the great river. Visit the state's largest red pine, whose trunk bends like the fledgling river. Climb the Aiton Heights Lookout Tower, an old fire tower a half-mile from the road, for a panoramic view of the forest and lakes. Then, be sure to visit Douglas Lodge. Built in 1905, this three-story pine-log building with its stone walkway and whole-log interior beams exudes stately charm. Visit the bookstore, take in dinner at the restaurant, or simply lounge in the armchairs before the massive fieldstone fireplace, where just a few minutes can be positively therapeutic. *The park lies about 20 miles north of Park Rapids on US 71, or 30 miles southwest of Bemidji on the same highway; 218-266-2100.*

◆ BEMIDJI

Bemidji's claim that it is the first city on the Mississippi suffers a bit from overstatement. Better, perhaps, to say first tourist and pulpwood town on the Mississippi. Bemidji is home to the original statue of the mythical logger **Paul Bunyan and Babe the Blue Ox.** *(See page 295 for more on Paul Bunyan.)* Built in 1937–38 for a celebration, the large road art (Paul is 18 feet tall) is angular and sort of, um, dorky in a campy sort of way. The logging hero also gives his name to Bemidji's Paul Bunyan Playhouse, Minnesota's oldest summer theater. Near town, on the

north shore of Lake Bemidji, is **Lake Bemidji State Park**. In the 1,700-acre park is a virgin pine forest. Bald eagles are a common sight. A 1,200-foot boardwalk winds over a bog. In summer, you're likely to see one of the seven orchid species, such as the stemless lady's-slipper, along the trail. *218-755-3843.*

■ CHIPPEWA NATIONAL FOREST *map page 285, B&C-3&4*

Chippewa National Forest comprises 1.6 million acres of what was some of Minnesota's most magnificent big pine country. Much of that timber was logged, but some of the magnificence remains, nonetheless. Within the borders of the forest are more than 700 lakes, including giants such as **Cass, Winnibigoshish,** and perhaps the state's best known musky lake, **Leech.** The musky, a large and often fickle relative of the northern pike, has the unnerving habit of following a lure to the boat only to sink into the green darkness at the last moment like treasure dropped overboard. For its reticence and scarcity it is often called the fish of 10,000 casts. During two days of muggy weather in 1955, Leech Lake gave lie to that sobriquet when unprecedented numbers of muskies up to 40 pounds decided spontaneously, simultaneously, and inexplicably to commit suicide on anglers' baits and lures. Nothing like it has happened since.

The forest harbors one of the country's greatest concentrations of **nesting bald eagles**—nearly 200 pairs. The eagle frequently builds one-ton nests of branches and limbs in the tops of giant white pines looking for all the world like boreal beaver lodges. Look for nests and nesting eagles in tall pines near water. The Leech Lake Reservation runs Che-Wa-Ka-E-Gon Gift Shop on US 2 in Cass Lake, with Ojibwa birch-bark crafts, maple syrup, and really wild wild rice, not the paddy rice common in stores. Near Cass Lake is the forest headquarters and Norway Beach Visitor Center. Both were built with local logs during the 1930s. Naturalist programs at the center during the summer teach visitors about natural features and native wildlife. **Camp Rabideau** is a Civilian Conservation Corps camp from the 1930s, one of only three still existing in the country (once there were 2,650). About half of its original 25 buildings still stand. Minnesota 46, a National Forest Scenic Byway, is called the **Avenue of the Pines** because it travels through old-growth red-pine forest. **Minnesota 38** north of Grand Rapids, also a National Forest Scenic Byway, winds through rolling, forest lake country. Campgrounds are scattered throughout the national forest. Many bike routes follow unpaved forest roads.

A rugged river in the Warroad area.

For hikers, the 22-mile **Cut Foot Sioux Trail** leads to the **Turtle Mound**, a well-known Indian "effigy mound," and to Farley Tower, an old fire lookout. The 13-mile **Simpson Creek Trail** offer opportunities to see eagles and osprey. The 21-mile **Suomi Hills Trail** near Marcell leads to trout, bass, and panfish lakes. A short trail winds through the **Lost Forty**, a stand of virgin pine left uncut because of a surveyor's error. A five-mile round-trip hike near Marcell leads to several log buildings on the shore of **Trout Lake**. The buildings, constructed in the 1920s, were once part of a private retreat. The **North Country Scenic Trail** runs 68 miles from just west of Walker on Leech Lake to just east of Remer.

The U.S. Forest Service offers naturalist programs in cooperation with more than a dozen resorts. For National Forest information, including the names of participating resorts, call or visit ranger stations in Blackduck, Cass Lake, Deer River, Marcell, or Walker. *218-335-8600.*

Lying mostly outside the national forest is the 28-mile **Heartland Trail,** which runs from Walker southwest to **Park Rapids.** Blacktopped for bicycles, the trail passes woods and farmland. An unpaved portion continues north to Cass Lake. A parallel mowed path is suitable for horseback riding, hiking, mountain biking and, in winter, snowmobiling. Three miles north of Park Rapids is the **Rapid River**

White Oak Rendezvous and Festival in Deer River.

Logging Camp, a re-created logging camp with a nature trail. Sit down to a lumberjack meal and watch the logging demonstrations. The Heartland Trail also passes through the tiny town of **Akeley,** which claims to have the largest Paul Bunyan statue in the world.

■ GRAND RAPIDS *map page 285, C-5*

Though Grand Rapids (pop. 7,980) lies at the western end of the Mesabi Range, it is in character a logging town, built in the heart of Minnesota's tall timber, on the Mississippi River, which carried logs to mill. The story of those days of lumberjacks is told expertly at the **Forest History Center,** operated by the Minnesota Historical Society. Walk through a logging camp, built to look as one of more than 300 logging camps might have appeared in Minnesota in 1900. Sit down at a table in the mess hall and talk to the cook over a cup of coffee. Visit the blacksmith, saw filer, or stable hand. In the history center itself are exhibits on the glory days of Minnesota logging, when lumberjacks sawed giant white pines by hand and moved the logs by sled or rail to river banks. Rare movie footage shows the last log drive in state history—down the north-flowing Littlefork River in 1937. "Whitewater men" walk logs and ride them on the river current. Wanigans—floating cook shacks and bunkhouses—slam down the rollicking rapids on the river. The drive, which began with spring melt, ended in midsummer on the Rainy River, where the logs were loaded on rail cars and hauled the rest of the way to the mill at International Falls. With the last log, a way of life in the woods passed forever from the scene. The center also tells the tale of Paul Bunyan, brainchild of William B. Laug-head, a copywriter for the Red River Lumber Company, which published the first Bunyan story as an advertising gimmick in 1914. There is information, too, on a real giant in the timber industry: Frederick Weyerhaeuser, once the most powerful figure in the U.S. lumber industry. *2609 County Road 76; 218-327-4482.*

The **Central School History Center,** a commanding Richardsonian Romanesque building (1895) in the town square, tells other stories of the town and region. The five period rooms of the **Itasca County Museum** depict Indian life, upper Mississippi exploration, pioneer days, and early commerce in town. The third floor of the former school is devoted to **Judy Garland,** born Frances Ethel Gumm in Grand Rapids June 10, 1922. The movie-star-to-be gave her first singing performance when she was two years old at her father's Grand Theater, a block from the Mississippi. Garland spent her childhood here before her family moved to California. The museum includes movie stills, movie posters, recordings, and taped interviews.

Blandin Paper Company, a major industry in town, provides tours of its paper mill. *Call 218-327-6226.* The **Mississippi Melodie Showboat,** moored on the big river, puts on summer shows of song, dance, and comedy. The **White Oak Society** has re-created a 1798 North West Company fur post just northwest of Deer River. The post is not regularly open to the public, but it is the site of an annual "rendezvous," a reenactment of the fur trade the first weekend in August. *218-246-9393, www.whiteoak.org.*

■ CUYUNA RANGE *map page 285, D&E-4&5*

Much of the iron of the Cuyuna Range lay deep below the surface, accessible only by underground mines. The soil covering the deposits was treacherous—swampy, sandy, laden with ground water. Shafts and drifts often collapsed, burying equipment and killing miners. In 1924, miners working the Milford Mine inadvertently tunneled into the bed of Foley Lake. The lake suddenly inundated the mine, entombing 41 in Minnesota's worst mining disaster. The handful of survivors told harrowing tales of escape. One of the most dramatic came from 14-year-old Frank Hrvatin, who was tramming ore when a terrific wind began to roar through the bowels of the mine. He realized immediately what had happened. Hrvatin and several other miners scrambled 40 feet up a ladder to a higher level of the mine and ran 200 yards down the dark passage toward the main shaft. The wind snuffed their carbide lamps. It blew so strongly it seemed to be trying to expel them from the earth. Running as hard as he could, Hrvatin kept clicking his flint to relight his head lamp. Suddenly, something as solid as a post struck his head, and his lamp flew off. It was still burning. He grabbed it and kept running.

Far down the tunnel Hrvatin saw a frail light. As he got closer, he saw it was Emil Kaino, standing at the main shaft. "Hey, what's the matter?" Kaino said. "Something's wrong. Something's wrong!"

"Save your breath and start climbing," Hrvatin yelled. "We know what's wrong."

Still, they had to climb 135 feet to the surface—seven men on the ladder. As they climbed they felt the water and mud rushing behind them.

"Can't climb any longer," said the old man right above Hrvatin.

"If you can't climb, get the hell out of the way," shouted the last man on the ladder.

ladder. Below, in the dark shaft, the mud caught up to the last man, burying him to the waist. Hrvatin could hear him shout and struggle. He pushed the old man farther up the ladder to make room for the men below.

They finally burst to the surface, exhausted and terror-stricken, and they sprawled on the surface. Everyone came running to see what the hell was the matter. Within 15 minutes the whole thing was over. Hrvatin walked to the mine entrance and peered into the shaft. There was the mud only 15 feet from the top. Bubbling, bubbling, bubbling, bouncing, bouncing. He knew then they were all gone. All dead. He'd never see any of them again.

He didn't want to go home. He stayed at the mine three hours. It seemed like only minutes. Finally he changed from his diggers into his street clothes. A friend met Hrvatin at the mine in his Model T and drove him home to Crosby four miles away. People in town were crazy for the news.

"Where's Pop?" his mom asked.

"In the mine, underwater," Hrvatin said. "He's drowned."

The Cuyuna mines are quiet now. The natural ore has played out. But you can imagine the ore cars rumbling deep underground and shadows dancing in the ghostly light of carbide lamps at the Croft Mine Historical Park, an underground museum just north of Crosby. Dioramas, machinery, artifacts, and historic buildings tell of past mining on the Cuyuna Range. *218-546-5466.*

The mining area makes up much of the 5,000-acre **Cuyuna Country Recreation Area**. With six natural lakes and 25 water-filled pits, the area is popular for canoeing and fishing for largemouth bass, sunfish, northern pike, and some trout. Some of the old mine pits are exceptionally deep. The old Portsmouth open-pit mine, nearly 400 feet deep, is ringed by clifflike shores. The clear water draws *218-546-5926.*

East of the Cuyuna Range, just south of **McGregor** on Minnesota 65, is **Rice Lake National Wildlife Refuge**. A haven for birdwatchers, the 18,000-acre refuge attracts flights of migrating waterfowl. Each spring in grassy openings, sharp-tailed grouse engage in dramatic courtship dances, similar to those of the prairie chicken. Other species spotted here but uncommon in most of Minnesota are great gray owls, nesting magpies, and tundra swans.

■ BRAINERD LAKES *map page 285, F-3/4*

A friend and I were enjoying a relaxing weekend at the lake cabin—fishing, taking walks in the woods, some canoeing on a nearby stream—when she asked if we could go into **Brainerd** (pop. 12,350) for the afternoon.

She had her reasons, I figured, so we drove the 30 miles into town. I never saw anyone so disappointed. "I never realized it was so ugly," she said. Only then did I realize that she expected that this 19th-century railroad and lumber town should somehow have survived transmogrification by 20th-century tourism with a shred of interest or charm intact. Little did she expect a withered downtown surrounded by acre upon acre of highway sprawl, strip malls, fast-food joints, amusement parks, and sunburned crowds.

Embedded in this sprawl is the **Paul Bunyan Amusement Center**, with yet another Paul statue. This one towers 26 feet—sitting yet!—and talks. His blue buddy is here too, along with kids' rides, lumbering exhibits, tame animals, and mini golf. (One Paul we've missed so far is Paul Bunyan's "grave" in Kelliher in northern Minnesota's peatlands, where a monument reads: "Paul Bunyan, Born 1794, Died 1899; Here Lies Paul, And That's All.") *218-829-6342.*

Paul Bunyan statues seem to stand everywhere in northern Minnesota. This one is in Bemidji.

THAT FAMOUS TOWN

*T*he town of Lake Wobegon, Minnesota, lies on the shore against Adams Hill, looking east across the blue-green water to the dark woods.

It is a quiet town, where much of the day you could stand in the middle of Main Street and not be in anyone's way—not forever, but for as long as a person would want to stand in the middle of a street. It's a wide street; the early Yankee promoters thought they would need it wide to handle the crush of traffic. The double white stripe is for show, as are the two parking meters. Two was all they could afford. They meant to buy more meters with the revenue, but nobody puts nickels in them because parking nearby is free. Parking is diagonal.

Merchants call it "downtown"; other people say "up town," two words, as in "I'm going up town to get me some socks."

Most men wear their belts low here, there being so many outstanding bellies, some big enough to have names of their own and be formally introduced. Those men don't suck them in or hide them in loose shirts; they let them hang free, they pat them, they stroke them as they stand around and talk. How could a man be so vain as to ignore this old friend who's been with him at the great moments of his life?

—Garrison Keillor, *Lake Wobegon Days,* 1985

Nearby is the **Northland Arboretum**, with flower and plant displays in summer and several miles of cross-country ski trails in winter. *Highway 210 North; 218-829-8770.* Also in Brainerd is the **Crow Wing Country Historical Society Museum,** a restored sheriff's house and remodeled jail house with exhibits on settlers, logging, mining, and railroads. *320 Laurel Street; 218-829-3268.* **The Colonel's Brainerd International Raceway,** seven miles north of Brainerd on Minnesota 371, offers top-caliber road and drag racing. *218-824-7220.*

The charm of the Brainerd area, however, is found in the surrounding countryside. Within 25 miles of town are nearly 500 lakes. Many are secluded potholes, reachable only by a dirt road and offering good fishing for bass and bluegills. Some are large and popular, ringed with resorts and cabins, such as the group of lakes near Cross Lake referred to simply as the **Whitefish Chain.** There on a bay of

Upper Whitefish Lake, about four miles northeast of Jenkins, is the **Driftwood Resort** *(see page 316)*, with the **Minnesota Resort Museum.** The museum tells the story of Minnesota's resort industry, with exhibits that include boats, furniture, tackle, and a model of a small cabin typical of early resorts, when anglers wanted simply a place to eat and sleep. Ironically, resorts flourished in the early 1900s, after loggers had cleared the most beautiful of the state's forests. The railroads left in the wake of one industry provided access for another. Indeed, the railroads solicited tourists as passengers for their trains. *800-950-3540.*

Ride a bike on the **Paul Bunyan Trail,** which follows the old Burlington Northern right-of-way from Brainerd to Bemidji, linking the resort communities of **Nisswa, Pequot Lakes,** and **Pine River.** For now, the trail is tarred between Baxter and Hackensack. Shop for Indian moccasins, souvenir T-shirts, and other knickknacks you'd never dream of buying at home.

Minnesota is laced with tens of thousands of miles of streams. Many, including the Mississippi, are excellent for canoeing. But two in the Brainerd area bear special mention for their gentle current, wooded shores, and sandy bottoms: the **Pine** and **Crow Wing.** The Pine River heads up in the lakes and marshes north and west of its namesake town, flows east through the Whitefish Chain, and then runs about 20 miles to the Mississippi. (These final miles are best for paddling.) The Crow Wing begins near Park Rapids and loops south and east to join the Mississippi at **Crow Wing State Park.** It is canoeable throughout its length. Canoes are available to rent from outfitters in **Menahga** and **Sebeka.** Staff at the state park can provide canoing information and will also tell you about the historic abandoned village at the park. *218-829-8022.*

■ MILLE LACS *map page 285, F-4*

If Minnesota had a state religion it would be worship of the walleye. Its sacred icon would be the giant walleye road art in **Garrison,** and its cathedral would be **Mille Lacs Lake,** the 132,000-acre lake suited like few others to the natural production and sustenance of the state fish.

The big lake developed with the mentality of a fishing camp. Small cabins and fishing resorts ring the lake. They buzz with activity during the spring, summer, and fall as thousands of anglers motor off toward the lake's watery horizon, trolling spinners and worms, and jigging minnows in pursuit of the walleye. Adoration of the walleye has always puzzled me a bit. They strike at a lure with the ferocity of a bird pecking at seed and put up the fight of an old log. But their meat is firm, flaky, and tasty, and in a lake such as Mille Lacs they commonly grow to 10 pounds.

Walleyes are not the only game fish that swim these waters. Mille Lacs offers up big northern pike and, since the state started a stocking program several years ago, some trophy-sized muskies. Large smallmouth bass also live here.

The good fishing hasn't exactly been a secret. When French explorer Daniel Greysolon, Sieur Duluth, reached Mille Lacs in 1679, he found the shore ringed with Dakota encampments. The Dakota, and later the Ojibwa, built their lives on the harvest of the lake's fish and abundant wild rice, and the maple syrup from the surrounding forest. When the Ojibwa signed treaties turning the area over to the federal government, they apparently retained rights to hunt, fish, and gather in the ceded area. In recent years, controversy has erupted among Indians, state government, and white sportsmen as tribes have elected to reassert these rights and govern their own hunting and fishing.

The new **Mille Lacs Indian Museum** tells the long history of Woodland Indians on the shore of Mille Lacs. Located on the Mille Lacs Ojibwa reservation 10 miles north of Onamia on US 169, the museum, with a copper roof and curving

(above) A mighty muskie of Baudette. (right) Darrien and Dorothy Stevens of Bagley hand-harvest wild rice in the same manner their Native American ancestors did.

bank of windows, is a stunning collaboration between the Minnesota Historical Society and the Mille Lacs Ojibwa. Tribal elder and bead work expert Batiste Sam designed the band of blue tile oak leaves that runs along the outside of the building. The centerpiece is the Four Seasons Room, a life-sized diorama depicting seasonal activities 200 years ago: collecting maple syrup in spring, fishing and gathering berries in summer, ricing in autumn, hunting and trapping in winter. Other exhibits show how Ojibwa have maintained their culture and traditions, even as their land base has shrunk and political autonomy has been threatened. Our Living Culture shows an array of modern powwow outfits made especially for the exhibit. A computer display demonstrates the Ojibwa language. *320-532-3632.*

Nestled in the hardwood-covered hills along the southwest shore of the lake is **Mille Lacs Kathio State Park.** Its sprawling 10,000 acres take in several shallow wild-rice lakes. Bald eagles, ospreys, and various hawks and owls are common in the mix of lake, marsh, and woodland. The park has a large trail system: 35 miles for hiking, 27 miles for horseback riding, 18 miles for skiing, and 19 miles for snowmobiling. Camping is also available. Humans have occupied this area for at least 4,000 years. In the park is an important prehistoric site where archeologists have recovered copper tools and weapons from Minnesota's Old Copper Indians and pottery from later Woodland groups. Burial mounds were common throughout the area. *320-532-3523.*

The park embraces the upper reaches of the **Rum River.** The Dakota named the river *Mde Wakan* (Spirit Lake) for its source at Mille Lacs Lake. Later residents, in a rather dismissive play on words, transmogrified "spirit" into "rum." Nonetheless, the Rum is a beautiful stream, unrelentingly riffly in its middle reaches—superb water for both canoes and smallmouth bass.

■ LITTLE FALLS AND ST. CLOUD *map page 285, F, G&H-3&4*

World famous aviator **Charles A. Lindbergh,** first to fly solo across the Atlantic in 1927, spent his childhood summers on the banks of the Mississippi, in a modest family retreat just south of Little Falls. Today the house, built in 1906, is preserved with original furnishings and family possessions. The house lies within the 600 wooded and grassy acres of **Charles A. Lindbergh State Park.** *320-632-3154.* The park is named not for the pilot, but for his father, a progressive Republican congressman. Just southeast of the park on Morrison County 52, the **Charles A. Weyerhaeuser Museum**, depicts early life in the area.

Downstream is "busy, gritty, Granite City." **St. Cloud** (pop. 48,810) was built, literally, from the granite in the many quarries that have operated in the area since shortly after the Civil War. The first quarry operated on the present site of the **Minnesota State Reformatory**, whose perimeter is secured by a wall of massive dark granite. A replica of a working granite quarry is on display in the **Stearns County History Museum**, which describes the river town's Germanic roots. *235 33rd Avenue South; 320-253-8424.* **St. Cloud State University** overlooks the west bank of the Mississippi River. You can visit the planetarium in the Math and Science building. On the east bank, in Riverside Park, are the **Munsinger Botanical Gardens**, with more than 50,000 types of flowers and bushes. It includes the **Virginia Clemens Rose Garden**, with more than 1,000 rose bushes of 200 varieties. *320-255-7238.* In the St. Cloud Civic Center is the **Minnesota Baseball Hall of Fame Museum.**

With more than 1,500 acres of wooded, rolling hills, **Lake Maria State Park** just off I-94 west of Monticello gives you room to stretch your legs. In fact, it provides space and solitude enough for backpacking. Seventeen remote campsites dot the area around Slough, Bjorkland, and Putnam lakes. Fourteen miles of hiking trails wind through the park. *612-878-2325.*

From St. Cloud to the Twin Cities the **Mississippi** runs broad, swift, and riffly. Flanked by wooded bluffs, it is a component of the state Wild and Scenic Rivers system, and provides excellent fishing for smallmouth bass, walleyes, northern pike, and even muskies.

■ WESTERN LAKES *map page 285*

Like a great curved galaxy of water, lake country sweeps from the Twin Cities westward, out toward the border with North Dakota, and finally northward, curving back toward the headwaters of the Mississippi. Figuratively and literally, the lakes are a bulwark against the prairie to the west: the lakes and hills and humid forest shielded the belly of the state from prairie wildfires. As a result, the demarcation between forest and prairie is surprisingly sharp. Driving west on US 10, you pass from the wide-open horizons near Hawley to the closed-in woodlands of Detroit Lakes in a mere 20 miles.

■ GOPHER PRAIRIE *map page 285, G-2*

Interstate 94 runs along this thin edge between prairie and woodland on its way west. One of the towns it passes, about two hours west of the Twin Cities, is **Sauk Centre** (pop. 3,580), boyhood home of Sinclair Lewis, first U.S. novelist to win the Nobel Prize. Lewis was of two minds about his home. On the one hand, he would write that his home was "the newest empire of the world . . . a land of dairy herds and exquisite lakes, of new automobiles and tarpaper shanties and silos like red towers, of clumsy speech and a hope that is boundless." On the other hand, he would savage his hometown as the thinly disguised Gopher Prairie in his most famous novel, *Main Street,* published in 1920. Novelist Pearl S. Buck, after a visit to Lewis's boyhood home, wondered, "I could only see him bursting out of those walls, and out of the town it stood for, loving it so much that he hated it for not being all he wanted it to be and knew it could be." Confided one Sauk Centre resident who knew Lewis: "I think his *Main Street* gave him the chance he always wanted, i.e. to make Sauk Centre suffer for the lonely, intolerable boyhood he had spent here."

Wheat harvesting in the Detroit Lakes area.

GLACIAL LAKES

Mile-long freight trains cross the plains throughout Minnesota.

Indeed, it was a lonely, intolerable life. His doctor father was cold and authoritarian. His mother died when he was six. Lewis was an awkward, small child, the constant butt of jokes and pranks. Despite a love of reading and talent for writing, he did poorly in school. His later success could only have astounded those who knew him as a child. In Buck's words, "What accidental combination of elements produced him?"

Those elements are the subject of the **Sinclair Lewis Interpretive Center**, next to I-94 in town. Exhibits include Lewis's manuscripts, photos, and letters. Nearby, on what is now designated 812 Sinclair Lewis Avenue, is the author's **boyhood home,** a modest, gray-clapboard affair with muted green shutters and a bit of gingerbread. The house contains original furnishings and family memorabilia. About three blocks away, on the original Main Street, is the **Palmer House**, where Lewis worked as a night clerk. It appears in *Main Street* as the Minniemashie House. Built in 1901, the Palmer House forms the cornerstone of downtown. The hotel, with 22 guest rooms, was recently refurbished with turn-of-the-century decor, including stained glass windows and vaulted ceilings. Despite townsfolks' outrage over the satire and perceived personal attacks in *Main Street,* they knew a good

IS THIS MY LIFE?

Minnesota's famed writer, Sinclair Lewis, wrote these lines describing Sauk Centre, here called Gopher Prairie.

*H*ad she really bound herself to live, inescapably, in this town called Gopher Prairie? And this thick man beside her, who dared to define her future, he was a stranger! She turned in her seat, stared at him. Who was he? Why was he sitting with her? He wasn't of her kind! His neck was heavy; his speech was heavy; he was twelve or thirteen years older than she; and about him was none of the magic of shared adventures and eagerness. . . .

She told herself how good he was, how dependable and understanding. She touched his ear, smoothed the plane of his solid jaw, and turning away again, concentrated upon liking his town. It wouldn't be like these barren settlements.

A mile from Gopher Prairie the track mounts a curving low ridge, and she could see the town as a whole. With a passionate jerk she pushed up the window, looked out, the arched fingers of her left hand trembling on the sill, her right hand at her breast.

And she saw that Gopher Prairie was merely an enlargement of all the hamlets which they had been passing. Only to the eyes of a Kennicott was it exceptional. The huddled low wooden houses broke the plains scarcely more than would a hazel thicket. The fields swept up to it, past it. It was unprotected and unprotecting; there was no dignity in it nor any hope of greatness. Only the tall red grain-elevator and a few tinny church-steeples rose from the mass. It was a frontier camp. It was not a place to live in, not possibly, not conceivably.

The people—they'd be as drab as their houses, as flat as their fields. She couldn't stay here. She would have to wrench loose from this man, and flee.

Something large arose in her soul and commanded, "Stop it! Stop being a whining baby!" She stood up quickly; she said, "Isn't it wonderful to be here at last!"

—Sinclair Lewis, *Main Street,* 1920

thing when they saw it: each summer the town celebrates Sinclair Lewis Days. *320-352-5201.*

Lewis's best known novels—*Main Street, Babbitt, Arrowsmith, Elmer Gantry,* and *Dodsworth*—were published during the 1920s. His later books never achieved the same success. Lewis died a lonely alcoholic in Rome in 1951. His ashes were flown back to Sauk Centre and buried alongside the remains of his relatives in the Greenwood Cemetery, a mile east of town.

■ MINNESOTA VIKINGS *map page 285, G-1*

By one account, 18th-century Scandinavians who settled western Minnesota were simply coming to the land their ancestors discovered 500 years earlier.

In 1898 Kensington farmer Olaf Ohman reported that as he pulled a stump on his property he came upon a 200-pound slab of rock 30 inches long, 15 inches wide, and about six inches thick. It was covered with mysterious carvings that appeared to be "runes," ancient Scandinavian writing.

Thus began the legend of the **Kensington Runestone,** now on display in its namesake museum in **Alexandria,** *206 Broadway; 320-763-3160.* The stone was soon translated: "8 Goths and 22 Norwegians on exploration journey from Vinland over the west. We had camp by 2 skerries one day's journey north from this stone. We were and fished one day. After we came home [found] 10 red with blood and dead. AVE [Ave Maria] save from evil. Have 10 of our party by the sea to look after ships 14 days' journey from this island. Year 1362."

Scandinavian scholars dismissed the find. They said characters on the stone were too modern to be authentic. But the stone captured the imagination of Hjalmar Holand of Wisconsin, who spent the rest of his life trying to demonstrate the authenticity of the stone. Among the evidence he cited was the existence of Viking "mooring stones" in the area, especially on the shore of Big Cormorant Lake west of Detroit Lakes. Holes bored in these large boulders supposedly held rings to moor Viking ships.

Despite Holand's enthusiastic promulgation of the theory of early Viking exploration of America, it's been a difficult notion to swallow that Norsemen could sail longboats from Hudson Bay, up the tortuous Red River, up a riffling tributary such as the Buffalo River, and then through a chain of lakes to the perfectly landlocked Big Cormorant. Most scholars have chalked up the stone to a clever hoax, perpetrated by Ohman or on Ohman. Nonetheless, the Runestone continues to attract supporters, including Cornell University linguistics professor Robert Hall, who has written two books claiming the tablet is authentic.

Alexandria is known for more than its reputed Vikings. It's the home of **Theatre L'Homme Dieu,** a regional summer theater providing stage experience for college students and professional actors.

■ PARKS AND WILDLIFE *map page 285, F&G-1&2*

Tucked in the cluster of lakes and hills north of Alexandria are several state parks. Immediately north of town is **Lake Carlos State Park,** situated on the shore of its namesake. Lakes in the area, including Carlos, are kettle lakes, formed when the glacial deposits buried chunks of ice the size of icebergs. As the blocks melted, the land collapsed, forming a basin that filled with water. Lake Carlos itself is clear and deep (150 feet). It provides good fishing for walleyes, northern pike, large-mouth bass, and crappies. Other activities in this 1,400-acre park include camping, hiking, horseback riding, cross-country skiing, and snowmobiling. *320-852-7200.*

Cooling off during the short, hot Minnesota summer.

Hidden among the back roads just west of Urbank is a state secret. **Inspiration Peak**, the highest portion of the glacial Leaf Hills, rises 400 feet above the surrounding countryside. The vista was well known to Sinclair Lewis, but unknown then, as it is now, to many Minnesotans. From the prairie-covered crest of the hill, he wrote, "there's to be seen a glorious 20-mile circle of some 50 lakes scattered among fields and pastures, like sequins fallen on an old paisley shawl." Lewis chided Minnesotans for not knowing the "haunts of beauty" in their own back yards. The hike to the top is rather easy. The view is particularly impressive when the hardwoods are ablaze.

Once a private retreat, 1,900-acre **Glendalough State Park** embraces oak-covered hills, grassy fields, and several undeveloped lakes. This new park, now under development, will provide catch-and-release fishing with restrictions on motors and on-board electronics. Bike trails and canoe camping are also planned. *218-864-0110.*

North of Underwood, at a dam on the Otter Tail River, sits **Phelps Mill**. The mill began operation in 1889, grinding flour for area farmers. Though idle since 1931, the mill, now owned by Otter Tail County, is open for inspection by the

In the wintertime, lakes freeze over and become playgrounds of a different sort. Here, a snowmobile race takes place on Mille Lacs Lake.

public. Signs describe the milling process. The **Phelps Mill Store**, which sits across the street, makes up the other half of town. William O. Douglas, associate justice of Supreme Court, was born in nearby Maine, two miles north.

Maplewood State Park is the largest park in the region. Its rolling, wooded hills overlook the surrounding farmland. Several clear lakes provide fishing for walleyes, northern pike, and panfish. It's a favorite with wildlife watchers, with an abundance of woodland animals, such as white-tailed deer, beavers, raccoons, and herons and other wading birds. It has a campground, several campsites for backpackers, and trails for hiking (25 miles), horseback riding (15 miles), cross-country skiing (17 miles), and snowmobiling (14 miles). *218-863-8383.*

What The Land Meant

My mother grew up in these hills, just a few miles southwest of Wadena in west-central Minnesota. Fall, winter, and spring she and her brother walked two miles down a dirt road to a one-room country schoolhouse, even on the cold days when the mail carrier made his rounds by sleigh. In summer, they would work on the farm. It was a small thing, just 160 acres. The ground that wasn't swamp or gravel would raise a crop of corn or small grains or hay. A couple of dozen cows grazed in the oak woods on either side of the road.

Like so many of her generation, my mother left the farm as soon as she could, taking a room with relatives and going to work in the city. But many years later, when I was a youngster, we'd return to the farm. Sometimes we'd take the train. It was long enough ago they would serve lunch in the dining car, with real plates, heavy silverware, and stiff white linen. A black waiter poured water and brought our menus. My uncle met us at the Wadena train station in a '56 Chevy and drove us home to the farm.

It was an exotic place for a kid from the suburbs. My grandfather would walk for miles through the woods and marshes as he checked his traps for muskrats and mink. I hunted for snakes around the haystacks and looked for cats in the barn. I was no farmer, though. I never did get the knack for squeezing milk from an udder or sliding my hand beneath a laying hen without getting pecked.

I went back recently. Wadena remained a tidy town. It wasn't much for tourists, but it managed to keep its movie house downtown. The homes are solid and neat, and modern schools sit on the west edge of town. I parked in front of the train station, of that classic design that could be mistaken for nothing else. Boards covered the windows. Weeds grew around the foundation. The tracks, still shiny, stretched east and west into the distance, but it was clear no passengers had stepped down to the platform for years. The platform, for that matter, was once lovely, made of bricks set in a tight herringbone. But the years and the weeds had loosened the brick. I plucked one free, and laid it in my trunk.

I drove out to the farm. I was last there several years ago, when my aunt and uncle auctioned off most of the farm equipment and many of their possessions before moving to town. Someone else owned the place now and by appearances did not live there full time. The barn had been torn down. The pig shed was gone and the corn crib stood empty. Grandpa's garden overflowed with weeds. Of a row of apple trees, only one remained standing. It was crooked, and small for its years. "Stone fences, wooden gates, barns, sheds, and trees all merge together in the landscape," wrote artist Wanda Gág, originally of New Ulm, where her childhood home still stands. "There is . . . a seeming intelligence of inanimate things, a unique grace and power as if this tree has meant a great deal to the land for so many years." Rooted in memory perhaps more firmly than in the land itself, the lone tree meant a great deal.

And what have we meant to the land, and the land to us? I looked down to the patch of woods where Grandpa and I used to hunt. It didn't seem half so far away as it once did, lying just beyond a field that has been groomed by a steel plow and planted in corn. We have made the land and, far more profoundly, it has made us. It has defined us—as hunters, as farmers, as miners, as city dwellers. It has defined our culture. The land is our identity, our tie to our ancestors, our image and name.

I think of a man named Mazomani, a Dakota leader who died in the 1862 war. His name in English means "Iron Walker," and his people were called Wahpetonwan, "Dwellers in the Leaves." His grave lies on a hillside in what is now Upper Sioux Agency State Park, a bit to the south of my own home ground. It is a fine place to be buried, with a long view overlooking the converging valleys of the Yellow Medicine and Minnesota rivers and the graves of people who have lived on this land for thousands of years. On a clear day, when the sky shines as bright and clear as a magnificent lens, a spirit in death could view the many places it had walked in life. It seems to me Indian tribes had sacred sites, not so much because they believed them to be sacred, but because they believed them to be *their* sacred sites. The land gave identity to a people. It held not only the remains of ancestors and relatives, but also their common memories.

With such a view, I believe Iron Walker must feel at home. As I gaze at this gnarled old apple tree, for the moment, so do I.

■ FERGUS FALLS *map page 91, F-2*

Fergus Falls, as its name implies, owes its existence to the water power provided by the Otter Tail River, which falls nearly 300 feet as it tumbles out of the glacial hills. The town itself is as neat as mathematics, with solid houses and tidy lawns. While the downtowns of many small towns have packed up and moved to the suburbs, the center of Fergus Falls appears vital and active, with coffee houses, restaurants, a theater (converted to a community theater), and an attractive river walk. The **Otter Tail County Historical Society Museum** holds dioramas and changing exhibits on local history. 110 *West Lincoln; 218-736-6038.* The county, by the way, contains more than a 1,000 lakes.

■ DETROIT LAKES *map page 285, D/E-1*

Detroit Lakes is a prosperous tourist town set in a cluster of resorts and lakes— more than 400 lakes within 25 miles. The name derives from détroit, or narrows, on the lake that now bears that name. Exhibits in the **Becker County Historical Society Museum** in town describe local history. Detroit Lakes City Park and the mile-long beach fill up on summer weekends. The Fourth of July celebration is a huge draw. So is WE Fest, the first weekend in August, on Sioux Pass Ranch three miles south of town on Minnesota 59. The celebration draws top country music performers. *(See page 334.)*

Northwest of Detroit Lakes on Becker County 29 is **Tamarac National Wildlife Refuge,** a 43,000-acre wildlife area with forests, wetlands, abundant wild rice, and many mammals and birds, including trumpeter swans, bald eagles, and loons.

Like giant lawn mowers, combines scoop up wheat—the golden bounty of the plains

TRAVELERS INFORMATION

Listings

Area Codes.....................312	Food & Lodging Map..........314
When to Come/Climate........312	Lodging Chains...............315
Getting Around...............313	General Information Numbers...332
Food & Lodging by Town.......314	Festivals & Events.............333
Food & Lodging Price Key......314	Great Outdoors..............335

NOTE: Compass American Guides makes every effort to ensure the accuracy of its information; however, as conditions and prices change frequently, we recommend that readers also contact the local visitors bureaus for the most up-to-date information—see "General Information Numbers," page 332.

■ AREA CODES

Minneapolis 612
Outlying north and northwestern Minneapolis suburbs 763
Outlying south and southwestern Minneapolis suburbs 952
St. Paul and eastern suburbs 651
Northern Minnesota 218
West-central Minnesota 320
Southern Minnesota 507

■ WHEN TO COME / CLIMATE

Minnesota is more than 400 miles tall, so climate varies from north to south. Expect winter to set in a month earlier and leave a month later in the north than in the south. That noted, here are some generalizations:

Summer is short and sometimes hot. For activities such as swimming and boating, visit in June–August; temperatures occasionally reach the 90s, rarely higher.

Autumn is glorious but also short, with nights turning chilly in mid-September. Tours to check out autumn foliage are popular along the North Shore, throughout the hardwood-covered hills near the Glacial Lakes, and in the southeastern hill country. Colors peak in the north as October begins, and a couple of weeks later in

TEMPS (F°)	AVG. JAN.		AVG. APRIL		AVG. JULY		AVG. OCT.		RECORD	RECORD
	HIGH	LOW	HIGH	LOW	HIGH	LOW	HIGH	LOW	HIGH	LOW
Bemidji	12	-11	49	28	80	56	66	44	107	-50
Duluth	16	-2	39	29	78	55	53	35	106	-41
Int'l Falls	10	-10	50	27	79	54	52	32	103	-49
Minneapolis	20	2	56	36	84	62	60	40	108	-41
Moorhead	15	-3	51	30	83	59	58	35	114	-48
Rochester	21	3	55	34	81	60	60	38	108	-42
St. Cloud	17	-5	53	32	82	58	58	36	107	-40
Windom	20	0	55	34	84	61	61	37	106	-32

PRECIPITATION (INCHES)	AVG. JAN.	AVG. APRIL	AVG. JULY	AVG. OCT.	ANNUAL	
					RAIN	SNOW
Bemidji	0.7	1.7	3.3	1.9	23	44
Duluth	1.2	0.8	3.9	2.4	30	79
International Falls	0.8	1.5	3.9	1.9	24	64
Minneapolis	0.8	2.2	3.8	1.9	27	52
Moorhead	0.6	1.7	3.1	1.5	19	38
Rochester	0.8	2.6	4.1	2.1	29	46
St. Cloud	0.7	1.9	3.6	2.0	26	48
Windom	1.0	2.2	3.6	1.4	28	37

the south. For up-to-date color information, call the Office of Tourism's **Fall Color Hotline**, 800-657-3700. Late October brings cold rains or snow flurries. November is dreary and cold.

Winter is Minnesota's best season if only because it's had more practice than any of the others. In northeastern Minnesota, where winter is longest and snow heaviest, expect lasting snow from December into late March. In the south, snow usually covers the ground from late December to late February. January is the coldest month, bringing subzero weather to the entire state. In the north, January nights of minus 20 degrees F are common.

Spring is brief and unpredictable. If you're planning a fishing or boating trip, keep in mind that far northern Minnesota lakes are usually ice-free at the start of the general fishing season in mid-May.

■ GETTING AROUND

Most out-of-state travel passes through Minnesota's largest airport, Minneapolis–St. Paul International Airport, which serves as the hub for Northwest Airlines. Buses and taxis run through major cities, but the most practical option for travelers is usually a rental car.

FOOD & LODGING

■ FOOD & LODGING BY TOWN

Restaurant prices:
Per person, not including drinks, tax and tips:
$ = under $10; $$ = $10–20; $$$ = over $20

❖

Room rates:
Per night, per room, double occupancy:
$ = under $70; $$ = $70–130; $$$ = over $130

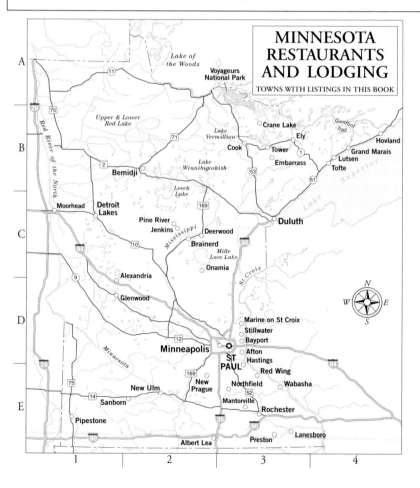

MINNESOTA RESTAURANTS AND LODGING

TOWNS WITH LISTINGS IN THIS BOOK

Hotel & Motel Chains

Best Western. 800-528-1234

Choice Hotels. 800-4-CHOICE

Country Inns. 800-456-4000

Days Inn. 800-325-2525

Hilton Hotels. 800-445-8667

Holiday Inn. 800-465-4329

Marriott. 800-228-9290

Radisson Hotels. 800-333-3333

Sheraton. 800-325-3535

Super 8. 800-800-8000

Albert Lea *map C-2*

■ RESTAURANTS & LODGING

Victorian Rose Inn. *609 W. Fountain St.; 507-373-7602, 800-252-6558* **$$**
A comfy B&B in a beautifully restored 1898 Queen Anne Victorian with stained glass windows, turrets, lace, gingerbread, and period antiques. All rooms have private baths.

Alexandria (Glenwood) *map C/D-1/2*

■ RESTAURANTS & LODGING

Arrowwood—A Radisson Resort.
3.25 miles north of town on County 22 in Alexandria; 320-762-1124 **$$**
Arrowwood is a full service resort and conference center, with golf course, boats, skiing, supervised children's activities. **The Lake Cafe**, overlooking the lake, offers Scandinavian and American food. **Luigi's** aims at families, with make-your-own pizza and ice cream.

Peter's Sunset Beach. *2.5 miles south on Minnesota 104 to Pezhekee Road; 1.5 miles west to Lake Minnewaska, Glenwood; 320-634-5223* **$$**
This classic lakeside resort with tennis, golf, marina, private beach, and skiing is especially popular with vacationing families. Consisting of a main lodge, annex, 12 cottages, and 9 town houses, the resort can accommodate up to 175 guests.

Bemidji *map B-2*

■ RESTAURANTS & LODGING

Birchmont Lodge. *4 miles north on County 21. 218-751-1630* **$$**
Full-service and fashionable resort with an excellent restaurant, two lodges, several cabins, with tennis, golf, waterskiing, supervised children's activities. The beach stretches a quarter of a mile.

Finn 'N Feather. *Rt. 3, Lake Andrusia 1.5 miles south on US 2, 71, then 10 miles east on County 8); 218-335-6598* **$$ - $$$**
A family-oriented lakeside resort with 19 cottages (all with kitchens, 2 to 4 bedrooms). Tennis, golf, beach, canoes, paddle boats, swimming pool, and whirlpool.

FOOD & LODGING

Brainerd and Vicinity *map C-2*
Deerwood, Onamia, Pine River

■ RESTAURANTS & LODGING

Breezy Point. *18 miles north on US 371; 5 miles east on County 11; 800-432-3777* **$$ - $$$**
Breezy Point is a classic resort on Pelican Lake, with private beach, golf, tennis, marina, skiing, supervised children's activities. Bands play in the Marina Lounge. The **Marina Restaurant** offers a full menu. Especially good are the barbecued ribs and chicken.

Cragun's Lodge, Spa, Resort and Conference Center. *4.75 miles north on Minnesota 371; 6 miles west on County 77; 800-272-4867* **$$ - $$$**
A large resort and conference center on Gull Lake with tennis, golf, marina, private beach, skiing, and supervised children's games and activities. The **Hungry Gull Restaurant and Lodge Dining Room** serves delicious homemade breads and desserts.

Driftwood Resort. *4.5 miles northeast of Jenkins on County 15, near Pine River; 218-568-4221* **$$**
An old-fashioned family resort on Whitefish Lake with tennis, golf, boats, and plenty of children's activities (this is definitely a kid-oriented resort—they even offer pony rides). Watercolor lessons throughout summer and frequent guest talent shows. It is also home of the Minnesota Resort Museum, which tells the tale of this most important industry.

Grand View Lodge. *14 miles north on Minnesota 371; 1 mile west on County 77; 800-432-3788* **$$$**
The Grand View grew around a lodge built on Gull Lake in 1919. Today the resort, with a quarter-mile-long private beach, offers tennis, 36 holes of golf, marina, skiing, and supervised children's activities.

Izaty's Golf & Yacht Club. *3 miles east of town on Minnesota 27; 1 mile north on Izatys Rd. in Onamia; 800-533-1728* **$$$**
Named for the ancient Dakota Indian village on the shore of Mille Lacs Lake, Izaty's is a full-service resort on the lake, with marina, pools, golf, supervised children's activities. Mille Lacs is one of the walleye state's best walleye lakes.

Madden's on Gull Lake. *4.75 miles north on Minnesota 371; 7.75 miles west on County 77; 800-642-5363* **$$ - $$$**
Madden's grew from a golf course clubhouse. Today it provides 45 holes of golf, tennis, marina, private beach, skiing and supervised children's activities.

Ruttgers Bay Lake Lodge. *5 miles south of Deerwood on Minnesota 6; 800-450-4545* **$$ - $$$**
Begun by the Ruttgers family in 1898, the resort has attracted family vacationers ever since. Accommodations include cabins, condos and villas, with a long sandy beach and pine forest. Activities include tennis, golf, marina, skiing, supervised children's activities.

Detroit Lakes and Vicinity *map C-1*

■ RESTAURANTS & LODGING

Fair Hills. *Rte. 1, 11 miles southwest on US 59; 3 miles west on County 20; 218-847-7638* $$ - $$$
Fair Hills was just a farmhouse in 1906 when its owners began taking in boarders. It has since grown to a resort of more than 90 units, with tennis, golf, marina, private beach, skiing, and supervised children's activities. No liquor.

Maplelag. *About 7 miles east of Callaway on Little Sugarbush Lake; 218-375-4466* $$ - $$$
Cross-country ski resort with rustic and modern cabins, more than 50 kilometers of tracked ski trails, skating rink, sauna, and steam rooms. Ask owner Jim Richards about his collections of fish decoys and railroad signs.

Duluth *map C-3*

■ RESTAURANTS

Grandma's Saloon & Deli. *522 Lake Ave. S.; 218-727-4192* $ - $$
A fixture near the entrance to the Duluth harbor: burgers, sandwiches, and other casual fare at good prices. The decor is casual and whimsical. A large deck overlooks the lake.

Pickwick. *508 E. Superior St.; 218-727-8901* $ - $$
One of the city's best restaurants, with a dark and relaxing interior, and a view of Lake Superior. The menu is classic American. Be sure to order onion rings.

■ LODGING

Fitger's Inn. *600 E. Superior St.; 800-726-2982* $$ - $$$
This stone-walled inn occupies part of the old Fitger's brewery. Spacious guest rooms have writing desks, wing chairs, and modern baths. Most rooms overlook Lake Superior; just outside the front door lies a beautiful walking trail along the shore. Shops and atheater nearby.

Radisson Hotel Duluth - Harborview. *505 W. Superior St.; 218-727-8981* $$
On the edge of downtown, the Radisson provides a towering view of Duluth, the harbor, the North Shore hills, and the lake. Heated pool, sauna, whirlpool.

Embarrass *map B-3*

■ RESTAURANTS & LODGING

Finnish Heritage Homestead.
4776 Waisanen Rd., Embarrass; 218-984-3318 or 800-863-6545 $
Cozy inn furnished with antiques.

FOOD & LODGING

Grand Marais *map B-4*
Cascade River, Gunflint Trail, Lutzen

■ RESTAURANTS & LODGING

Bearskin Lodge. *275 Gunflint Trail, E. Bearskin Rd.; 218-388-2292 or 800-338-4170* $$ - $$$
Started as a rustic fishing camp on a secluded bay in 1925, Bearskin has grown into a popular year-round resort. In summer, fishing for northern pike, walleyes, and smallmouth bass is excellent. In winter, guests have access to 65 miles of groomed Nordic ski trails.

Birch Terrace. *Half mile west of Grand Marais on US 61; 218-387-2215* $$
A charmingly decorated north-woods manor that overlooks the lake and town. Try Lake Superior trout or steak.

Bluefin Bay. *Tofte; 800-258-3346* $$ - $$$
This large, modern motor lodge directly on the shore of Lake Superior has quickly gained a reputation for good food (especially seafood) and fine accommodations. With the lodge are townhouses and condominiums. Tennis court, volleyball court, golf, gym, pool, and sauna.

Cascade Lodge. *9 miles northeast of Lutsen on US 61; 800-322-9543* $$ - $$$
Long renowned for some of the best dining along the shore, the Cascade has become particularly popular in winter because of the excellent cross-country skiing nearby in Cascade River State Park. Rustic main lodge (circa 1930) and cabins with fireplaces are available.

Gunflint Lodge. *143 S. Gunflint Lake; 800-328-3325* $$$
The main lodge is decorated with voyageur artifacts, wooden carvings, and other rustic crafts. Still popular with fishermen, Gunflint Lodge has broadened its clientele by offering kayaks and canoes in summer, and ski trails and sled dog trips in winter.

Lutsen Resort. *1.5 miles southwest of Lutsen on US 61; 800-258-8736* $$
Lutsen is one of the original large North Shore resorts, known for its downhill skiing. The large dining room in the pine lodge overlooks the lake and mouth of the Poplar River.

Naniboujou Lodge and Restaurant.
About 14 miles northeast of Grand Marais on US 61, on the mouth of the Brule River; 218-387-2688 $$
The Naniboujou has been a North Shore landmark since it was built as a private club in the 1920s, to serve members that included Babe Ruth and Ring Lardner. The Depression scaled back plans, but what was built is impressive nonetheless. The stunning dining room, with its painted ceiling and massive fieldstone fireplace, is decorated with Cree Indian designs. For dinner, try Lake Superior fish or chicken with fresh tomatoes.

Hastings *map D-3*

■ RESTAURANTS & LODGING

Rosewood Inn. *620 Ramsey St.*

Thorwood Inn. *315 Pine St.; 888-846-7966 or 651-437-3297* **$$ - $$$**
Two Victorian mansions built in the 1880s and restored as bed-and-breakfasts by innkeepers Pam and Dick Thorsen. All rooms have private baths; some have fireplaces and whirlpools. Rosewood is the more luxurious (and larger-with its ornate parlors, grand piano, and bay windows. Six blocks away from each other, both are within walking distance of the Mississippi.

Minneapolis *map D-3*

■ RESTAURANTS

Anthony's Wharf. *201 SE. Main St.; 612-378-7058* **$$ - $$$**
Located on the historic Mississippi riverfront, site of old St. Anthony, across the river from downtown. Specializes in seafood.

Aquavit. *IDS Center, 80 S. Seventh St.; 612-343-3333* **$$$**
An adventure in sophisticated dining. Traditional northern European fare, such as meatballs, venison, seafood and caviar, prepared with a nouvelle twist.

Black Forest Inn. *1 E. 26th St.; 612-872-0812* **$ - $$**
German decor and German food with patio dining in summer. Mainstays such as sauerbraten and red cabbage are excellent. The place is always busy.

The Blue Nile. *2027 E. Franklin Ave.; 612-338-3000* **$$**
Ethiopian culture and cuisine, with lamb, chicken, seafood, beef, and many vegetarian dishes. Live African and world music.

Bobino Cafe and Wine Bar. *222 E. Hennepin Ave.; 612-623-3301* **$$**
Innovative treatment of seafood and chicken in a bistro atmosphere you'd expect to find on the West Coast. Try the tapas and imported cheeses.

Buca di Beppo-Minneapolis.
11 S. 12th St.; 651-638-2225 **$$**
Intimate and usually crowded cellar with huge helpings served family-style. Go with a large or very hungry group and expect to wait. Try the spaghetti marinara, green beans (yes! green beans) and mashed potatoes, and chicken marsala. Other Bucas—different atmosphere, same family-style servings—are located in **Eden Prairie** *(7711 Mitchell Rd.; 612-724-7266),* **Burnsville** *(14300 Burnhaven Dr.; 612-892-7272),* and **St. Paul** *(2728 Gannon Rd.; 651-772-4388).*

Cafe Brenda. *300 First Ave. N. (Third St.); 612-342-9230* **$ - $$**
This warehouse district restaurant has very good vegetarian food in an attractive setting.

Minneapolis *(continued)*

Cafe Un Deux Trois. *Foshay Tower, 114 S. Ninth St. (between Second and Marquette Ave.); 612-673-0686* $ - $$
A lively French bistro.

Campiello. *1320 W. Lake St. (Lagoon Ave.); 612-825-2222* $$ - $$$
Whimsically decorated trattoria. The open kitchen turns out wood-fired pizzas, terrific roasts, and pastas.

Capital Grille. *Lasalle Plaza, 801 Hennepin Ave.; 612-692-9000* $$$
A downtown steakhouse with the atmosphere of money. The dining room is dark. Heads of wildlife trophies ring the room. The Grille specializes in the best cuts of steak and two-pound lobsters.

Christos. *2632 Nicollet Ave. S.; 612-871-2111* $ - $$
Greek food, from hummus to octopus, and great service in a light, casual atmosphere. The seafood is superb.

D'Amico Cucina. *100 N. Sixth St.; 612-338-2401* $$$
Northern Italian food with a bit of California. Specialties include artfully prepared wild mushrooms, gnocchi, and roast game. The restaurant is housed in the Buttler Building, a landmark in the popular Warehouse District.

Famous Dave's Bar-B-Que. *Calhoun Square, 3001 Hennepin Ave.; 612-822-9900*
4264 Upton Ave. S.; 612-919-1200 $$
Big portions of ribs and other barbecue are served in a restaurant done-up as an old juke joint. Portions are big. Come hungry and ready to be sloppy. More than a dozen other restaurants in this chain are filled with antiques, signs, posters and other memorabilia.

Figlio. *3001 Hennepin Ave. S.; 612-822-1688* $ - $$
The dining room, which overlooks Hennepin and Lake, is a popular nightspot for the Uptown crowd or for watching the Uptown crowd, which seems pretty bizarre by tame Midwestern standards. The food is good, too, tending toward California-Italian in style. You can dine outside in summer.

The 510 Restaurant. *510 Groveland Ave.; 612-874-6440* $$$
Pricey and stylish, with a grand dining room, the 510 ranks as one of the Twin Cities' classiest restaurants. Recommended: a terrific Caesar salad, lamb, seafood, and sweetbreads.

Giorgio's. *2451 Hennepin Ave. (24th St.); 612-374-5131* $ - $$
A tiny neighborhood trattoria almost always packed with patrons seeking authentic, garlic-drenched Tuscan fare. The risotto is a particular favorite.

Goodfellow's. *40 S. Seventh St.; 612-332-4800* $$$
A creative menu, ample stock of high-quality wines, and classy atmosphere make Goodfellow's, in the midst of downtown, one of the Twin Cities' best.

Jax Cafe. *1928 University Ave. NE; 612-789-7297* $$ - $$$
A tradition in northeast Minneapolis, serving steak, prime rib, seafood. The restaurant overlooks a garden with an artificial trout stream and pond, from which you can pick your own trout dinner. A pianist plays weekends.

Joe's Garage. *1610 Harmon Pl.; 612-904-1163* $$
Unusual burgers, including lamb and tuna—just what you'd expect in chic Loring Park, near the Guthrie and the Walker. In good weather, try the rooftop.

Kikugawa. *43 SE Main St.; 612-378-3006* $ - $$$
Japanese cuisine on the riverfront, across the Mississippi from downtown.

Kincaid's Steak, Chop and Fish House. *8400 Normandale Lake Blvd. (Bloomington); 612-921-2255* $$$
One of the Twin Cities' top-rated steakhouses. As the name suggests, it's well-known for beef and seafood.

Lord Fletcher's on the Lake. *3746 Sunset Dr., Spring Park; 952-471-8513* $$
Specializes in beef and fish. Old English decor on the shores of Lake Minnetonka, west of Minneapolis. The Lord Fletcher's experience is best if you can manage to arrive by boat.

Loring Cafe and Bar. *1624 Harmon Pl.; 612-332-1617* $$$
A stylish place in downtown's hip Loring Park, the bar has outdoor seating overlooking the park, while the cafe faces a courtyard. Dabble in the appetizers, and try the sun-dried tomato pizza.

Lucia's. *1432 W. 31st St.; 612-825-1572.* $$
An eclectic menu where soups, salads, and homebaked breads shine, in a sparse, informal setting with an adjoining wine bar.

Mayslack's. *1428 NE Fourth St.; 612-789-9862* $$
Since Stan Mayslack, erstwhile professional wrestler, opened his bar and restaurant, it has become a northeast Minneapolis classic for its huge, spicy, roast beef sandwiches.

The Moghals. *1123 W. Lake St.; 612-823-2866* $$
This modest restaurant prepares a variety of Indian dishes including scorching curries and delicious tandoori.

Murray's. *26 S. Sixth St.; 612-339-0909* $$$
Murray's well-known specialty is the "silver butter knife" steak for two. It's not cheap, but it may be the best steak you find in the Twin Cities. Not up for beef? The salmon and walleye are good too.

Napa Valley Grille. *Mall of America (Bloomington); 612-858-9934* $$$
An innovative restaurant that emphasizes fine wine is not what you'd expect in a shopping mall, but that is what you get at Napa Valley. How's this for not-your-ordinary mall fare: grilled ostrich fillet, served with garlic- and goat-cheese-roasted red potatoes, braised apples and cabbage. Choose from hundreds of California wines.

FOOD & LODGING

Minneapolis *(continued)*

New French Cafe. *128 N. Fourth St.;*
612-338-3790 $$ - $$$
Intimate and informal setting in remodeled building from about 1900 in the city's warehouse district. Specialties: rack of lamb, seafood. The bakery next door serves up some of the best baguettes and pastries in town.

Nye's Polonaise Room. *112 Hennepin Ave. E.; 612-379-2021* $$
A Minneapolis institution that has refused to change—and with good reason. The dark '60s decor and heavy food (kielbasa, sauerkraut, and prime rib) continue to please a long-time clientele. After dinner, hang around the piano bar.

Origami. *30 N. First St. (First Ave.); 612-333-8430* $$
Sushi-lovers flock to this stylish warehouse district storefront where the food is beautifully prepared and the saki selection quite impressive.

Palomino Euro Bistro. *825 Hennepin Ave.; 612-339-3800* $$
Serving the business crowd on the Hennepin Mall, this European-styled restaurant specializes in Mediterranean food, including game, in season. Try the garlic chicken or prime rib.

Ping's Szechuan Bar and Grill. *1401 Nicollet Ave. S.; 612-874-9404* $ - $$
Chinese menu, including Peking duck and Szechwan dishes. This restaurant, with a clean, sophisticated interior, overlooks a stylish and newly refurbished neighborhood just south of downtown.

Pracna on Main. *117 Main St.; 612-379-3200* $ - $$
Housed in the 1890 building once occupied by Frank Pracna's saloon, Pracna on Main started the riverfront revival on the site of the old St. Anthony milling district. Outdoor dining provides a wonderful view of St. Anthony Falls and the Minneapolis skyline. The menu is common fare, from pasta to burgers.

Rainbow Chinese Restaurant and Bar. *2739 Nicollet Ave. S.; 612-870-7084* $
Excellent food, huge menu, and a convivial bar have made the Rainbow a success in ethnically diverse south Minneapolis.

Rainforest Cafe. *Mall of America (Bloomington); 612-854-7500* $$
The tropical birds, fish, and exotic foliage are enough to distract you from the food, which runs toward standard fare such as pasta dishes and burgers.

Sawatdee Thai Restaurant. *607 Washington Ave. S.; 612-338-6451* $ - $$
This restaurant and its namesake in the Lowertown area of St. Paul, *285 E. Fifth St., 612-222-5859,* probably did as much as any place to popularize Thai food in the Twin Cities. Take advantage of the luncheon buffets.

Shuang Cheng Restaurant. *1320 Fourth St. SE.; 612-378-0208* $
A modest spot in the heart of Dinkytown, next to the university, but the kitchen treats seafood and chicken with authentic Chinese flair.

Singapore Chinese Cuisine. *1715 Beam Ave. (Maplewood); 651-777-7999* $-$$
The Singapore specializes in the spicy chicken and seafood dishes of Malaysia. Try the chicken satay and anything with squid. A more typical Chinese-American menu is also available.

Tacos Morelos. *14 W. 26th St.; 612-870-0053* $-$$
A recent immigration of Mexicans to south Minneapolis has resulted in the opening of new markets, shops and restaurants, including this cozy taqueria.

Village Wok. *610 Washington Ave. SE.; 612-331-9041* $
Good Chinese food and lots of it from a huge menu at almost unbelievably low prices have made this a favorite with University students and those who simply like the campus atmosphere.

Whitney Hotel and Grille. *150 Portland Ave.; 612-339-9300* $$$
The dining room is dark, subdued, and private. The menu is all-American.

■ LODGING

Crown Plaza Northstar. *618 Second Ave. S.; 612-338-2288* $$$
A recent $4 million renovation gave this 17-story hotel a rich look and feel, with dark wood and Victorian details. There's a good restaurant, and guests can use the pool of the nearby Minneapolis Club.

Hotel Sofitel. *5601 78th St. W., Bloomington; 612-835-1900* $$
A bit of France in mall land, Hotel Sofitel provides some of the best food and lodging in Bloomington. The three restaurants here are all good: Chez Colette for heavy country cooking, Le Cafe Royal for more sophisticated dining, and La Terrasse for casual dining. Hotel guests have access to the pool and spa.

Hyatt Regency. *1300 Nicollet Mall; 612-370-1234* $$$
A full-service hotel in the heart of downtown. For a small fee, guests can use the Regency Athletic Club, with tennis and racquetball courts, weight room, running track, Jacuzzi, and sauna. All guests can use the large swimming pool.

The Marquette. *710 Marquette Ave.; 612-333-4545* $$$
A high-quality hotel in the IDS Tower, Minneapolis's tallest building. All rooms are spacious corner rooms and some have steam baths. Guests have access to a gym facility. .

Nicollet Island Inn. *95 Merriam St.; 612-331-1800* $$$
A quaint hotel and restaurant, located in a historic stone building on picturesque Nicollet Island, in the heart of the city's milling district, with striking views of St. Anthony Falls and the Minneapolis skyline. This restaurant takes cooking seriously and has *nouveau* tendencies that are a pleasure to experience.

Whitney Hotel and Grille. *150 Portland Ave.; 800- 233-1234* $$$
Contained in a renovated flour mill, the stately hotel overlooks the historic milling district. Some rooms provide stunning views of the river.

FOOD & LODGING

Moorhead *map C-1*

■ RESTAURANTS & LODGING

Tree Top. *403 Center Ave.; 218-233-1393*
$$
For more than 40 years the Tree Top has provided some of the best dining in the Moorhead area at a reasonable price, with a view of the Red River Valley from the seventh floor of what is now the Metropolitan Federal Building. Favorites are the prime rib, shrimp fettucini, and homemade soup.

New Prague & Vicinity *map E-2*

■ RESTAURANTS & LODGING

Minnesota Horse & Hunt. *2920 E. 220th St., Prior Lake; 952-447-2272* **$$ - $$$**
A sprawling log cabin with an unusual game menu.

Schumacher's New Prague Hotel. *212 W. Main St.; 952-758-2133* **$$$**
Hotel built in 1898 resembles country inns of Germany, with imported antique Bavarian wainscoting and chandeliers. Schumacher's restaurant (**$$$**) specializes in Czech, German, and Polish sausages and game such as roast duck, pheasant in heavy cream, and fresh trout.

New Ulm *map E-2*

■ RESTAURANT

Veigel's Kaiserhoff. *221 N. Minnesota St., New Ulm; 507-359-2071* **$$**
The perfect place for a Bavarian restaurant: New Ulm is perhaps Minnesota's most German town. The barbecued ribs are a specialty.

Northfield *map E-3*

■ RESTAURANT

The Tavern. *212 Division St.; 507-645-5661* **$ - $$**
Located in the Archer House hotel, this pleasant restaurant overlooks the river and serves breakfast, lunch, and dinner. In summer sit outside on the patio.

■ LODGING

Archer House. *212 Division St.; 507-645-5661* **$$**
A downtown hotel, built in 1877, on the bank of the Cannon River. Today it provides a stylish anchor for the city's downtown. The rooms retain their historic atmosphere—but *do* have whirlpools.

Pipestone *map E-1*

■ RESTAURANTS & LODGING

Calumet Inn. *104 W. Main St.;*
507-825-5871 **$ - $$**
This historic structure was originally
built as a joint hotel and bank. Its recent
renovation restored the original character, and made the bank and vault into a
lounge and wine room. The dining
room recaptures the elegance of a bygone era. You can choose between antique and modern furnished rooms.

Red Wing *map E-3*

■ RESTAURANTS

Liberty's. *Corner of Third and Plum Sts.;*
651-388-8877 **$ - $$**
Twenty-years ago this popular eatery
started out as a pizza delivery outfit. The
menu still includes pizza but you'll also
find choice steaks, pastas, and Mexican
entrees. The dining room and bar are
decorated with mementoes of Red
Wing's past.

Marie's Casual Dining. *217 Plum St.,*
651-388-1896 **$ - $$**
A low-key place to stop for a grilled
cheese sandwich—or lobster.

Port of Red Wing. *In the St. James Hotel;*
651-388-2846 **$$ - $$$**
Downstairs from the hotel lobby, this
restaurant and bar, with its quarried
limestone walls, affords a pleasant, warm
atmosphere. The menu offers nicely prepared American-Continental fare. Open
for lunch and dinner.

Staghead. *219 Bush St.; 651-388-6581* **$$**
This coffeehouse-cum-restaurant offers
innovative cooking, friendly staff, and
pleasant ambiance. The dinner menu
changes weekly and may include wild
mushroom risotto or pork tenderloin
with applewood smoked bacon, and a
side of parsnip mashed potatoes. Lunch-
es are no less imaginative with a variety
of sandwiches, pastas, and fresh fish.

■ LODGING

Pratt-Taber Inn. *706 W. Fourth St.;*
651-388-5945 **$$**
This Italianate house, built in 1876 near
the center of town, has been converted
to a bed-and-breakfast and decorated
with 1850s and 60s furnishings. Food is
good and the setting on a quiet small-
town street is restful.

St. James Hotel. *406 Main St.; 651-388-*
2846 or 800-252-1875 **$$ - $$$**
Renovation of the classic St. James
Hotel, built in 1875, launched the refur-
bishing of downtown Red Wing and
created a rich and scenic main street.
The rooms are richly decorated in antiques and period pieces. The hotel has
two excellent restaurants and a variety of
shops in the lobby.

FOOD & LODGING

Rochester and Vicinity *map E-3*
Mantorville, Preston, Wabasha

■ **RESTAURANTS**

Michael's Restaurant and Lounge. *15 S. Broadway, Rochester; 507-288-2020* **$$**
The restaurant has long been known for an excellent and varied menu of Greek and American food, including steaks, seafood, fresh fish, and roast duck. The lounge serves lighter meals, including pastas, gyros, and espresso.

Hubbell House. *Highway 57, Mantorville; 507-635-2331* **$$**
The Hubbell House has such a reputation that many Twin Citians make a special trip to eat in this country inn, which serves excellent steaks and seafood, including local walleye. Built in 1854, now decorated with Civil War–era antiques, including a land grant signed by none other than Abraham Lincoln.

■ **LODGING**

Anderson House Hotel. *333 W. Main St.; Wabasha; 507-565-4525 or*

800-535-5467 **$ - $$**
Not only does this comfy hotel have handmade quilts and home-baked cookies, but where else can you rent a cat to take to your room? Dating back to the mid-1800s, this is the oldest country inn in Minnesota and its filled with antiques and memorabilia.

Grand Old Mansion. *501 Clay St., Mantorville; 507-653-3231* **$**
A 1899 restored Victorian with antiques, a large doll collection, private baths, and a full breakfast.

Historic Jail House Inn. *109 Houston 3 NW., Preston (24 miles southeast of Rochester); 507-765-2181* **$$ - $$$**
Formerly the Fillmore Country Jail, this 12-room inn has undergone extensive renovation to the point guests would hardly suspect its earlier incarnation (unless they stayed in the Cell Block Room, where the bars are still intact). The rooms are sunny and comfortable.

Root River Valley *map E-3*
Lanesboro, Wykoff

■ **RESTAURANTS & LODGING**

Carrolton Country Inn. *RR 2; Lanesboro; 507-467-2257* **$$**
Nine guest rooms in a 100-year-old farmhouse. Guests prepare their own breakfast each morning, then spend the day exploring the surrounding valley.

Historic Wykoff Jail Haus. *Wykoff, 507-352-4205* **$-$$**
Kids who stay here love to tell their friends that they slept behind bars on vacation. One "cell" of this two-room jailhouse (now comfy B&B) is still out-

fitted with the original bunk beds. (The other room has a nice double bed and pretty antiques.) Breakfast, fortunately, is standard regional fare.

Mrs. B's Historic Lanesboro Inn and Restaurant. *101 Parkway;, Lanesboro; 507-467-2154, 800-657-4710.*
Best known for five-course dinners ($$$) prepared with local ingredients. Reservations only. The intimate and popular bed-and-breakfast ($ - $$) is situated in a limestone building on the banks of the Root River, in one of the loveliest valleys and towns in Minnesota.

St. Croix River Towns *map D-3*
Afton, Bayport, Marine on Rush City, St. Croix, Stillwater

■ RESTAURANTS

Bayport Cookery. *328 Fifth Ave. N. (US 95), Bayport; 651-430-1066* $$$
Features a prix fixe menu, which is often extraordinary, in an intimate storefront.

Dock Cafe. *425 Nelson Ave. E. (Main St.), Stillwater; 651-430-3770* $- $$
A casual, lovely spot on the St. Croix River offering standard American fare. Dine on the patio in summer to take in the best views around.

Grant House Cafe. *80 W. Fourth St., Rush City; 320-358-3661* $
1940s style decor and simple dinners, good in the "home cooking" sort of way.

Lowell Inn. *102 N. Second St., Stillwater; 651-439-1100* $$$
An impressive old hotel in a colonial style, on the bank of the St. Croix River, the Lowell Inn is perhaps *the* place in the area for special occasion dining. An indoor trout pool is fed by springs that run from the hillside on which the hotel sits. Not surprisingly, the restaurant is known for its brook trout.

■ LODGING

Afton House. *3291 S. St. Croix Trail, Afton; 651-436 8883* $$
An 1867 country inn situated a short walk from the a picturesque waterfront on the river. The small historic district of town makes for pleasant walking. The restaurant ($$) specializes in seafood.

Ann Bean Mansion. *319 W. Pine St., Stillwater; 651-430-0355* $$$
A spacious mansion (11-foot ceilings) built by a lumberman in 1878, this inn has its original oak woodwork and is furnished with plenty of antiques. All five large rooms have private baths.

Asa Parker House. *17500 N. St. Croix Trail, Marine on St. Croix; 651-433-5248* $$$
Situated in one of the quaintest villages along the St. Croix, this 1856 house provides historic accommodations and a renowned breakfast. You can even take a canoe for a paddle on the national Wild and Scenic River at your doorstep.

FOOD & LODGING

St. Paul *map D-3*

■ RESTAURANTS

À la Française. *823 University Ave.;*
651-291-2661 $
Another highly recommended Viet-namese restaurant in St. Paul's increasingly Asian neighborhood. À la Française provides a huge menu of seafood, chicken, beef, pork, and vegetarian dishes. Big portions in an informal setting. French-style bakery inside the restaurant.

The Barbary Fig. *720 Grand Ave.;*
651- 290-2085 $$
An informal spot with spicy North African cuisine and outdoor dining in summer, the Barbary Fig is one of the many reasons Grand Avenue is as appealing as it is. Try the vegetarian couscous or fish and eggplant dishes.

Cafe Latte. *850 Grand Ave.; 651-224-5687*
$
This stylish cafeteria along the busiest stretch of Grand Avenue provides a full range of meals, but it's best at serving up dessert—especially anything chocolate.

Cafe Minnesota. *345 W. Kellogg Blvd.;*
651-297-4097 $
Situated in the monumental and artistic Minnesota History Center, this isn't your typical museum-cafe. Innovative entrees, served cafeteria-style, include many vegetarian choices.

Caravan Serai. *2175 Ford Pkwy.;*
651-690-1935 $ - $$
Recline on carpet and pillows and dine on lamb or tandoori chicken in the relaxing middle ground between sitting and reclining. Besides wonderful Middle Eastern food, the Caravan Serai offers music and dancers on occasion.

Carol's Calico Kitchen. *9100 N. Highway Dr. (Lexington); 651-786-7477* $$
Carol's look like a small-town cafe, but this one actually delivers on the promise of home cooking, from hamburgers on homemade buns to cream pies with flaky crusts.

Cossetta's Italian Market and Pizzeria.
211 W. Seventh St.; 651-222-3476 $
Worth a visit for the smell alone. Stop for pizza, pasta, salads, or sandwiches or to pick up Italian meats, olives, cheeses, sauces, and other groceries for dinner at a friend's.

Dakota Bar and Grill. *1021 E. Bandana Blvd.; 651-642-1442* $$ - $$$
Good food in one of the area's best-known jazz clubs, in Bandana Square, a converted railroad yard building. Fish is always changing and always tasty. The Dakota has one of the best Caesar salads around.

Dixie's on Grand. *695 Grand Ave.;*
651-222-7345 $ - $$
Southern and some Caribbean specialties such as chicken-fried steak and black-bean soup with a lively bar on Grand Avenue.

Fabulous Fern's Bar and Grill. *400 Selby Ave.; 651-225-9414* **$$**
A casual place fronting the historic and refurbished portion of Selby Avenue (near the cathedral), Fern's does a wonderful job on its daily fish specials. Also good is the Southwestern flank steak.

Forepaugh's. *276 S. Exchange St.; 651-224-5606* **$$ - $$$**
French specialties in a converted mansion in historic Irvine Park. The house retains its many rooms, so the atmosphere is cozy and intimate even when busy—which is usually.

Gallivan's. *354 N. Wabasha St.; 651-227-6688* **$$**
Steak, prime rib, and seafood in a downtown location. The decor, heavy on the wood, is traditional and relaxing.

Keys. *767 Raymond Ave.; 651-646-5756* **$**
The number of regulars here testifies to the good food, big helpings, and convivial (and often crowded) surroundings. A great place for breakfast, if your arteries can stand big pancakes drenched in butter, and spicy Italian hash.

Khyber Pass Cafe. *1399 St. Clair Ave.; 651-698-5403* **$ - $$**
Authentic Afghan food, good lamb and vegetarian dishes. The setting is informal, with a touch of Middle Eastern decor in a quiet residential district.

La Cucaracha Mexican Restaurant. *36 S. Dale (Grand); 651-221-9682* **$ - $$**
Mexican food—what else?—in an informal setting, with a cozy bar. Try the chicken mole and a Negra Modelo beer.

The Lagoon Restaurant. *540 Rice St.; 651-292-1351* **$**
One of many good, cheap Vietnamese restaurants along or near University Avenue and the State Capitol. Try the hot and spicy mock duck.

Lake Elmo Inn. *3442 Lake Elmo Ave. N., Lake Elmo; 651-777-8495* **$$**
Built in 1881 as a hotel and stage stop, the Lake Elmo Inn retains the atmosphere of a country inn. It's popular for special occasions. The menu, including the dessert list, is extensive. Especially good are the lamb and roast duckling.

Leeann Chin Chinese Cuisine. *214 E. Fourth St.; 651-224-8814* **$$**
Cantonese, Mandarin, and Szechwan food, in the old Union Depot downtown.

Lexington. *1096 Grand Ave.; 651-222-5878* **$$ - $$$**
More formal than most Grand Avenue restaurants, the Lexington is a white linen kind of place serving traditional American dishes, such as steak, prime rib and seafood. It does offer a few offbeat choices, such as chicken fettuccini rosa or Asian-inspired appetizers.

Lindey's Prime Steak House. *3610 Snelling Ave. N.; 651-633-9813* **$$$**
Don't even think of visiting this odd little throwback to the '50s unless you love steak, because that's all they serve—large, sumptuous steaks, potatoes, and a rather minimal salad (who, after all, would go out to eat lettuce?). The restaurant occupies a sort of sprawling

FOOD & LODGING

rambler, finished in knotty pine, set in a wooded neighborhood in Arden Hills, just north of St. Paul.

Mancini's Char House. *531 W. Seventh St.; 651-224-7345* $$ - $$$
An old-fashioned nightclub and steak house, perfectly at home in this old Italian neighborhood. Try steak or lobster.

Mi Tierra. *175 Concord St.; no phone* $
One of the best of the many small family-owned Mexican restaurants on St. Paul's West Side: simple, traditional dishes such as burritos and enchiladas in authentic style, with excellent fresh salsa and cilantro on the side. It's a fun visit on Cinco de Mayo.

Moscow on the Hill. *371 Selby Ave.; 651-291-1236* $$
Authentic Russian food and drink in an intimate bar on historic Ramsey Hill. Live Russian music on the weekends.

Muffuletta. *2260 Como Ave.; 651-644-9116* $$
Varied menu from French to Italian in a pleasant neighborhood and relaxing decor. Move outdoors during the summer. The sumptuous Sunday brunch is popular.

No Wake Cafe. *Harriet Island; 651-292-1411* $$
This delightful cafe, a mainstay of the St. Paul riverfront and known for delicious soups, breads, and regional favorites such as wild rice dishes, has moved on board a 1946 tugboat.

Pazzaluna. *360 St. Peter St.; 651-223-7000* $$$
Specializing in regional Italian seafood, steak, veal, gnocchi and deserts, Pazzaluna is a good choice after an evening at the Ordway Music Theatre—but make reservations first.

Ristorante Luci. *470 Cleveland Ave. S.; 651-699-8258* $$
Superb Italian pastas and regional dishes in a sparse, small—and very busy—cafe. Save room for one of the fruit tarts.

Ruam Mit Thai. *475 St. Peter St.; 651-290-0067* $$
Hot Thai curries and other flavorful sauces in a cozy downtown setting. Recommendations include the toam yum soup and roast duck curry.

Saint Paul Grill. *St. Paul Hotel, 350 Market St.; 651-224-7455* $$$
Long regarded as the most elegant dining room in all of St. Paul, with high-backed booths, window seats, and a lovely view of Rice Park. Recommended: steaks, grilled chicken breast, fish.

Saji-Ya. *695 Grand Ave.; 651-292-0444* $$
A favorite St. Paul hangout for sushi fans, the Saji-Ya also provides Japanese atmosphere, including teppanyaki cooking at your table on some evenings.

Sakura Restaurant and Sushi Bar. *350 St. Peter St.; 651-224-0185* $$$
Cozy up around the sushi bar or sit around the low dining tables traditional in Japan for dinner. The sushi is fresh

and surprising in its variety. For dinner, try any of the seafood or the beef.

Table of Contents. *1648 Grand Ave.; 651-699-6595* **$$**

Here's an unusual idea: The Hungry Mind bookstore to feed your mind, adjoining the Table of Contents restaurant to nourish your body. The menu is creative and varies. Try the fish specials or the thin-crust pizzas.

Taste of Thailand. *1671 Selby Ave.; 651-644-3997* **$-$$**

The surroundings are as nondescript and humble as they come, but the food really stands out. Try the spring rolls, chicken pad pak, and pad thai. The sauces are tangy but not too fiery.

W. A. Frost & Company. *374 Selby Ave.; 651-224-5715* **$$**

Elegant setting in an elegant neighborhood where F. Scott Fitzgerald brushed up against St. Paul's wealth. Specialties include chocolate silk pies. W. A. Frost is at its best in summer, with dining on the lush patio. But outdoor tables are at a premium. Eat early or late or be prepared to wait.

■ **LODGING**

Covington Inn. *Harriet Island; 651-292-1411* **$-$$$**

Housed on a 1946 tugboat, the new Covington Inn is a floating bed and breakfast. The Harriet Island location, though worlds apart from downtown in atmosphere, is just a 5-minute drive away. Adjacent to the wonderful **No-Wake Cafe.**

Embassy Suites. *175 E. 10th St.; 651-224-5400* **$$$**

Embassy attempts the impossible—to bring a Mediterranean atmosphere (and climate, one hopes) to downtown St. Paul. The atrium of the hotel is decorated with tropical plants, waterfalls, and Spanish tile. Guests can use the indoor pool, whirlpool, and sauna.

Saint Paul Hotel. *350 Market St.; 800-292-9292* **$$ - $$$**

Overlooking Rice Park, one of the prettiest settings in downtown, the stylish St. Paul Grill and Hotel provides perhaps the city's best lodging and food.

S a n b o r n   *map E-2*

■ **LODGING**

McCone Sod House Bed and Breakfast. *12598 Magnolia Ave.; 507-723-5138* **$$**

Get a hint of what it meant to be a pioneer on the prairie by staying overnight in a re-creation of the sod house built by early white settlers. Take the experience a step further by dressing in period costume and reading at night by oil lamps.

FOOD & LODGING

Voyageurs National Park *map A-2*

■ RESTAURANTS & LODGING

Kettle Falls Hotel and Resort.
Voyageurs National Park; 888-KF-HOTEL,
218-875-2070 $ - $$$

This historic hotel is lovingly called the "Tiltin' Hilton" because of the sloping floor in the famous LumberJack Saloon. The rooms retain their rustic charm with antique washstands and shared baths. Family style dining features local walleye and wild rice. You can dine out on the hotel's wrap-around porch in summer. Winter access to the hotel is by snowmobile or ski plane only.

Ludlow's Island Lodge. *Catch boat to island at 3 miles north on County 24; 3 miles east on County 78; 2 miles east on County 540; 218-666-5407* $$$ (weekly)

This resort and conference center is located on an island and two adjacent beaches in Lake Vermilion. Cabins, tucked into woods of birch and pine, have fireplaces, decks, and wood interiors. Tennis, marina, private beaches, supervised children's activities.

Nelson's Resort. *7632 Nelson Rd., Crane Lake; 218-993-2295* $$

The resort, on Crane Lake, provides access by boat to the large lakes and islands of Voyageurs National Park. The restaurant menu includes homebaked bread and pastries. The resort rents or provides boats, canoes, a naturalist program, bicycles, sauna, and a private beach.

■ GENERAL INFORMATION NUMBERS

Minnesota Department of Natural Resources.
651-296-6157 or 888-646-6367; camping reservations: 800-246-2267
www.dnr.state.mn.us

Minnesota Office of Tourism.
651-296-5029 or 800-657-3700;
www.exploreminnesota.com

Greater Minneapolis Convention and Visitors Association.
612-661-4700; www.minneapolis.org

St. Paul Convention and Visitors Bureau.
800- 627-6101; www.stpaulcvb.org

Minnesota Historical Society.
www.mnhs.org

National Park Service. www.nps.gov

■ FESTIVALS & EVENTS

Minnesotans put on hundreds of festivals, fairs, and similar events during the year. The following are some of the better known or more unusual. For a more complete listing, call the Minnesota Office of Tourism 651-296-5029 or 800-657-3700 for the current Minnesota Explorer, which contains a calendar of events.

■ JANUARY

Duluth: John Beargrease Sled Dog Marathon. 500-mile dogsled race up the North Shore and back. *800-4-DULUTH*

St. Paul: Winter Carnival. Parades, sports events, and other festivities in St. Paul's traditional city festival. *651-223-4700.*

■ FEBRUARY

Mora: Vasaloppet Cross-Country Ski Race. A long-standing and popular marathon ski race. *800-368-6672*

New Ulm: Fasching. A traditional German festival of food and music, the Saturday before Ash Wednesday. *507-354-8850*

Walker: International Eelpout Festival. A fishing tournament and other shenanigans honoring Minnesota's ugliest and most reviled fish. *800-833-1118*

■ MARCH

Finland: St. Urho's Day. A faux-Finnish festival celebrating the day St. Urho drove the grasshoppers out of Finland. Official color purple. Sound familiar? *218-353-7359*

St. Paul: St. Patrick's Day Parade. A big parade in the more Irish of the Twin Cities. *651-292-3225*

Winona and Wabasha: Eagle Watch. Bald eagles gather by the dozens along the Mississippi River during the winter. These river towns respond with tours and other activities for eagle watchers.

■ APRIL

Hibbing: Last Chance Curling Bonspiel. For those of you who couldn't get enough of curling during the winter season. *800-444-2244*

■ MAY

St. Paul: Cinco de Mayo. Traditional Mexican celebration on the West Side, the heart of St. Paul's Latino population. *612-222-6347*

St. Paul: Macalester College Scottish Country Fair. Traditional Scottish games, food, and music (Warning: There will be bagpipes!) *612-696-6239*

■ JUNE

Duluth: Grandma's Marathon. One of the state's most popular marathons run along the shore of Lake Superior. *800-438-5884*

Redwood Falls: Minnesota Inventors Congress. Exhibits of inventions of all kinds by adults and students, with food, arts and crafts. *800-468-3681*

St. Paul: Grand Old Days. Parade and plenty to eat along convivial Grand Avenue. *612-224-0486*

■ JULY

Bemidji: Paul Bunyan Water Carnival.
Water show, parade, concert, fireworks
near or on the lake. *612-297-6899*

Chisholm: Minnesota Ethnic Days. Festival at Ironworld celebrating the diversity
of Minnesota's Iron Range with food,
music, and crafts. *800-372-6437*

Minneapolis: Minneapolis Aquatennial.
Parades, sports events, and other entertainment in the city's traditional midsummer festival. *612-331-8371*

St. Paul: Taste of Minnesota. Several-day
Fourth of July extravaganza on the State
Capitol mall, with free bands, food, and
fireworks. *612-297-6899*

**Walnut Grove: Laura Ingalls Wilder
Pageant.** This event tells the story of the
Ingalls family and their life on the
prairie during the late 1800s, from the
eyes of the author of the "Little House"
books. *507-859-2174*

■ AUGUST

Detroit Lakes: WE Country Music Festival.
Big-name country groups perform for
thousands in a weekend-long outdoor
concert. *800-542-3992*

Duluth: Bayfront Blues Festival. Big-name
blues bands have made this concert exceptionally popular. *800-438-5884*

Grand Rapids: Tall Timber Days. A test of
lumberjack skills, with ax throwing, log
rolling, log chopping, pole climbing —
and a big parade as well. *800-355-9740*

Minneapolis: Uptown Art Fair. Crowds of
up to 250,000 gather in Uptown for this
street exhibition of arts and crafts.

St. Paul: Minnesota State Fair. More than
a million visitors join in during a 12-day
traditional state fair, which lasts through
Labor Day. *612-642-2200*

Shakopee: Renaissance Festival. Seven
weekends of food, games, crafts, and entertainment with a 16th-century theme.
612-445-7361 or 800-966-8215

Zimmerman: Bluegrass Festival. Outdoor
weekend concert. *612-856-9998*

■ SEPTEMBER

Cambridge: Potato Festival. Potato performers, games, potato carving and
recipes, potato exhibit, and potato print
art work. *612-689-4229*

**Eveleth: Iron Range Snowmobile Grass
Drags.** Snowmobile drag racing on grass
on the Sunday of Labor Day Weekend.
218-744-1940

Mora: Kanabec Fall Festival. Artists,
games, storytelling, food, and entertainment. *320-697-1665*

New Prague: Dozinky Harvest Festival.
Czechoslovakian and German foods,
music, arts, crafts, and entertainment.
612-758-4360

Northfield: Defeat of Jesse James Days. A
re-enactment of the James gang raid and
defeat. But it's better now with a parade,
arts fair, rodeo, and no live ammunition.
507-645-5604

**Rollag: Western Minnesota Stream
Threshers Reunion.** One of the largest
threshing bees in the country, honoring
the traditional process of separating the
grain from the straw. *701-232-4404*

■ OCTOBER

Albert Lea: Big Island Rendezvous and Festival. A re-enactment of a fur-trade-era rendezvous, with costumes, music, and food. *507-373-3938*

Minneapolis-St. Paul: Twin Cities Marathon. Twenty-six mile route follows some of the most scenic avenues and neighborhoods in the two cities. *612-673-0778*

New Ulm: Oktoberfest. German music, dance, food, and drink in this traditional festival. *507-354-4217*

■ NOVEMBER

Minneapolis: Two Rivers Art Expo. Juried exhibition and sale of arts and crafts, with children's activities, food, and music. *612-348-7000*

Shakopee: Autumn Festival. Artists and crafters from across the country gather in 19th-century costumes; food and entertainment. *402-331-2889*

■ DECEMBER

Minneapolis: Holidazzle Parade. Evening parades down Nicollet Mall in downtown. *612-338-3807*

Taylors Falls: Lighting Festival. Lighting of the village, with horse-drawn hay rides, craft fair, and winter walks. *612-465-3125*

Winona: Swan Watch. Bus tour to Weaver Bottoms on the Mississippi to view thousands of migrating tundra swans, in conjunction with a wildlife art show and sale. *507-452-2272*

■ THE GREAT OUTDOORS

■ CANOEING & KAYAKING

What better place to paddle a canoe or kayak than the Land of 10,000 Lakes? Check the Minnesota Office of Tourism and Department of Natural Resources 888-646-6367 or 651-296-6157; check online at www.dnr.state.mn.us for names of outfitters. The DNR can provide maps and other information about these and other river trips.

■ GOLF

Golf has become one of Minnesota's most popular outdoor sports, with more than 450 public and resort courses, including scores of new courses in recent years. The golf explosion perhaps has perhaps been most dramatic in the resort area surrounding Brainerd in north-central Minnesota, where the golf holes—465 of them—now outnumber the lakes. Courses have been carved from the woodlands by some of golf's top designers, such as the Legacy Courses at Cragun's Golf Resort, designed by Robert Trent Jones Jr., and Deacon's Lodge, by Arnold Palmer. But the golf boom has affected the rest of the state as well, with new courses appearing on the prairies in southern Minnesota, woodlands near the Twin Cities, and the North Shore of Lake Superior. For a directory of more than 70 public and semi-private courses in the state, contact the Minnesota Office of Tourism, or check its website for even more listings.

MINNEAPOLIS MUSIC

Minneapolis still likes to think of itself as an oasis of cool in the artistically staid steppes of the upper Midwest. Certainly the city's visual arts, theater and filmmaking action could justify its denizens' unwavering self-perception as much more than a cold Omaha. But the backbone of the area's counterculture remains the music scene.

No doubt Minnesota has something fundamentally tuneful going for it: the state has produced the painterly intensity of Bob Dylan, the drunken brilliance of the Replacements, the twisted but undeniable genius of ⚥, and the Trashmen, a '60s surf band with a major cult following.

And despite Minnesota's unremitting whiteness, black music has long supplied the local music scene with heaps of vitality. As Prince, ⚥ was hands-down the chief architect and proprietor of Minneapolis' rocking soul sound, but just as significant over the long haul has been the work of Jimmy Jam Harris and Terry Lewis, former members of Prince protégés the Time, now proprietors of the area's hit-making Flyte Tyme Productions studio. The likes of Janet Jackson and Mariah Carey come here seeking the Jam-and-Lewis team's platinum touch, though their efforts remain almost exclusively invisible, tucked away in their area studio.

Minneapolis hasn't been *the* hot spot for music since the mid-'80s, but the city's music community has never lost either its extraordinary vitality or its down-to-earth attitude. Radio-rocking power-pop stars Semisonic are the area's latest hitmakers, but a plethora of less nationally renowned acts populate a decidedly humming scene. It's one dominated by earnest, honest rock bands that write their own songs, though eclectic jazz-international-funk hybrids show up, and a for-real hip hop crowd—ostensibly led by the perfectly populist Rhyme Sayers Syndicate—has emerged in recent years. Indeed, smart, hard-working bands pop up everywhere like weeds through spring snow; small labels and independent record stores survive (if not thrive); and a wonderful variety of venues serve up live music 24-7-52—well, almost.

The still-beating heart of the music community remains **First Avenue,** as reliably well run, innovative, and vibrant as ever. A big old bus depot in the middle of downtown, the club is really a two-for-one deal: its annex is the **Seventh Street Entry,** a hole-in-the-wall that started hosting underground bands back when hardcore and punk were new—the first time. Between the two of them, First Avenue and the Entry regularly offer 30-odd jazz, blues, international, but mostly rock bands each week. *701 First Ave. N.; 612-338-8388.*

The **400 Bar,** located in the heart of the earthy-crunchy West Bank, is another venerable venue. Its regular crowd of foreign university students gives way to grungers some nights, neo-hippies on others, and longtime devotees of the local folk scene about once a week. *400 Cedar Ave.; 612-332-2903.* Close by, the low-key **Cedar**

Cultural Center is a P.C. (no smoking/no alcohol) kind of place that's intriguingly if infrequently booked. *416 Cedar Ave.; 612-338-2674.* Five blocks up Cedar, the **Cabooze** is a sturdy old biker blues bar that's become the reggae and Phish crowd's territory. *917 Cedar Ave.; 612-338-6425.* **The Quest** is hosting an increasing number of national acts. *110 Fifth St. N.; 612-338-3383.*

Other smaller venues have burgeoned in recent years, filling various niches and garnering their own loyal subjects. Places like the venerable faux-wood-paneled **Lee's Liquor Bar**, *101 Glenwood Ave., 612-338-9491,* and the **Foxfire Coffee Lounge**, *319 First Ave. N.,* both downtown; the **Terminal Bar** in near northeast Minneapolis, *409 E. Hennepin Ave.; 612-623-4545;* the **Turf Club** in St. Paul, *1601 University Ave.; 651-647-0486;* and the **Blue Nile** in South Minneapolis, *2027 Franklin Ave.; 612-338-3000,* among others, have added their flavors to the melange that makes Minnesota extra musically tasty.

Finding interesting live rock music at night in downtown St. Paul—hell, finding live *humans* at night in downtown St. Paul—is more than a challenge. The thing the elder twin does have going for it is a small but resilient jazz club called the **Dakota**— a classy, expensive host to locals and a steady stream of big-name players willing to venture north—in slightly out-of-the-way Bandana Square, *1021 E. Bandana Blvd.; 651-642-1442.* There's also the new local-music-history-themed **Minnesota Music Cafe**, *East Side St. Paul, 449 Payne Ave.; 651-776-4699,* and scruffy, fun Turf Club.

If you visit the Twin Cities in summer, you'll catch the indie music scene in full post-spring-thaw tilt. Walker Art Center sponsors a low-key, grassy Monday night series of music and movies in **Loring Park.** *Call 612-332-1617.* **Cedarfest,** in August on the West Bank, is a packed, joyous outdoor gathering featuring buckets of hip acts from near and far; and the **Mill City Music Fest** is a multi-day, multi-stage blowout that takes over Minneapolis' Warehouse District for Labor Day Weekend.

For a break from the music, you might wander down the eclectic row of bars on the West Bank:—Red Sea, the 400 Bar, Five Corners Blues Saloon, *501 Cedar Ave.,* Whiskey Junction, *901 Cedar Ave.,* and the Cabooze are within a mile of each other along Cedar. Or head over to South Minneapolis to visit the genuinely hip **Bryant-Lake Bowl**—if there isn't something uniquely, pleasing wacky going on in the theater (as there is more often than not) you can always drink expensive, delicious beer and throw a few games. *810 W. Lake St.; 612-825-8949.*

The Minneapolis/St. Paul music scene is hardly fickle as some, but the moods of the moment are nonetheless best accessed through the periodicals that track it. *City Pages,* the stalwart Wednesday weekly, has listings of everything, and the dominant daily *Star Tribune* manages a spot of hipness with its Friday "Free Time" section.

—Michael Welch

RECOMMENDED READING

Breining, Greg. *Fishing Minnesota.* 1993. Anecdotes and advice for catching most any kind of fish in Minnesota's lakes and streams.

Breining, Greg. *Paddling Minnesota.* 1999. Descriptions and maps for 125 canoe and kayak trips around the state.

DeGroot, Barbara, and Jack El-Hai. *The Insiders' Guide to the Twin Cities.* The Insiders' Guides Inc. (Manteo, NC) and Saint Paul Pioneer Press (St. Paul), 1995.

Densmore, Frances. *Chippewa Customs.* St. Paul: Minnesota Historical Society Press, 1979. Densmore wrote the classic study of the society, economy, arts, and spiritual beliefs of the Ojibway from time she spent with these people in the early 20th century.

Dunn, James Taylor. *The St. Croix: Midwest Border River.* St. Paul: Minnesota Historical Society Press, 1979 (reprint ed.). Dunn wrote the definitive history of settlement and logging in the St. Croix River valley.

Gruchow, Paul. *Journal of a Prairie Year.* Minneapolis: University of Minnesota Press, 1985. Stories and facts about the tallgrass prairie that once covered southern and western Minnesota.

Hampl, Patricia. *A Romantic Education.* Boston: Houghton Mifflin Company, 1981. A St. Paul woman comes to a truer understanding of her home by traveling to her Czeckoslavakia homeland. This memoir includes rich and telling portraits of St. Paul.

Keillor, Garrison. *Lake Wobegon Days.* New York: Viking Penguin, 1985. Keillor's unforgettable small-town characters provide the insight and gentle humor without Sinclair Lewis's sharp bite—set in the mythic Minnesota town that time forgot.

Lass, William E. *Minnesota: A History.* New York: W. W. Norton & Company, 1983. A concise and readable overview of the state's history.

Leschak, Peter M. *Letters from Side Lake: A Chronicle of Life in the North Woods.* Minneapolis: University of Minnesota Press, 1992. A humorous and descriptive account of building a log home and making a place in the north woods community.

Lewis, Sinclair. *Main Street.* New York: Harcourt, Brace, & World, Inc., 1920. Meet Carol Kennicott, the Lewis protagonist who leads us on a satirical examination of the pettiness and smuggness typical of small town life in early Minnesota. *Babbitt.* New York: Harcourt, Brace, & World, Inc., 1922: Minnesota's Nobel Prize-winning satirist introduces us to George F. Babbitt, of Zenith City, whose smug narrowmindedness, uninformed opinions, and soulless sentimentality defines babbittry.

Madson, John. *Where the Sky Began: Land of the Tallgrass Prairie.* Boston: Houghton Mifflin, 1982. Madson, in his literate and colorful way, describes the tallgrass prairie, landscape that once covered southwestern Minnesota and much of the Midwest. *Up on the River.* New York: Nick Lyons Books, 1985. The inimitable Madson presents a portrait of the upper Mississippi River.

Meier, Peg. *Bring Warm Clothes.* Minneapolis: Neighbors Publishing, 1981. *Too Hot, Went to Lake.* Minneapolis: Neighbors Publishing, 1993. Two books loaded with a charming, often humorous collection of photographs from Minnesota's past.

Mohr, Howard. *How to Talk Minnesotan.* New York: Penguin Books, 1987. Follow this hilarious tour of the idiosyncrasies of Minnesota speech, mannerisms, attitudes, and habits. It sure beats some of that other stuff you could read. You bet.

Northrup, Jim, *Walking the Rez Road.* Stillwater: Voyageur Press, 1993. Through poetry and short fiction, centering on his protagonist Luke Warmwater, Northrup provides an often humorous account of life on northern Minnesota's Fond du Lac Reservation.

Nute, Grace Lee. *The Voyageurs' Highway.* St. Paul: Minnesota Historical Society, 1969. The classic description of the fur trade that led to the European exploration and settlement of northern Minnesota and southern Canada.

Ojakangas, Richard W., and Charles L. Matsch. *Minnesota's Geology.* Minneapolis: University of Minnesota Press, 1982. The virtues of this volume include clear explanations and plenty of photographs of places to visit.

Olson, Sigurd. *The Singing Wilderness.* New York: Alfred A. Knopf, 1956. Olson remains the unsurpassable chronicler of Minnesota's northern wilderness.

Pond, Samuel W. *The Dakota or Sioux in Minnesota as They Were in 1834.* St. Paul: Minnesota Historical Society Press, 1986. Though not a scholarly description of Minnesota's Indians, Pond's is certainly readable, interesting, and wonderfully insightful.

Rölvaag, O. E. *Giants in the Earth.* New York: Harper & Row, 1927. Per Hansa and his family cross the prairies of Minnesota to settle in South Dakota. This is a classic story of the struggle of humans against an unfamiliar nature, and husband against wife.

Waters, Thomas F. *The Streams and Rivers of Minnesota.* Minneapolis: University of Minnesota Press, 1977. Watershed by watershed, Waters describes the landscape of Minnesota. Along the way, he conveys plenty of interesting and useful information—from history to the location of good stream fishing.

Wilder, Laura Ingalls. *On the Banks of Plum Creek.* New York: Harper & Row, 1937. One of several "Little House" books, this tells the story of the pioneer family in southern Minnesota.

WPA Guide to Minnesota, 1938. St. Paul: Minnesota Historical Society Press, 1985. a reissue of a classic guide to Minnesota, produced by the Federal Writers' Project during the Depression. The information is date, of course, but that's half the fun. Much of the information and characterizations of the state are as interesting and relevant as ever.

I N D E X

accommodations 314-332
Aerial Lift Bridge, Duluth 229-230
Afton 207, 328; Afton State Park 207
Agassiz National Wildlife Refuge 281
Akeley 292
Albert Lea 132, 315
Alexandria 305, 315
American Swedish Institute 192-193
Amish 118, *120*
Anderson House Hotel, Wabasha 114, *117*, 326
Angel Hill Historic District 211
Arches Museum of Pioneer Life 116
Ard Godfrey House 184
area codes 312
Arrowhead Bluffs Museum 114
Arrowhead Trail, Hovland 249
Assumption Catholic Church 162
August Schell Brewing Company, New Ulm 72
Aurora 268-269
Austin 132
Avenue of the Pines 289

Bandana Square 175
Banning State Park 222
Baptism River 242
Barn Bluff, Red Wing 106
Basilica of St. Mary 190, *193*
Battle Creek Park 153
Battle of Wood Lake 74
Baudette 278
Bayport 207, 327
Beargrease Sled Dog Marathon 242, *280*
Beaver Bay 241
Beaver Creek Valley State Park 118, 122

Becker County Historical Society Museum 310
Bell Museum of Natural History 196
Beltrami, Giacomo Constantino 283
Bemidji 287, 315; state park 287
Big Stone Lake 66
bird watching 110, 111, 124, 132, 201, 289, 294
Blackduck 279
Blandin Paper Comany 293
Blue Earth County Heritage Center, Mankato 71
Blue Mounds State Park 81-*82*
Bluestem Prairie Preserve 65, 92
Bornemann House, St. Peter 71
Boundary Water Canoe Area Wilderness 255-260
Brainerd 295-297, 316
Bronko Nagurski Museum 261
Brooklyn Park Historical Farm 201
Brown County Historical Museum 72
Brownsville 118
Brule River 248
buffalo *62, 82*
Buffalo River State Park 92
Bunker Hills Regional Park, Anoka County 200
Burlington Bay 237
Butterwort Cliffs Scientific and Natural Area 246

Caledonia 118
Calumet Inn, Pipestone 80, *81, 324*
Calvary Episcopal Church 84
Camden State Park 78
Camp Rabideau 289
Canal Park, Duluth 229

Cannon Falls 105, 106
Cannon River Valley 105
canoeing 98, 105, 126, 204, 210, 214, 215, 222, 226, 255, 257, 300; outfitters 336
Carleton 127
Carleton Peak 245
Carley State Park 123
Carlos Avery State Wildlife Mangement Area 201
Carpenter St. Croix Valley Nature Center 206-207
Carver, Jonathan 140-142, 283
Cascade Lodge 318
Cascade River State Park 246
Cass Lake 289-290
Cass, Lewis 283
Castle Danger 239
Cathedral of St. Paul 170-*173*
Catlin, George 78-79, 101
Cedar Creek Natural History Area 201
Central School History Center, Grand Rapids 292
Cherokee Park, St. Paul 167
Children's Theater, Minneapolis 192
Chippewa City 247
Chippewa National Forest 289-291
Chisholm 271
City Hall and Courthouse, St. Paul 164
Civil War 41-42
climate 18-20, 58, 157, 312
Como Park, St. Paul..175
Concord St., St. Paul.. 167
Concordia College 92
Conly Sod Castle, Jasper *80*
Cook 314
Cook County Museum 247
Coteau des Prairies 78
Coulee Country 117-118

Crane Lake 314, 332
Crocus Hill, St. Paul 174
Crookston 92
Croft Mine Historical Park 294
Crosby House, Duluth 233
Crosby Manitou State Park 243
Cross River 243, 245
Crow Wing Country Historical
  Society Museum 296
Crow Wing River 297
Cut Foot Sioux Trail 289
Cuyuna Country Recreation Area
  294
Cuyuna Range 293-294

Dakota Indians 21-24, 27-29,
  30, 32-38, 66-67, 70, 78, 110,
  146; Dakota War 73-74
Deerwood, 314, 316
Defeat of Jesse James Days,
  Northfield 126
Democratic-Farmer-Labor Party
  (DFL) 51
Depot Museum, Duluth 232,
  237
Depot Square, Duluth 230, 232
Detroit Lakes 310, 317
Devil Track river canyons 247
DeWitt-Seitz Marketplace,
  Duluth 229
Dodge County Courthouse 125
Douglas State Trail 125
Driftwood Resort 297, 316
Duluth 227-235, 317-318

E. St. Julien Cox House, St. Peter
  71
E. S. Hoyt House, Red Wing 109
Eagle Mountain 245
Eastman, Seth 62
Echo Trail 257
Ed's Museum 120
Elba 123
Eli Wirtanen Farm 269
Eloise Butler Wildflower Garden
  and Bird Sanctuary 194

Embarrass 268, 317
Enger Tower 234
Erdrich, Louise 60
Eveleth 270, 281, 334

Faribault 127; Woolen Mill
  Company 127
Faribault, Jean Baptiste 152
Farmamerica, Waseca 131
Farmer's Market, St. Paul 166
farming 40, 57; diary 84
Featherstonhaugh, George W. 36,
  62
Fergus Falls 310
festivals and events 333-335
Finland 243, 333
Finnish Farmsteads 268
Finnish Heritage Homestead 268,
  317
Finntown Kaleva Hall, Virginia
  269
fishing 67, 78, 89, 98, 105, 123,
  126, 147, 149, 198, 199, 205,
  210, 211, 225, 277, 298
Fitger's on the Lake 233, 317
Fitzgerald, F. Scott 170; This Side
  of Paradise 174
Fleming Field 178
flour milling 51
Flying Cloud Airport 198
Folsom, Henry Carmen 211
food & lodging, by town 314-
  335; map 314
Forest History Center, Grand
  Rapids 292
Forest Resource Center 119
Forestville 120; Mystery Cave
  State Park 120
Forpaugh's, St. Paul 167, 329
Fort Belmont 83
Fort Ridgely 73, 74; State Park
  74
Fort Road, St. Paul 167-169
Fort Snelling State Park 147-148
Fort Snelling, 24, 35, 142-148,
  152, 156

Fountain 119
Freeborn County Historical
  Society Museum and Pioneer
  Village 132
French and Indian War 24, 32
Frontenac 110; State Park 110
fur trade 24, 30-33, 35-36

Gabbert Raptor Center 175
Galtier Plaza 165
Galtier, Father Lucian 156
Gammelgarden Museum, Scandia
  210
Garland, Judy 292
Gehry, Frank O. 186
geography 18-20,
geology 17-18
George H. Crosby Manitou State
  Park 243
Germans 49-50
Giants Ridge, Biwabik 269
Gibbs Farm Museum 175
Gilbert, Cass 160, 232, 271
Glacial Lakes 282-311; map 285
Glacial Lakes State Park 75, 77
Glacial Lake Agassiz 66, 88-89,
  98, 278
Glacial River Warren 66, 98, 141
Glendalough State Park 307
Glensheen 233-234
Goodhue County Courthouse
  109
Goodhue County Historical
  Museum 109
Goodhue, James Madison 39, 47-
  48, 204
Gooseberry Falls State Park 239-
  240
Gooseberry River 239
Governor's Residence, St. Paul
  174
Grand Avenue, St. Paul 174
Grand Marais 247, 318
Grand Mound 261-263
Grand Old Mansion, Mantorville
  125, 326

Grand Portage 250-253;
    Indian Reservation 252;
    National Monument 252;
    State Park 253
Grand Rapids 292-293
Grand Round, Minneapolis 194
Granite Falls 74, 75
Grant House, Rush City 215
grasslands 58-65
Great Lakes Aquarium 250
Green Giant Company 67, 70
Greysolon, Sieur Daniel Duluth
    24, 30-31, 227, 298
Gull Lake 316
Gunflint Trail 247, 318
Gustavus Adolphus College 71
Guthrie Theater 190

Hampl, Patricia   *A Romantic
    Education* 170
Hanley Falls 75
Harbor Museum 237
Harmony 118
Harriet Island 166-167
Hastings 104, 318
Hawk Ridge Nature Reserve 234
Hawkins Mine, Nashwauk 273
Hay Creek 122
Hay Lake School 210
Hayes Lake State Park 281
Heartland Trail 290
Hegman Lake 257
Helen Allison Savanna 201
Hennepin Avenue, Minneapolis
    190-191
Hennepin Parks 199
Hennepin, Father Louis 24, *30-
    31*, 116, *140*, 187, 283
Heritage Hall 92
Heritage Hjemkomst Interpretive
    Center, Moorhead 91
Heritage Village 110
Heron Lake Environmental
    Learning Center 83
Hibbing *272-273*
Hidden Falls-Crosby Farm
    Regional Park 152

High Bridge, St. Paul 167
Hill Annex State Park, Calumet
    273
Hill, James J. 45-46, 170-171,
    186
Hinckley Fire 216-220
Historic Orpheum Theatre,
    Minneapolis 190
Historic State Theatre,
    Minneapolis 190
Historic Wykoff Jail Haus 120,
    327
Homer 115
Honeywell 52
Hormel Museum 133
Houston 119
Houston County Museum
    Complex 118
Hubbard, Rensselaer D. 71
Hubbell House, Mantorville 125
Hubert H. Humphrey
    Metrodome 188
Hull-Rust-Mahoning 272
Humphery, Hubert 25

Indian Mounds Park   152
information numbers   332
Inspiration Peak 307
International Falls 261
International Wolf Center 257
Iron Range 263-273;
    driving tour 266-273
Ironwold USA 271
Irvine Park, St. Paul 167
Isle Royale 252
Itasca State Park 287;
Itasca County Museum 292

J. C. Hormel Nature Center 133
Jackson 83
James J. Hill House 172
Jay Cooke State Park 235
Jeffers Petroglyphs 85-87
Jenkins 316
Johannes Erickson Log House
    museums 210
John A. Latsch State Park 115

John Rose Minnesota Oval 200
Joseph R. Brown Wayside 74
Judge C. R. Magney State Park
    248
Julius C. Wilkie Steamboat Center
    115

Kabetogama Peninsula 261
Kadunce 247
Kandiyohi County Museum 75
Karpeles Manuscript Museum
    233
Keillor, Garrison
    Lake Wobegon Days 296
Kellogg Park 166
Kensington Runestone 305
Kettle Falls Hotel 261, 332
Kettle River 221-222
Kiesling House 72
Knife River 237

La Crescent 118
labor movement 51
Lac qui Parle Mission 75
Lac qui Parle Wildlife
    Management Area 75
Lake Bemidji State Park 287
Lake Benton 78
Lake Bronson State Park 94
Lake City 111
Lake Elmo Park Reserve 178
Lake Harriet 194-195
Lake Louise State Park 133
Lake Maria State Park 301
Lake Minnetonka 199
Lake of the Woods 274-277, 278
Lake Pepin 110-111
Lake Superior & Mississippi
    Railroad 234
Lake Superior 17-18, 28, 33, 52,
    103, **223-225**, *224, 231,*;
    Hiking Trail 237; Maritime
    Visitors Center 230; Railroad
    Museum 232, Zoological
    Gardens 234
Lake Vermillion 332
Landmark Center 162-*165*

Lanesboro 119, 327
Lass, William E. 35, 44, 47, 70,
   89, 143, 283-284, 286
Latch Island 115-116
Lawther Octagonal House,
   Red Wing 109
Le Sueur 67, 70; Museum 70
LeDuc-Simmons Mansion,
   Hastings 104
Leech Lake 289
Lester River 236
Leveaux Mountain 246
Lewis, Sinclair 227, 307;
   Main Street 302-305
Lilydale Regional Park 152
Lindburgh, Charles A. 25, 300-
   301
Little Crow, *43*-45
Little Falls 300-301
Livingston-Burbank-Griggs villa
   172
Lock and Dam 1 152
Lock and Dam 2 105
logging **38-39,** 129, 202-204,
   213, 236-237
Longyear Drill Site 269
Lowell Inn, Stillwater 209, 327
Lower Sioux Agency 73
Lucy Wilder Morris Park 187
Lumbertown USA, Gull Lake
   296
Lutsen Resort 246, 318
Lyndale Park Gardens 195

Mabel 118
Madson, John 58, 117;
   Where the Sky Began 94
Maiden Rock 110-111
Mall of America, Bloomington
   198
Manitou River 243
Mankato 65-66, 71-72
Mantorville 125, 326;
   Opera House 125
Maplewood State Park 308
maps Glacial Lakes 285; greater

Minneapolis / St. Paul; Histo-
   ry & Natural Features 19;
Minneapolis (downtown)
   188; Northern Reaches 276;
   North Shore and the Arrow-
   head 226; overview 11; Red
   River Valley 91; restaurants &
   lodging 314; St. Croix River
   Valley 205; St. Paul (down-
   town) 158; Southeast 97;
   Southwest 59
Marine on St. Croix 210, 328
Marshall 78
Marshall's Great River Vineyard
   111
Mauer Brothers Tavern, Elba 123
Mayo Clinic 25, 70, 123, *125*
Mayo, Dr. W. W. 70, 123, *124*
Mayowood, Rochester 124
McCarthy Beach State Park 273
McCone Sod House 83
McGrew, James *73*
Mears Park 165
Mendota 152
Merchants National Bank 115
Merriam Park, St. Paul 174-175
Mesabi Iron Range 25, 50-51,
   264-265, 270-272
metric conversions 312
Mickey's Diner 162
Mille Lacs 29, 45, 297-300
Mineral Springs Park 130
mining 263-273, 293-294
Minneapolis 31, **180-201;** down-
   town 188-191; food & lodg-
   ing 320-325; map 188;
   nightlife 322-323; parks
   194-195; public library and
   planetarium 190; suburbs
   196-201; *see also Twin Cities*
Minneapolis City Hall 189
Minneapolis Grain Exchange 189
Minneapolis Institute of Art 192
Minneapolis Sculpture Garden
   190

Minneapolis music scene 322-
   323
Minnehaha Falls *16,* 195
Minneopa State Park 71
Minnesota Baseball Hall of Fame
   Museum 301
Minnesota Brewing Co. 169-170
Minnesota Children's Museum
   162
Minnesota History Center 162,
   164
Minnesota Iron Mining Company
   263
Minnesota Landscape Arboretum
   198
Minnesota Mining and
   Manufacturing (3M) 52
Minnesota Museum of American
   Art 164
Minnesota Opera 164
Minnesota Orchestra 188
Minnesota Resort Museum 297
Minnesota River Valley 66-77,
   141; Upper 75
Minnesota State Capitol 160
Minnesota State Fair 175, *56,*
   175, 176, 178, 179
Minnesota State Reformatory 301
Minnesota Valley National
   Wildlife Refuge 67
Minnesota Valley State Recreation
   Area 67, 199
Minnesota Vietnam Veterans'
   Memorial 160
Minnesota Zephyr 209-210
Minnesota Zoo 196
Mississippi River 18, 24, 148-
   153; history 98-103, 282-
   287; Upper 75-77
Mississippi Melodie Showboat
   293
Mohr, Howard 296; *How to Talk*
   Minnesotan 107
Monson Lake State Park 75
Moorhead 65, 91, 324
Morton Gneiss 75

Mountain Iron 270
Mower County Historical Center 133
Munsinger Botanical Gardens 301
Murphy's Landing, Shakopee 199
music scene 336-337
Myre Big Island State Park 132

Naniboujou Motor Lodge 248-249, 318
Native Americans 20-38, 78, 143, 261-262, 283
Nerstrand Big Woods State Park 129
New Prague 324
New Ulm 65, 72-73, 324
Niagara Cave 119
Nicollet Island 184, 186
Nicollet Island Inn 323
Nicollet Mall 188
Nicollet, Joseph 70, 140
Norrish Octagon House, Hastings 104
North Country Scenic Trail 290
North Shore 223-273; map 226-227
North Shore Drive 236-253
North Shore Mountains Ski Trail System 246
North Shore Scenic Railroad 232
Northfield 126, 324
Northfield Historical Society Bank Museum 126
Northland Arboretum 296
Northern Vineyards Winery 209
Northrup Auditorium 195
Northwest Angle 274
North West Company 33, 35, 215, 249-250, *252*

O. L. Kipp State Park 116
Oberg Mountain 246
Ojibwa Indians 24, 26-29, 32-38, 298, 299
Old Copper Complex 20-21

Old Mill State Park 93
Oliver H. Kelley Farm 201
Olmstead Country History Center 124
Olof Swensson Farm Museum 75
Olson House, Hastings 104
Olson, Sigurd F. *The Singing Wilderness* 206
Onamia 316
Orchestra Hall, Minneapolis 188, *190*
Ordway Center for the Performing Arts 165
Otter Tail County Historical Society Museum 310
Our Lady of Lourdes Church 184, *185*
Owatonna 129
Owatonna Arts Center 129

Paleo-Indians 20
Palisade Head 242
Palmer House 303, 305
Park Point, Duluth 230
Park Rapids 290
Parrant, Pierre *144,* 153, 156
Paul Bunyan 287, 290, 292, *295;* Arboretum 295-296; Amusement Center 295; Trail 297
Paulucci Space Theatre 273
peatlands 278-281
Phelps Mill 307-308
Pickwick Mill 118
Pig's Eye 156, 157
Pig's Eye Lake 153
Pigeon Point 253; River 253
Pike, Lt. Zebulon 24, 33-35, 142, 283
Pillsbury "A" Mill 184
Pincushion Trails System 247
Pine River 297, 316
Pine City 215

Pipestone 78-82; 324
Historical Museum 80
Pipestone National Monument

21, 60, 78
Planes of Fame, Minneapolis 198
Point Douglas 206
politics 55
Polk County Museujm 92
Pond, Samuel W. 23, 36, 43-44, 61, 143, *146*
Prairie Island Dakota Reservation 110
prairies 58-91, *68-69, 87*
Pratt-Tabor Inn, Red Wing 109
Pringle House, Hastings 104
Public Library and James J. Hill Reference Library 165

railroads 45-47, 75, 102, 157, 166, *303*
Rainy Lake 253, 261
Ramsey County Historical Society 164
Ramsey Hill, St. Paul 174
Ramsey, Alexander 160, 206; house of 167
Reads Landing 110, 111
recommended reading 338-339
Red Lake Indian Reservation 281
Red River Valley 88-95; attractions 91; early life 89-90; map 91
Red Wing **106-110,** 325
Redwood River 78
Rice County Museum of History 127
Rice Lake National Wildlife Refuge 294
Rice Park 162-165
River Bend Nature Center 129
Riverwalk, Lake Pepin 111
Rochester 123-126, 326
Rolette, Joe 35-36, 71
Rölvaag, O. E. 81, 126; *Giants in the Earth* 50, 63-64
Root River Trail 119
Root River Valley 119-122; 326; South Branch 120
Roseau 281

Rothsay 63
Rum River 300
Rush City 215

St. Anthony Falls 24, 31, 51, 101, 140-142, **182-187**, 195
St. Cloud 300-301
St. Cloud State University 301
St. Croix Dalles 211-214
St. Croix River 202 223; map 205, 327
St. Croix State Park 221
St. James Hotel, Red Wing 106, 325
St. Louis County Courthouse 232, Historical Society 232, 269
St. Louis River 235
St. Olaf 127
St. Paul 45, 103, **156-179**; Como Area 175-177; Chamber Orchestra 164; downtown 158-166; food & lodging 328-331; Lowertown 165; map 158; Rice Park 162-165; suburbs 178; University Ave. 169; West Side 166-175; *see also Twin Cities*
St. Paul Curling Club 174
St. Paul Hotel 165, 331, 331
St. Paul Saints 175-176
St. Peter 70-71
St. Peter's Church 152
Sakatah Hills State Park 72
Sakatah Singing Hills State Trail 72
Sanborn 83, 331
Sauk Centre 302
Scandia 210-211
Schech's Mill 118
Schoolcraft, Henry Rowe 283-284, 286
Schubert Club Musical Instrument Museum 164
Science Museum of Minnesota 166
Scott, Dred 41

Severin, Timothy 30, 31, 33-34, 66, 284
Sibley, Henry H. 36, 104, 152, 153
Sibley State Park 77
Silver Bay 242
Silver Lake 124
Simpsons Creek Trail 290
Sinclair Lewis Interpretive Center 303
Sioux Uprising *see also Dakota War*
Sioux *see Dakota*
Sisu Heritage Homestead Tours 268
Skyline Parkway Drive 234
skyways 162, *181*
Snake River 215, 221
Solomon G. Comstock House 92
Soudan Underground Mine State Park 267
Southeastern Hills 96-126; map, 97
Southwest State University Anthropology Museum and Planetarium 78
Spirit Mountain Recreation Area 235
Split Rock Point 241; State Park 241, Lighthouse Historic Site *238*, 241, *241*
Sprague House, Red Wing 109
Spring Grove 118
Spring Lake Park Reserve 153
Springbrook Nature Center, Fridley 200
Stadium Village, Minneapolis 196
State Capitol, St. Paul 158
Steam Engine Museum, Mabel 118
steamboats 99-103, 115, 118, 148, 156
Stearns County Heritage Center 301
Stillwater 207-210, 327-328

Stone Arch Bridge, Minneapolis 186
Straight River 131
Summit Avenue, St. Paul 170-175
Sunrise 214
Suomi Hills Trail 290
Susie Islands 252
Swan Lake 72

T. B. Sheldon Memorial Auditorium 108
Taconite Harbor 243
Tamarac National Wildlife Refuge 310
Target Center 190
Taylor's Falls 211-214
Temperance River 245
Tettegouche State Park 242
Thief Lake State Wildlife Management Area 281
Thomas Sadler Roberts Bird Sanctuary 195
Thomsonite Beach 247
Tom's Logging Camp Museum 236-237
Tower 267
Tracy 83
Traverse des Sioux, St. Peter 70
Treaty Site History Center 70
trout fishing 122-123
Trout Lake 290
Trout Run Creek 122
Turtle Mound 290
Twain, Mark 98-103, 111, 136-137, 148
Twin Cities 57, 136-155; history 140-148; map 138-139; *see also St. Paul and Minneapolis*
Twin Lakes State Wildlife Management Area 93
Two Harbors, North Shore 237

U.S Dakota War 42-48, 147; sites 73-74; *see also Dakota Indians*

U.S. Hockey Hall of Fame, Evelth 269
Union Depot, St. Paul 166
University of Minnesota Duluth 234; Minneapolis 196; St. Paul 167, 175
University Theatre, Minneapolis 195
Upper Mississippi River Wildlife and Fish Refuge 114
Upper Sioux Agency 309

Valleyfair Family Amusement Park 198
Vasa 106
Verendrye (La), Sieur Pierre Gaultier 32-33, 277
Vermilion Lake 268; Range 264; River 104
Victorian Rose Inn, Albert Lea 132, 315
Village of Yesteryear, Owatonna 130
vineyards 111, 209
Virginia 269; Heritage Museum 269
Virginia Clemens Rose Garden 301
Voyageurs' Highway 253
Voyageurs National Park 258-259, 260-261, 332

W. A. Frost & Co. 174, 331
Wabasha 114, 228
Wadena 308-309
Walker Art Center 190
Walnut Grove 83
Warren, William W. 28, 29, 32, 37
Waseca 131
Washington County Courthouse, Stillwater 209
Washington County Historical Museum 209
Wayzata 200
Weaver 114
Weaver Bottoms 114
Weisman Art Museum 196
Welch 105
West Bank, Minneapolis 196
Western Lakes 301-302
Wheels Across the Prairie Museum, Tracy 83
White Oak Society 293
Whitefish Chain 296-297
Whitewater River 123
Whitewater State Park 123
Wild, John Casper 35
Wild River State Park 214
Wild Wings Gallery, Lake Pepin 111
Wilder, Laura Ingalls 64, 83

Wilderness Drive 287
Wildflower Waysides 133
Willard Munger State Trail 222
William O'Brien State Park 210
Willmar 75
wine 111
Winona 114-115
Wirth Park 194
Wolf Ridge Environmental Center 243, 245
Wolsfeld Woods Scientific and Natural Area 200
Wood Lake Nature Center 196
Woodland Tradition 21
Woodward, William F. 84
Worthington 82
Wykoff 120

Yellow Medicine County Museum 75
Yellow Medicine River 75, 309

Zippel Bay State Park 278
Zumbro River 126

COMPASS AMERICAN GUIDES

Critics, booksellers, and travelers all agree: you're lost without a Compass.

"This splendid series provides exactly the sort of historical and cultural detail about North American destinations that curious-minded travelers need."
— *Washington Post*

"This is a series that constantly stuns us; our whole past book reviewer experience says no guide with photos this good should have writing this good. But it does."
— *New York Daily News*

"Of the many guidebooks on the market, few are as visually stimulating, as thoroughly researched, or as lively written as the Compass American Guides series."
— *Chicago Tribune*

"Good to read ahead of time, then take along so you don't miss anything."
— *San Diego Magazine*

NEW FROM COMPASS:

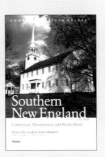

Vermont
$19.95 ($27.95 Can)
0-679-00183-2

Southern New England
$19.95 ($29.95 Can)
0-679-00184-0

Georgia
$19.95 ($29.95 Can)
0-679-00245-6

Pennsylvania
$19.95 ($29.95 Can)
0-679-00182-4

Compass American Guides are available in general and travel bookstores, or may be ordered directly by calling (800) 733-3000. Please provide title and ISBN when ordering.

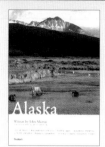

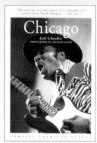

Alaska (2nd edition)
$19.95 ($27.95 Can)
0-679-00230-8

Arizona (5th edition)
$19.95 ($29.95 Can)
0-679-00432-7

Boston (2nd edition)
$19.95 ($27.95 Can)
0-679-00284-7

Chicago (2nd edition)
$18.95 ($26.50 Can)
1-878-86780-6

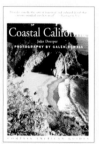

Coastal CA (2nd ed)
$19.95 ($29.95 Can)
0-679-00439-4

Colorado (5th edition)
$19.95 ($29.95 Can)
0-679-00435-1

Florida (1st edition)
$19.95 ($27.95 Can)
0-679-03392-0

Hawaii (4th edition)
$19.95 ($27.95 Can)
0-679-00226-X

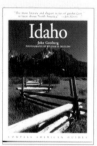

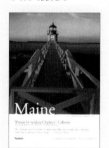

Idaho (1st edition)
$18.95 ($26.50 Can)
1-878-86778-4

Las Vegas (6th edition)
$19.95 ($29.95 Can)
0-679-00370-3

Maine (3rd edition)
$19.95 ($29.95 Can)
0-679-00436-X

Manhattan (3rd ed)
$19.95 ($29.95 Can)
0-679-00228-6

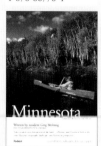

Minnesota (2nd ed)
$19.95 ($29.95 Can)
0-679-00437-8

Montana (4th edition)
$19.95 ($29.95 Can)
0-679-00281-2

New Mexico (3rd ed)
$18.95 ($26.50 Can)
0-679-00031-3

New Orleans (3rd ed)
$18.95 ($26.50 Can)
0-679-03597-4